More Praise for Job*Shift*

"A remarkable book, providing the reader with keen insight into the jarring reality that is upon us, and considerable help for both individuals and organizations in coping with its implications."
—*Santa Barbara News Press*

"For those anticipating the Information Age and all its fallout, Bridges suggests that it's already here. . . . Job*Shift* keenly points out the tremendous changes in the work world and shows how workers can safely make it through the turbulence."
—*Fort Worth Evening Star-Telegram*

"Companies are turning more and more to contingency workers, organizational hierarchies are flattening, and flexibility is the rule. Bridges's book helps workers and managers adapt to this new way of work."
—*Orange County Register*

"I highly recommend it. I bought it as much for my children as for myself, since they, more than I, will live and work in this ever-changing world."
—*San Bernardino Sun*

"Traditional management duties wil'
facts as the eight-hour day, leaves
tirement. . . . Bridges's ideas may
realistic."
—*American Demographics*

D1153509

"Bridges contends that jobs were t~~he way~~ ~~of putting~~ repetitive situations in which responsibilities were narrowly and rigidly defined. But when the market changes as swiftly as it does now, jobs get in the way."
—*Industry Week*

"Fascinating, lively, and very useful . . . William Bridges remains one of America's leading authorities on the profound structural changes altering the way we work."
—James Sullivan, Vice Chairman, Chevron Corporation

"A great book—a real breakthrough . . . Job*Shift* is *the* guidebook for work in the 21st century."
—Noel M. Tichy, coauthor of *The Transformational Leader*

Other Books by the Author

Transitions: Making Sense of Life's Changes

Managing Transitions: Making the Most of Change

The Character of Organizations: Using Jungian Type in Organizational Development

Surviving Corporate Transition: Rational Management in a World of Mergers, Layoffs, Start-ups, Takeovers, Divestitures, Deregulation, and New Technologies

A Year in the Life

JobShift

How to Prosper in a Workplace without Jobs

William Bridges

Addison-Wesley Publishing Company

Reading, Massachusetts   Menlo Park, California   New York
Don Mills, Ontario   Wokingham, England   Amsterdam   Bonn
Sydney   Singapore   Tokyo   Madrid   San Juan
Paris   Seoul   Milan   Mexico City   Taipei

Many of the designations used by manufacturers and sellers to distinguish their products are claimed as trademarks. Where those designations appear in this book and Addison-Wesley was aware of a trademark claim, the designations have been printed in initial capital letters (e.g., Chrysler).

Library of Congress Cataloging-in-Publication Data

Bridges, William, 1933–
    JobShift : how to prosper in a workplace without jobs / William Bridges.
      p.   cm.
    Includes bibliographical references and index.
    ISBN 0–201–62667–5
    ISBN 0–201–48933–3 (pbk.)
      1. Unemployment—United States.   2. Occupations—United States.
    3. Labor market—United States.   I. Title.   II. Title: Job shift.
    HD5724.B715   1994   94–18642
    650.1—dc20   CIP

Cover design by Chris St. Cyr and Suzanne Heiser
Cover art by Dave Cutler
Text design by Deborah Clark
Set in 10.5-point New Baskerville by Weimer Graphics

2 3 4 5 6 7 8 9-DOH-9998979695
Second printing, November 1995
First paperback printing, September 1995

Addison-Wesley books are available at special discounts for bulk purchases by corporations, institutions, and other organizations. For more information about how to make such purchases in the United States, please contact the Corporate, Government, and Special Sales Department at Addison-Wesley Publishing Company, 1 Jacob Way, Reading, MA 01867, 1–800–238–9682.

Contents

Preface

As I write this, the morning newspaper has yet another story of new "job losses"—several stories, actually. We are told that the recession has been over for quite a while but the percentage of the workforce that is "jobless" has not fallen the way it has at the end of previous recessions. The Clinton administration is trying to "create jobs," although its critics claim that some of the new taxes and regulations will "destroy jobs." We hear that the only way to protect our "jobs" is to increase our productivity, but then we discover that reengineering our work processes, utilizing self-managed teams, flattening our organizations, and turning our routine work over to computers always makes many "jobs" redundant.

When I was growing up, we used to read predictions that by the year 2000 everyone would have to work only thirty hours a week and that the rest would be leisure time. But as we approach the year 2000, it seems more likely that half of us will work sixty hours a week and the rest of us will be unemployed. As the captions to the picture puzzles in children's magazines used to ask, "What's wrong with this picture?"

It's not that the president or his critics don't care what happens to us. It's not that the organizations that once asked for our loyalty, and grew because of our efforts, have double-crossed us. The fault does not lie even with that dreaded monster "overseas competition," which has been blamed for everything from unemployment to falling living standards. It's a shame that these things are not the culprits: if they were, our task would be simpler.

The reality is much more troubling, for what is disappearing today is not just a certain number of jobs, or jobs in certain industries, or jobs in some part of the country—or even jobs in America as a whole. What is disappearing is the very thing itself: *the job*. That much-sought-after, much-maligned social entity is vanishing today like some species that has outlived its evolutionary time. In Part One of this book, "The Late, Great Job," we will study the social, economic, and technological forces that have put the job on the list of endangered species.

A century from now our descendants will look back and marvel that we couldn't see more clearly what was happening. How fixated we were on this game of "musical jobs," they will say, in which, month after month, scores and scores of people had to drop out. They will sympathize but say that our suffering came from trying to play by the old rules. To our counterparts at the end of the twenty-first century, today's struggle over jobs will seem like a fight over deck chairs on the *Titanic*.

Now, this is not another one of those the-economy-is-sinking jeremiads—far from it, for I believe that the modern world is on the verge of a huge leap in creativity and productivity. But *the job* is not going to be part of tomorrow's economic reality. Although there will always be enormous amounts of work to do, this book suggests that the work will not be contained in the familiar envelopes we call jobs. In fact, many organizations are today well along the path toward being "dejobbed."

The job is a social artifact, although it is so deeply embedded in our consciousness that most of us have forgotten its artificiality or the fact that most societies since the beginning of time have done just fine without jobs. The job concept emerged early in the nineteenth century to package the work that needed doing in the growing factories and bureaucracies of the industrializing nations. Before people had jobs, they worked just as hard but on shifting clusters of tasks, in a variety of locations, on a schedule set by the sun, the weather, and the needs of the day. The modern job was a startling new idea—to many people, an unpleasant and even socially dangerous one. Its critics claimed that it was an unnatural and even inhuman way to work. They predicted that most people wouldn't be able to live with its demands. Americans even once talked about the job as "wage slavery" and contrasted it with the farmer's and craftsperson's freedom and security. But what started as controversy became the ultimate orthodoxy: we're hooked on jobs.

Now the world of work is changing again. The very conditions (mass production and the large organization) that created jobs two hundred years ago are disappearing. Technology enables us to automate the production line, where all those jobholders used to do their repetitive tasks. Instead of long production runs where the same thing has to be done again and again, we are increasingly customizing production. Big firms (where most of the good jobs used to be) are "unbundling" their various activities and farming them out to little firms, who have created or taken over profitable niches. This "outsourcing" of work is not just happening in the support areas where it started—running the cafeteria, for instance, or providing building-maintenance services. Three out of ten large American industrial firms now outsource at least half their manufacturing. Public services are privatizing and government bureaucracies (the ultimate bastions of job security) are thinning. As the conditions that created jobs fade, we lose the need to package work into jobs. No wonder they're disappearing.

We all will have to learn new ways to work. Part Two of this book, "A Career Guide for the Twenty-first-Century Worker," will tell you how. While in some cases the new ways of working will require new technological skills, in many more cases they will require something more fundamental: the "skill" of finding and doing work in a world without clear-cut and stable jobs. It has become almost a truism that today's careers must be self-managed, but too often that statement simply means that you'll have to find your next job without outside help. The trouble is, that advice is already outdated. Today's workers need to forget jobs completely and look instead for work that needs doing—and then set themselves up as the best way to get that work done.

But as individuals we can go only so far. Part Three, "We're All in This Together," outlines what the dejobbed organization will

have to do to accommodate the dejobbed worker, as well as what
society itself needs to do to respond to the new worker's needs.
Part Three ends with a chapter (called "Getting Ourselves from
Here to There") on dealing with the discontinuities and disloca-
tions that will occur during this new transition period.

As I said, the papers carry daily accounts of layoffs, but they
also carry disturbing stories of a different kind: revisions of the
job-loss figures, debates over whether the recession was really so
bad after all, arguments that we may be overreacting. But the
data in such articles are dangerously selective. Consumer demand
may be "bouncing back" and manufacturers "may have no
choice but to add to their payrolls," according to one story.
"That is especially true in the auto industry . . . [where] many
laid-off workers are likely to be called back." That news will come
as a surprise to the hundreds of thousands of workers in auto and
auto-related manufacturing who have no chance of getting their
jobs back, even if the economy enters the biggest boom in twenty-
five years. Their jobs are gone for good.

Closer to the mark is a *U.S. News & World Report* cover story
called "Where Did My Career Go?" which appeared just a week
after the article just quoted. It showed that the current annual
rate of employment recovery is only 20 percent of the average
rate of recovery in recessions since 1950. It pointed out that
white-collar unemployment is higher today than during the recession's trough, and that 85 percent of those who've lost white-
collar jobs will never get them back—an all-time high for any
recession. It is not surprising that a recent Yankelovitch survey
found that two out of three Americans believe that job security is
worse today than it was in the recession's trough. And more than
half of them believe that the condition will "last for many years."

We need to understand the optimistic forecasts for what they
are: attempts to reassure badly shaken people, who know that
something big is going on but aren't quite sure what. And we
need to recognize that reassuring us is doing us no favor, for
without a clearer picture of reality we cannot prepare ourselves
for the future. The future is going to be very different from what
most of us grew up expecting, and most of us are no more ready

for it than eighteenth-century English villagers were for jobs in nineteenth-century English factories.

So let's get on to the real future. It's not a future with much of a political constituency, for most of us would like it to go away and let us get back to the world that we expected. If we must have uncertainty, we'd rather it would be over which party's plan for job creation is better, not over how to live without jobs entirely. But it is in our own self-interest to wake up: the political debates in Washington and the fifty state capitals rationalize and make us comfortable with our denial. Unless we see that, we'll be un-able—as individuals and as a society—to prepare for the future. Reality is the best land to live in, after all. Let's visit it now.

William Bridges
Mill Valley, California
June 1994

Acknowledgments

No intellectual project is a solo piece: it takes place in conversation and dialogue with others. I've been fortunate to have access to a number of people who were paying close attention to what was going on in the organizational world, and I would like to thank many of them here. I am sure that I am overlooking some, and I apologize for that oversight.

David Belsheim, Moore Business Forms and Systems; Sharon Bray, Lee Hecht Harrison; Larry Brunner, Procter & Gamble; Ray Burch, Skopos; Betsy Collard, Career Action Center; Jane Creech, Quantum; Bill Daniels, American Consulting and Training; Brent Dempster, Southern Life Assurance (South Africa); Kirby Dyess, Carlene Ellis, Tracy Koon, and Rich Martin, Intel; Debra Engle and Eddie Reynolds, 3Com; Bob Farnquist, Santa Clara County, California; Vicky Farrow, Sun Microsystems; John Iacovini, Kaset International; Garth Johnston, Colorado Issues Network; Michael Lindfield, Boeing Corporation; Fred Nichols, Xerox Corporation; Mark Powelson, KQED; Teresa Roche, Grass Valley Group; Jim Schroth and Sue Thompson, Levi, Strauss & Co.; Anne Sparks, Alumnae Resources; Noel Tichy and Andy McGill, University of Michigan; Warner Woodley, Chris Edgelow, and Paul Giroux, Mainstream Access (Canada).

I also want to thank my colleagues Bonnie Carpenter and Candida Bierbower, who ran my organization while I wrote; my daughter and colleague, Sarah Bridges-Parlet, whose questions encouraged me to strengthen my argument; my agent, Jim Trupin, who did his usual "no-sweat, let-me-worry-about-it" business of finding a publisher; and John Bell, my editor at Addison-Wesley, who not only saw the value of what I was saying but kept finding ways to help me say it better.

I especially want to thank Mondi, who, back in 1973, encouraged me to write from my own experience and in my own voice. Her advice has been the guiding principle and her support has been my mainstay in every subsequent project.

And finally I want to thank my father, Ronald Bridges, whose values, shortcomings, and interests unwittingly set me on this subject more than fifty years ago. I am dedicating this book to him. Rest in Peace.

The Late, Great Job

America has entered the age of the contingent or temporary worker, of the consultant and subcontractor, of the just-in-time work force—fluid, flexible, disposable. This is the future. Its message is this: You are on your own. For good (sometimes) and ill (often), the workers of the future will constantly have to sell their skills, invent new relationships with employers who must, themselves, change and adapt constantly in order to survive in a ruthless global market.

—Lance Morrow, "The Temping of America,"
Time, 1993

Our organizational world is no longer a pattern of jobs, the way that a honeycomb is a pattern of those little hexagonal pockets of honey. In place of jobs, there are "part-time and temporary work situations." But this change is symptomatic of a deeper one, subtler but more profound: Today's organization is rapidly being transformed from a structure built out of jobs to a field of "work needing to be done."

Jobs are artificial units superimposed on this field. They are patches of responsibility that, all together, were supposed to cover the work that needed to be done. His job is to take care of this, hers is to take care of that, and yours is to take care of the other thing. Together, you all get the work done. And you usually did, although there were always scraps and pieces of work that

1

didn't quite fall into anyone's job description, and over time job responsibilities had to be adjusted and new jobs added to keep getting everything done.

When the economy was changing much more slowly, the discrepancies between the job matrix and the work field could be forgotten. If new technology opened up a new area in the work field, new jobs could be created to cover the new work that needed doing. If a new market opened up, new jobs could be created to serve it. If a new law or judicial ruling required an organization to do something different, new jobs could be created to handle it.

But jobs—those boxes on the organization chart, with regular duties, hours, and salaries—encourage hiring at the very time that organizations need to reduce their employee base. They encourage hiring by cutting work into "turfs," which in turn require more turfs (and more hiring) whenever a new area opens up. They further encourage hiring by giving managers a level of power commensurate with the number of turf areas for which they are responsible: the more areas, the more power. Jobs also discourage accountability, because they reward people not for getting the necessary work done but for doing their jobs.

Furthermore, jobs are rigid solutions to an elastic problem. We can rewrite a person's job description occasionally, but not every week! When the work that needs doing changes constantly, we cannot afford the inflexibility that the job brings with it. (A vice president of operations at a West Coast computer maker summarized the problem when he said to me, "I just can't move the boxes around the organizational chart fast enough anymore!") Jobs are no longer socially adaptive creatures, and so they are going the way of the dinosaur.

In Chapter 1 we'll ask, "Where have all the jobs gone?" We'll see that the question means two different things: first, fewer jobs today, and second, the work needing to be done (and there is more than enough of that) no longer fits a traditional job description. In Chapter 2 we'll trace "The Rise and Fall of the Good Job," and we'll see in the process that jobs are only one way to frame work—a historically unusual way at that. Invented about two centuries ago, they worked only so long as the socioeconomic forces that created them remained dominant. The "disappearance of jobs" is really a symptom of a deeper socioeconomic change, and no public job-creation program is going to bring jobs back from the dead. That's the bad news. The good news, as described in Chapter 2, is that there are already clear signs of what work arrangements will replace jobs.

Where Have All the Jobs Gone?

> *. . . we have to create a new organizational architecture flexible enough to adapt to change. We want an organization that can evolve, that can modify itself as technology, skills, competitors, and the entire business change.*
>
> —Paul Allaire, CEO, Xerox Corporation

Jobs Are Disappearing . . . and This Time for Good

During the 1980s, economists and labor experts kept telling us that the generation after the baby boomers was smaller and that there were going to be labor shortages in the '90s. It was a reassuring message, for the big post–World War II generation (called by some the demographic equivalent of a pig being digested by a boa constrictor) had clogged the career channels in many American organizations. So it came as a relief to hear that better times were ahead. But—surprise! It hasn't worked out that way. We've been in a particularly bad job market since the end of the '80s. President George Bush's failure to address the problem effectively—and even, for an agonizingly long time, to acknowledge it—cost him a second term. He kept waiting for the hiring "downturn" to reverse itself, as it always had in previous recessions. But this time it didn't.

Then a new statistic started to appear, though it was still overshadowed by the more familiar unemployment figures. It measured not the people who were out of work but the jobs that those out-of-work people would never be able to find because they had disappeared completely from the economic landscape. By the fall of 1992, only 18 percent of the lost jobs had returned, although at such a late stage in every other recession for a half century, all the previously lost jobs had come back again. In the summer of 1993 the Bureau of Labor Statistics announced that the ratio of permanently terminated workers to temporarily laid-off was 4 to 1, whereas at the recession bottom of 1975 it was 1.5 to 1, and at the bottom in 1982 it was 2 to 1. The message was clear: jobs are going away, not just until times improve but for good. James Medoff, a Harvard economist who has studied these figures in more depth than anyone else, has summed up the situation with discomforting bluntness: "Today, people who lose their jobs are history."

The disappearance of these jobs is going to change the lives of all Americans, the employed as well as the unemployed. Europe and Japan are also feeling the effects of this great socioeconomic sea change, and their situations will worsen in the years ahead. The job cuts are already well under way in Europe, and unemployment is stuck at a very high level. Even so, knowledgeable observers such as Gerhaard Schulmeyer, an executive at international conglomerate ABB, estimate that European companies are still overstaffed by 20 percent.

Japan probably won't hit the wall for another five to ten years, but Japanese companies are already beginning to break their patterns of lifetime employment. A recent survey of top Japanese executives showed that 41 percent of them think that Japan "must thoroughly revise the lifetime employment system." Toyota Motor Corporation, a fairly conservative company, recently made a startling announcement: It was creating a new category of temporary professional worker. Automotive designers (the cream of the automotive workforce) will be hired henceforth on one-year contracts and paid on the basis of individual contribution. Quite a change from jobs for life and pay based on seniority!

Today's transformation is so large that you have to go back almost two centuries to the coming of industrialism to find a comparable change. During that earlier period, work was packaged into "jobs" to fit the demands of a new kind of workplace, and the numbers of those jobs grew along with the appearance of large factories and bureaucracies. In our own time, those big workplaces are shrinking and being automated, and work is once again being repackaged to meet new economic realities. This time the transformation represents nothing less than the "dejobbing" of America. This dejobbing takes two forms: the quantitative and the qualitative.

Dejobbing: The Quantitative Aspect

In the quantitative sense, dejobbing is simply a numbers game: the same work that used to require a hundred workers a few years ago can be done by fifty today—and maybe by ten tomorrow. That is old news, of course. We've been turning manufacturing tasks over to machines for almost two hundred years. We've done that so effectively that the manufacturing sector of our economy today produces, with no more workers, five times as many goods as it did at the end of World War II.

Now, however, the process is moving so fast that immense shifts take place almost overnight. In the United States, the collapse of the Soviet Union and attempts to shrink the budget deficit have led to huge cuts in the defense budget and layoffs in the defense industry. Between 1990 and 1992, there were more than 1,000 mergers in that industry—all of which led to job losses. If you add the jobs lost since 1989 by workers in defense businesses (440,000) to those lost by U.S. military personnel (300,000) and civilians working for the Department of Defense (100,000), the total is two-and-a-half times the jobs lost during that period in the headline-making downsizings at GM, IBM, AT&T, and Sears. These job losses are particularly significant because the defense industry had provided the last wave of really good blue-collar jobs, with wages in aerospace companies averaging more than $18 an hour.

A recent editorial cartoon by Tom Toles caught the irony in all of this. It showed the Northern Hemisphere, with a voice from the middle of the former Soviet Union saying, "When the Communists were in power, we at least all had jobs." Across the ocean, from a United States plastered with "Base Closing" signs, comes the reply: "Tell us about it!" Far down in the lower-right corner, a tiny voice says out of the darkness, "We can't take this shock therapy!"

Nor is the disappearance of defense-industry jobs the last industrywide workout that we are likely to see. In simple numbers, the potential for consolidations and downsizings in the health industry dwarfs what has happened in defense. Everyone agrees that we are spending too much money for health services, although we conveniently forget that the lower costs, which we so clearly need, can come only at the price of very large job losses at hospitals, pharmaceutical companies, doctors' offices, and insurance companies.

It is not just blue-collar jobs that are disappearing. Proportionately, white-collar jobs are disppearing even faster, and still more of them are at risk. Had such a thing occurred a generation ago, we might have said that the common people had been taking it in the neck for too long, that now it was the "better-off" folks' turn. But times have changed. The white-collar folks *are* the common people today, representing six out of ten American workers. As they go, so goes America.

The quantitative side of dejobbing has reached its apex (or nadir, depending on where you stand) in the head-count–reduction mania of the past few years. Starting with the premise (which is true) that the average organization has more employees than it either needs or can afford, a conclusion is reached (which is false) that the answer is simply to reduce their number. What is really needed is to redesign the whole production system so that it is simpler and responds more directly to the needs of the customer or client—and so can be operated by fewer people. Then, and only then, can the organization decide whether its excess

people represent an opportunity for growth or whether it needs
to help them find work elsewhere. Instead of doing that, organization after organization has named numerical targets for "head-
count reduction." That is like an obese person with unhealthy
eating habits deciding against making dietary changes and opting
instead for liposuction.

Executives are given head-count–reduction targets by their
boards, and sometimes financial incentives are tied to reaching
the targets. IBM chose Louis Gerstner as its CEO not because he
understood the business so well that he could lead its redesign
but because he had shown that he could reduce head count and
other costs. The ability to "downsize" is so prized that when
Christopher Steffen, a tough financial guy from Chrysler, was
made chief financial officer at Kodak, analysts applauded. When
he left a few weeks later, Kodak stock fell. And when it was *ru-
mored* a few days later that he was going to IBM, IBM stock rose!

Dejobbing: The Qualitative Aspect

There is a qualitative shift going on too. It's not just that fewer of
the old-style jobs are left. It's that the work situations encouraged
by the new technological and economic realities are not jobs in
the traditional sense; and a great deal of what is being done in
today's organizations is done by people who do not have "a real
job." It is certainly suggestive that the private company that employs more Americans than any other—whose 560,000 employees dwarf other "giants" like GM (currently 365,000) and IBM
(330,000)—is the temporary-employment agency Manpower.
There is no doubt that, as the press has started to recognize,
America is being "temped." Temporary and part-time workers
are doing an increasing share of the work in American organizations, and the process has gone further than most people realize.
A confidential Bank of America memo leaked to the press estimated that "soon, only 19% of the bank's employees will work
full-time."

These members of what is coming to be called the contingent
or just-in-time workforce are not just clerical or assembly-line
workers. Temporary hires do sophisticated electrical engineering

for Silicon Graphics Corporation, they work as senior benefits analysts for Charles Schwab Corporation, and they do systems engineering for Parker Hannifin's aerospace group. Temporary professionals are increasing twice as fast as the temporary workforce as a whole—and temporaries as a whole have increased almost 60 percent since 1980. Those figures are probably low, since they do not count the professionals who are technically consultants but whose roles and relationships to the rest of the organization are more like those of temporary workers.

The San Francisco firm M^2 has built a successful and rapidly growing business out of providing temporary executives and project managers to all kinds of companies. As one of its principals, Claire McAuliffe, has pointed out, hiring a temporary executive to do a tough and badly needed task is just a small step away from IBM's bringing in Gerstner as CEO to put its house in order; hiring a temporary professional to supply necessary talent is not all that different from the White House's bringing in David Gergen to mend its damaged press relations.

Some organizations have taken the radical step of doing away with permanent employees entirely and started simply "leasing" all their workers from companies like Action Staffing, based in Tampa, Florida. Montgomery, Alabama's Home Corporation, the owner/ manager of apartment complexes scattered through ten states, has leased its entire five-hundred-person property-management staff (everyone from resident managers to groundskeepers) from Action Staffing. Action Staffing handles the complexities of state regulations and negotiates better group health insurance rates than Home Corp. could do on its own.

Why Is This Happening?

Ten years ago it was common to blame our job problems on overseas competition. However, many organizations, like Home Corp., are insulated from overseas competition, so that answer is clearly inadequate. Even in cases where jobs have been lost because goods can be made more cheaply overseas, the story is more complicated than we usually realize. When we talk about jobs going overseas, we're likely to leave out a very important part of the story: *production* leaves these shores, not *jobs* per se. For every one thousand American jobs lost in such a relocation, as few as a hundred may be gained by the overseas country that wins the relocated production facility.

Jobs do not follow the old physics principle of conservation of matter, where nothing ever disappears absolutely. Job loss is not a zero-sum game, where *they* win and *we* lose, because relocation is appealing only partly because pay is lower for the same job in Malaysia or Mexico than in the United States. An increasingly important factor in relocation is that it is easier to start from scratch in a location where people's attitudes are not compromised by decades of experience with traditional industrialism— and, of course, with jobs.

To understand where all our jobs have really gone, we need to understand how work is changing today and what those changes do to jobs. For as we noted in the introduction, the job is not a timeless fact of human existence. It is a social artifact. It is what Joel Barker would call a paradigm, a way to put boundaries around some significant area of human life and define how you need to act to succeed within those boundaries. Until we do that, we'll be unable to meet the challenge that we face—as individuals, as organizations, and as a nation. We'll only be arguing about how to turn back the clock.

Change and the Transformation of Work

We all know that change is more frequent today than in the past, but the reason why is not widely understood. Anyone who thinks about the speedup of change must sense that it has a lot to do with modern technology. You can see the link when you notice how short the new high-tech-product life cycles are becoming and how whole new industry sectors appear almost overnight. An example: Watchmaking changed relatively little for more than a century, and timepieces were sold in watch and jewelry shops. But new technology created this rapid sequence of events:

- Timex turned the watch into a tiny electric motor and shifted watch sales to drugstores.
- Casio made the watch into an information-generating piece

of electronic equipment and moved the watch business into electronics stores and departments.

■ And Swatch reinvented the watch as a piece of designer clothing, to be sold (where else?) in clothing stores.

We also read that scientific discoveries are coming along so fast now, that most of what we now know was discovered only in the past decade. And the big new discoveries have the power to change whole sectors of the economy. Who knows, for example, what the pharmaceutical business will look like when the potentials of genetic engineering have been realized? Who knows what digitized images will do to our communication, or what video telephones will do to our need for travel? When such possibilities are widely capitalized upon, what will that do to the airline business, or to airplane manufacturers? What will it do to the hotel and restaurant business, and to the construction industry and equipment makers that serve it?

But such effects notwithstanding, if new products were the only way that technology affected the world of work, the job would be relatively safe: jobs lost in one sector of the economy would be added in another. Technology affects jobs more directly in the way it changes how work is actually done. Those effects fall into three primary clusters.

Technology and Change 1: "Informating" the Workplace

Shoshana Zuboff coined the verb *to informate*, to describe the way information technology inserts "data" in between the worker and the product. The factory worker no longer manipulates the sheet of steel; he manipulates the data about the steel. Work that has been informated is no longer physical but is, instead, a sequence or pattern of information that can be handled and changed almost as if it were tangible. An order, once entered into a salesperson's laptop in a customer's office, becomes simply data, and it automatically triggers a chain of data events with a minimum of further human intervention,

■ in the purchasing department, where necessary materials and components are ordered;

■ at the suppliers' sites, where those orders are received and a

comparable chain of electronic events initiates the preparation
and shipment of what has been ordered;
- at the receiving dock, where the ordered goods arrive and
where the finished product is later sent out to the market;
- in the factory, where the product specifications are coded
into the computer-aided manufacturing (CAM) system and the
product is turned out by largely automated machinery;
- at the accounts payable and receivable departments, where
payment is made for the materials and an invoice is sent for the
products;
- and at a dozen other points along the production-delivery
route, such as the salesperson's electronic file, which will cal-
culate the commission due on the sale, and the factory's production records, which will dictate everyone's bonus at the end
of the year.

At each step along the way, people who used to fill out and file
papers are made redundant. (Seeing how Mazda Motors had informated its accounts-payable system woke Ford Motor Company
up to its possible savings. Mazda, which is admittedly a good deal
smaller than Ford, did with five—yes *five!*—employees what Ford
was using four hundred to accomplish.) Obviously, informated
work needs fewer people.

We knew that automation would change how work was done,
but until recently we still saw the future as an extension of the
past. We pictured the twenty-first-century workplace as inhabited
by dozens of little robots, humming around the floor doing hu-
manoid things with their mechanical little arms. Instead of simply
making products robotically, informated systems provide us with
services—like the ATM that gives us the cash we need at all hours
of the day and night. Instead of rooms full of R2D2s dashing
around retrieving things from files and mailing them to new locations, we have a computer network that gives employees a conti-
nent away access to the data in our electronic database. Instead
of electronic brains making enormously complex decisions (like,
should we send up the rocket or not?), computer programs make
ordinary decisions (like, should we loan the customer $100,000
or $150,000?). Instead of "smart machines" replacing all the

manual labor on the factory floor, they are replacing the mental labor in the middle-management offices. (No wonder that middle managers made up more than one in five of the layoffs in the current round of downsizing, even though they make up only one in ten workers.)

In showing how informated systems transform white-collar work, I don't want to leave the impression that informating has not changed how products are manufactured or that, in the process, it has not caused job losses in manufacturing. It has. At the Charlottesville, Virginia, GE Fanuc Automation plant, the production of circuit boards has doubled without an increase in employees. Wilson Chen, president of another circuit-board maker, Santa Clara, California's Solectron, has said, "If I had to produce this year's run with the old machinery, I would have had to nearly double my work force to 8,000 people."

We have hardly scratched the surface of the way informated work will affect our lives. Consider what the "smart card" (a card with an embedded programmable chip, already widely used in France and Japan) will do to clerical work at your bank. You hand your smart card to the cashier at a restaurant and she runs it through a scanner. The system not only records a charge—the way your present credit card does—but also instantaneously deducts the appropriate amount of money from your account, credits it to the restaurant's account, and records your new balance on the card's embedded chip. Just like that.

There is no list of charges at the end of the month (and no workers to prepare that list), no processing the check you write to pay your credit card bill (and no workers to handle that check), no payment from the credit card company to the restaurant (there go more workers at both ends of that transaction). One has to wonder how far the process will go. Will this electronic wizardry end up transforming wealth so completely into credit data that money too will finally disappear (and with it all the workers who used to manufacture it and handle it)?

But don't stop there. What happens to jobs when similar cards—or enhanced ones, based on optical-disk technology—can be encoded with your whole medical history, the medication

you currently take, your ten most recent blood-pressure read-
ings, the image of your last chest X ray, and all the details of your
medical insurance policy? All that record keeping and file storage
at your doctor's office and the insurance company and the hospital will be unnecessary, and so will the jobs of the people who ran
those departments. In a decade or so, we'll consider today's
medical-data practices as archaic as the hand-copying of medieval
manuscripts.

It's not just the clerical jobs that are being replaced by com-
puter-driven systems. WHDH-TV in Boston now does all its studio filming with six robotic cameras, coordinated by one
technician seated in front of a touch-screen PC. Standard shots
(those of news anchors, for example) are programmed into a
database. But the station's computers do much more. Virtually
every activity—from budgeting to videotape editing—is integrated into a computer network. In the process, the station has
become very profitable. Not coincidentally, it has only half as
many employees as it did in 1988.

The process of informating our labors goes on everywhere.
Colombian drug lord Pablo Escobar, describing the primitive
conditions in the prison from which he subsequently escaped, was
quoted by *Fortune* as saying, "We were fifteen prisoners, and
there were only three computers."

Technology and Change 2: The Business of Data

Technology also renders jobs obsolete by replacing the relatively
slowly changing world of "things" with the much more mercurial
world of "data." Things have to be assembled or processed from
raw materials by teams of workers; data are typed into a terminal
by a single worker—or even handwritten on or spoken into tomorrow's computers. Things require space for storage; we need
staffed stockrooms to maintain an inventory. Data take up almost
no space, can be maintained by users, and can be duplicated as
needed. We hear a lot today about "information workers" and
how different they are from the old-style workers of the mechanical age. No wonder.

Peter Drucker estimates that the new workers, who work with

data instead of things, "already number at least one-third and more likely two-fifths of all employees." This figure is significant, because our assumptions about jobs—the very concept of job itself—fitted the task-patterns dictated by the labor divisions necessary to run a mechanistic system. Long production runs, extended chains of command, fixed job descriptions—all these things made sense in the slower-moving factories and offices of the pre-electronic world. But today these things are too rigid. The structures, procedures, and roles of the past are too slow for a world driven and networked by electronic data, for as Safi Quereshy, the cofounder and CEO of AST Research, said recently, "The computer business is changing so quickly these days that sometimes we feel as if we're in the fresh-produce business." (If the recent genetically altered tomato lives up to its promise, vegetables may start having a longer shelf life than laptops.)

We still picture production on the model of a General Motors factory or a Chevron oil refinery, but such thinking is outmoded. As Nuala Beck has recently pointed out, the center of economic gravity has already moved from those "old" industries to the "new" ones of computers, biotechnology, and other data-based industries. Drawing on recent U.S. Census and Department of Labor statistics, she demonstrates conclusively that

a fact of life today is that more Americans work in the computer industry as a whole (equipment, semiconductors and computer services) than in the auto, auto parts, steel, mining and petroleum-refining industries combined. . . . More Americans work in biotechnology than in the entire machine-tool industry. . . . Twice as many Americans make surgical and medical instruments as make plumbing and heating products.

More evidence for the same extraordinary shift is found in the fact that in 1970, American corporations spent 11 percent of their durable-equipment outlays on information-processing equipment. In 1989 that figure had risen to 51 percent, and it is certainly higher still today.

Located along the growing edge of the economy and driven by the fastest-changing elements in modern technology, these "new" organizations have moved furthest away from traditional jobs. We'll see how they get their work done in the next chapter, but as a foretaste of their style and substance, consider this explanation (by a Silicon Valley manager to Rosabeth Moss Kanter) of how his job was defined.

> In my position, the nature of the duties can change a lot depending on the expertise and interest of the individual. For example, if I were really anxious to travel and instruct, I could look around for some topics that aren't well documented and make myself an expert on those topics, and tell management that someone needed to go out and teach a course in that. In general, there's more work to do than people to do it, so you look at your position and you say, there are lots of things that would be appropriate for me to do. If I have a conscience, I'll do what needs to be done. If I'm selfish, I'll do what I want to do. So there is a lot of flexibility.

That's not a job description in the conventional sense.

Technology and Change 3: Communications Technology as "Multiplier"

In 1815, on the eve of American industrialism, the United States fought the Battle of New Orleans even though a peace treaty had already been signed to end the War of 1812. At that time, it took so long for information to move from one place to another that change could spread only slowly. Steam engines might be used to pump water out of coal mines in England, but in America it would still be buckets for a long time. A crop could fail in Canada, a king could be executed in France, a war could erupt in Asia, and a famine could ravage Africa—while elsewhere things went along unaffected and unchanged.

But today the weather predictions for drought-ravaged Africa, the morning's gold price in Tokyo, the latest hitch in negotiations in the Middle East, the new unemployment figures from Washington, and the announcements of job cuts at a European multinational corporation and of new software from a small American startup—they all reach us simultaneously. Now add to those events all the changes made *in reaction to* those primary changes (and also communicated everywhere at once). Of course, those secondary changes in turn create changes in reaction.

In this way technology, and particularly communications technology, introduces a "multiplier effect" that interlocks the whole world such that time and distance no longer buffer us against the effects of change. In the past, if there were a thousand change events worldwide during any given period, only four or five of them would have been experienced in any one place. But today's world is a great, electronic spider web, where footsteps anywhere are felt by individuals everywhere, so that today we experience hundreds of those thousand changes. No wonder we say that there is more change today.

Reactions to Change Are Themselves Changes

The effect of technological change is amplified by the very strategies that organizations currently use to cope with that change.

- Because they have to make decisions more quickly, organizations are shortening their chains of command, flattening their hierarchies, handing the authority for many decisions to front-line employees. Each of those things is a change.

- Because organizations want to speed up production of goods and delivery of services, they turn over the redesign of their processes to cross-trained and self-managing teams. This changes not only what is done but also who has the power to determine what will be done.

- Because organizations want to unburden themselves of big, slow-moving inventories, they shift to just-in-time systems of materials handling—which changes procedures and processes throughout the organization.

- Because many organizations want to involve their suppliers more closely in operations, they put suppliers (and even customers) on their product development teams—which, incidentally, now are also peopled with individuals from different functions who have never worked together before. Again, a change for everyone involved.

A feedback loop is formed, so that as more change occurs around an organization, more change will take place within the organization, as it has to modify its structure, procedures, and culture to cope with it.

One of the most important change-driven changes is the simplification of product design and work processes so that everything can be done faster. The steering-column design of a Pontiac Grand Am, for example, has been radically simplified so that it contains 30 percent fewer parts. Something similar has happened to the Hewlett-Packard PC "server," the key PC in a network, which holds the system's common programs and documents. The old server was held together by fifty screws, all separately inserted and tightened. The new server is designed to simply snap together: no screws. It used to take up to twenty-five minutes to put together a server; now it takes an average of four minutes. And what does that do to jobs? It is certainly no secret that head count at HP is much lower than it was five years ago.

Another important change-caused-by-change is "outsourcing." Because they are beginning to recognize that their old do-it-yourself habits were unwieldy, more and more organizations are limiting their activities to those parts of the business where they have special competence and outsourcing the rest to external vendors. At first they gave up only peripheral activities like maintaining plant security or repairing company vehicles. But as the demand for world-class results and the need for organizational flexibility has grown, organizations have turned to outside sources for much more of what goes into the final product or service. It is no accident that, whereas enormously successful Toyota outsources the making of about 75 percent of its component car parts and fairly successful Ford outsources 50 percent, still-struggling GM outsources only 25 percent of its components.

Outsourcing has become standard operating procedure at a wide variety of organizations. DuPont no longer owns and maintains its copying machines; Lanier Corporation does. Continental Airlines uses EDS, and General Dynamics uses Computer Services Corp., to run information-services operations. Pitney-Bowes Management Services handles the mailrooms and copying services for Merrill Lynch, Sears, and Texaco. Dell Computer outsources almost all its manufacturing, doing only a little assembly in one plant. It also turns over all orders for its peripherals and computer supplies to a big distribution company called Merisel. Proving that nothing is sacred, the "merchant and *maker*" Brooks Brothers outsources the tailoring of most of its clothing.

Outsourcing can lead to surprising arrangements. In November 1990, Commodore Business Machines hired Federal Express to service its consumer products. If you call Commodore's twenty-four-hour consumer-assistance number, the voice on the other end actually belongs to a FedEx employee (though you won't know it), who will arrange for the machine to be picked up and replaced with a loaner the next morning (by another FedExer). The machine will, in all likelihood, be shipped to the FedEx hub in Memphis and back again after repair, via overnight air. Six months after the arrangement began, Commodore vice president Jim Reeder said that the result was better service at one-half the cost!

Or consider the guy who comes in and sets up the big Xerox photocopier that your company just bought. He's full of advice about the machine and thoughtfully sweeps up any developer powder he spills, but he's actually a truck driver, not a copier specialist. And he's not a Xerox employee, either. In fact, he works for Ryder System, the big truck-rental outfit. Ryder has subcontracted with Xerox not only to deliver but also to install its copiers.

One of the most interesting outsourcing arrangements involves a couple of unlikely organizations, both monasteries: the Holy Cross Abbey in Virginia and the Gethsemani Abbey in Kentucky. The monks' cloistered life precludes them from running a school or a public business, but with the help of a data-services broker with the wonderful name of Electronic Scriptorium, they have set themselves up to computerize technical and intellectual databases. For example, they have computerized 10,000 catalog cards for a Yale University library, created an index for the Johns Hopkins Medical Institutions Archives, and regularly help automate libraries preparing to install data-management software. "'There is some leftover romanticism,' that resists bringing modern technology into monastic life, says Brother Benjamin of

Gethsemani [to the *Wall Street Journal*]. But there is a long tradition, he adds, of monasteries 'using to the best advantage what's
available to society and sort of baptizing it along the way.'"

Delocalizing Work

In the same way that the new communications technology has
facilitated collaborations between a company and a network of
outsourcing vendors, it has also enabled collaborations between
different sites of the same organization—and with no more difficulty than linking two offices in the same building. The new technology allows mail-order firm PC Connection, for example, to
locate its headquarters in a remodeled mill in Marlow, New
Hampshire, where the owner wants to live, and locate its delivery
center in the more geographically convenient site of Wilmington,
Ohio; likewise, huge, Philadelphia-based Rosenbluth Travel can
locate its data-entry operations in Linton, North Dakota.

But not all such changes are driven by the profit motive. In the
summer of 1988, Hal Rosenbluth, Rosenbluth Travel's CEO,
read about the difficulties faced by midwestern farm families during that drought year. Wanting to help, he decided to relocate a
little of the company's bookkeeping to a place where new employment opportunities were desperately needed. He offered twenty
temporary data-entry jobs in Linton, North Dakota, but when
eighty people applied, he hired forty. Rosenbluth was amazed:
"There was virtually no absenteeism or turnover. The quality of
the work was extremely high." So he hired more and more. The
number reached one hundred and is slated to double again. The
temporary hires have become permanent employees too.

Why stop with North Dakota? How about County Cork, Ireland? Metropolitan Life has a group of 150 people analyzing your
medical claims there. And how about Bangalore, India? Well,
Texas Instruments established a software design operation there
to take advantage of the supply of Indian programmers.

You never know where your phone line will take you. If you
use Quarterdeck Office Systems software, for example, your call
for assistance with one of the company's programs may not go to
the company headquarters in California but to the customer-

service center in Dublin, Ireland. When your fingers do the walking, they can travel a long way these days.

The Demise of the Office

For millions of Americans, the job is at the office. The two entities go together like home and family. But the same technological forces that are making it possible to scatter operations around the world are making it possible to do away with offices to an extent that no one would have dreamed possible just a few years ago. Faxes and modems enable a person to take on assignments and turn in work as effectively from home as from the desk across the room. Cellular phones and laptops turn the salesperson's or service rep's car or hotel room into an office, complete with immediate access to all the customer information in the company database.

Arthur Andersen, the huge consulting and accounting firm, has already equipped one-third of its professional employees with laptop computers and cut them loose from their offices. Smaller firms can achieve even more flexibility. ValueQuest Ltd. is an investment-management firm that handles $500 million from the likes of the 3M pension plan and the California Public Employee Retirement System. Its two principals, Terrence B. Magrath and Katherine Busboom Magrath, ran the business last summer from their yawl on a lake on Cape Breton Island in Canada. Their PC was linked by radio to a cellular phone antenna on the island, so they could stay in touch with their company. Of course their company isn't your average Wall Street firm: it operates out of their home in Marblehead, Massachusetts.

Herman Miller Inc., a furniture designer, has responded to this delocalization process by creating an office with workstations that employees use on an ad-hoc basis. The firm has created ways to personalize this office of the moment (as it calls it) by providing each employee with a cart that contains his or her files, as well as a tackboard on the side for memos and personal photos.

Delocalizing the office would not have gone so far had it not coincided with another change in the organizational world: the need to save money on real estate expenses. Arthur Andersen's chief information officer, Bruce Turkstra, says (as most of those pushing office delocalization do) that the chief benefit is in getting people away from their desks and closer to the customer. But he also admits that "achieving a lower occupancy cost" was another motive. IBM has also started a space-saving program that will trim office space by a huge amount. Although no target was announced, John Breckenridge, the real estate service director for IBM's U.S. operations, said that cutting use by 5,000,000 square feet is a "conservative" estimate.

Employee numbers may not be affected by these changes, but the concept of office is so central to the work lives of many people that its disintegration is another strong solvent that blurs the outlines of the job. Former office dwellers who spend some of their work hours in a car, some at home, and some at a customer's work site (where offices may also be disappearing) need to develop a whole new work concept—not to mention new work habits.

Telecommuting, or working from home during regular business hours, has been the most-discussed possibility opened up by the new communications technology. And the number of telecommuters is large and growing. Some recent estimates put the number of workers who telecommute at least part time at more than six-and-a-half million. (An additional eight-and-a-half million work at home after hours.) We once thought that telecommuting might be the answer to everything from child care to traffic jams. But like so many things in our bottom-line era, telecommuting and the other office-saving measures are ending up being encouraged less by the social benefits than by the dollars they save. All the same, they represent a change-driven change made possible by the new technology, and a change that makes the traditional job a less and less meaningful concept.

Reengineering the Work

None of the changes of the past decade promises to have so much impact on the workplace and jobs as the redesign of work processes, called reengineering. In almost all businesses and institutions, work and the workers that do it are organized ineffectively. Often people are grouped by professional or clerical specialty, and the flow of any particular piece of work (e.g., an order being filled, a product being designed, a complaint being responded to) is likely to "island-hop" from one work area to another. Typically, there are big snags and bottlenecks where work piles up, and cracks and "Bermuda Triangles" where it sometimes disappears mysteriously. The result is that a piece of work takes a long time to complete.

Michael Hammer and James Champy, the two foremost apostles of reengineering, tell a story that illustrates the problem. IBM Credit is responsible for providing customers with financing for the products that IBM sells. Typically, requests for financing took six to fourteen days. All too often a competitor approved a credit request more quickly and IBM lost a sale. Hammer and Champy tell what happened:

> One day two senior managers at IBM Credit had a brainstorm. They took a financing request and walked it themselves through all five steps [in the approval process], asking personnel in each office to put aside whatever they were doing and to process this request as they normally would, only without the delay of having it sit in a pile on someone's desk. They learned from their experiments that performing the actual work took in total only *90 minutes.* The remaining six or more days were consumed by handing the form off from one department to the next.

The whole work process was redesigned as a result of this experiment, so that task sequences were done beginning to end by single generalists, instead of sequentially by multiple specialists. The result: "IBM Credit slashed its six-*day* turnaround to four *hours.* It did so without an increase in head count—in fact, it has achieved a small work force reduction. At the same time, the number of deals that it handles has increased 100-fold. Not 100%, but *100 times.*"

Reengineering is the systematic work-redesign process that helps organizations make similar savings in time and money, while enhancing quality. When Louisville's Capital Holding Corporation reengineered its back-office operations, it found that it could increase its business 25 percent while cutting its staff from

1,900 to 1,100. (It expects to go further, to 800.) Ford Motor
Company's North American accounts payable department
thought that it could do its tasks with 20 percent fewer people if it
used them more effectively. After a full-scale reengineering exercise, it found itself with 75 percent fewer people.

The purpose of reengineering is seldom staff reduction per se.
Saving time is at least as important. Hallmark Cards wanted to cut
the two years that it took to develop a new card; it took that long
because the designers, artists, financial people, and printers who
were working on the same card were separated into different departments rather than gathered as a single team.

The San Diego Zoo, on the other hand, reengineered its tasks
as part of a larger effort to show its animals in a new way: by
bioclimatic zones, like Gorilla Tropics (an African rain forest) and
Tiger River (an Asian jungle setting). But mammal and bird specialists, horticulturalists, construction workers, and maintenance
people—all of whom would have to cooperate on such a project—were separated into fifty different departments at the zoo.
To create the new environments, the specialists were reassigned
to cross-disciplinary teams. The result, in the words of Thomas A.
Stewart, who described the zoo's project in a *Fortune* article:
"Seven people run Tiger River; when it started there were 11,
but as team members learned one another's skills, they decided
they didn't need to replace workers who left."

In one sense, nobody at the zoo lost a job, but in another sense
everyone did. The old traditional jobs are gone, and in their place
is a fluid, cross-trained team, which does things that no job description can encompass. The new way also does it with four
fewer people, too. Make no mistake about it: reengineering
promises to alter the job world in a very big way, both qualita-
tively and quantitatively. A front-page *Wall Street Journal* article
on reengineering estimated that redesign of work processes
could, if done throughout the private sector in America, "knock
out between a million and two-and-a-half million jobs each year
for the foreseeable future"—as many as 25 million jobs in total.
It is harder to estimate what the remaining work situations would
look like. Probably not much like the jobs they replace.

The quantitative dejobbing going on today leads to qualitative dejobbing. Downsizing dissolves the outlines of conventional jobs, since it forces organizations to add new responsibilities and change existing ones. As the "stayers" pick up the pieces left behind by the "leavers," job descriptions make less and less sense. People report to one person in one area of their responsibility and another person in another. As the numbers fluctuate, old job identities are destroyed.

Turbulence Erodes Job Outlines

The numbers fluctuate far more than employment statistics show. In an important article titled "The Rise and Fall of Everybody," David Birch showed that although employment figures can change minimally over a period of time, there is an immense amount of turbulence within the apparently static situation. Comparing the situation to a thundercloud, where the billowy masses of white hide huge updrafts and downdrafts, he wrote that "inside [the apparently stable economic cloud] is a turbulent, swarming mass of companies, coming and going, rising and falling at extraordinary rates." Tracking workers within companies of different sizes, he found that "the turnover of jobs within each layer of the cloud [i.e., different-size companies] is very high. By 1986, almost 43% of the workers in the pool of 20–99 employee companies held jobs that were not there in 1982."

This turbulence exists even in parts of the economy that have good futures; remember that when you read Alvin Toffler, Nuala Beck, and others who identify information technology as the place where jobs are going to be created in the next decade. As I wrote that sentence, Apple Computer just laid off 16 percent of its workers. In the first half of 1993, thirty-four U.S. manufacturers of computer-related products announced layoffs totaling more than 21,000. At the same time, some computer companies are hiring. One study of the situation concluded: "The bottom line: People are more likely than in past years to lose the [computer-related] jobs they have, but have a better chance than in many areas [of the economy] of finding new ones."

Birch's research on such "turbulence" got a good deal of

attention, but that was because of one of his other findings: that small- to medium-size companies were the creators of employment in America, because while the Fortune 500 were shrinking, small firms were growing fast. That point is also important to our argument here, for the Fortune 500 companies are the bastion of jobs in the traditional sense, and the young, rapidly growing companies (often in the "newer" industries) have a great deal of work to do but fewer and fewer traditional jobs. Birch's basic point, however, is equally germane to our argument: the updrafts and downdrafts in employment create a fluid and turbulent situation. In such a situation, jobs naturally begin to disintegrate.

Jobs Are Change Inhibitors

With so much turbulence and so many changes that organizations must make to navigate the fast-moving currents of today's marketplace, many employees feel as though their organization has joined a change-of-the-month club. In interviews, they often remark that more of their energy goes into planning and managing change than turning out products and services. These changes would not take so much effort, however, if their organization's structure, procedures, values, and roles were more change-worthy.

Peter Drucker has recently said that "rapid knowledge-based change imposes one clear imperative: every organization has to build the management of change into its very structure." The difficulty is that the job is proving to be part of the problem, not part of the solution. That little packet of responsibility (job description), rewarded in accordance with a fixed formula (pay level), and a single reporting relationship (place in the chain of command) is a roadblock on the highway of change.

Throughout today's work world, we are witnessing a search for speed: faster product development, faster production, faster delivery, faster information processing, faster service, and faster implementation of all the changes necessary to keep up with changes in the marketplace. We are seeing a switch to a fast-break, no-huddle style of doing business. And jobs are disappearing as a result. This change-driven style of operations has emerged over the past decade, and recent events have simply capped the situation. Because conventional jobs inhibit flexibility and speedy response to the threats and opportunities of a rapidly changing market, many organizations are turning over even their most important tasks to temporary and contract workers or to external vendors. That way, when conditions change outside the organization, there is no turf guardian inside whose livelihood depends on not changing how things are done. There are problems using such dejobbed workers, of course, and we will discuss them in Chapter 7. But the fact that this strategy has pitfalls should not blind us to the fact that it represents one legitimate response to a serious problem.

The good times of the 1980s masked the changes in two different ways: First, the general economic expansion hid the fact that jobs were disappearing from organizations—you could, after all, get a new job if you lost an old one. Second, good times permitted many organizations to carry the extra baggage of their job structure without serious penalty, even though it had ceased to serve them well. Recession ended both of those situations, but it only triggered the change. Recession didn't cause it. The loss was caused by technological change and the amplifying feedback loop of responses to that change. Those new elements in the organizational world are not going to go away, so our task is to create effective and humane ways to live with them.

The Future Is Already with Us

When I first started circulating early versions of this book, reactions varied enormously:

At one end of the spectrum were people who thought the basic argument was crazy: "No more jobs? What'll everyone do—retire?" "Oh, come on! When the economy bounces back, companies will start hiring like crazy again."

There was a middle ground, ranging from "I don't want to hear this" to "I guess you're overstating the case to make your point—aren't you?" to "I never thought of it that way, but it makes sense."

I was ready for such reactions, because I had heard them whenever I spoke on the topic. I wasn't surprised that people denied the likelihood of a future they found threatening.

But the longer I worked on this project, the more I came to see that they weren't denying the future that would probably arrive, they were denying the present that was already with us. As Peter Drucker has reminded us, in predictable times we try to guess what will happen next, but in more turbulent times like ours, we need to ask, "What has already happened that will create the future?"

The disappearance of jobs is, with every passing month, more and more a "change that has already happened." It is also a change that can be exploited by individuals and organizations that know how to do so. Even if you are not innovation-minded, you need to deal with this change, for it is one of those shifts in the socioeconomic environment guaranteed to render obsolete the people and institutions that deny it.

The Rise and Fall of the Good Job

In most [pre–nineteenth-century English] households an adequate subsistence depended on a complex of various forms of task-work and wage labour. Regular, full-time employment at a single job was not the norm.

—R. W. Malcolmson

Less than half of the workforce in the industrial world will be in "proper" full-time jobs in organizations by the beginning of the twenty-first century.

—Charles Handy

The Job: The Building Block in American Organizations

In the preindustrial past, before factories routinized work, people worked very hard, but they did not utilize a job to frame and contain their activities. Then jobs became not only common but important; they were nothing less than the only widely available path to security and success. Now, however, they are disappearing from the economic landscape. Like some species caught in the flow and ebb of evolution, jobs emerged under one set of conditions and now begin to vanish under another.

It is hard for us to see these changes clearly, for we are too close to them. Marshall McLuhan used to say, "If you want to know about water, don't ask a fish." Jobs are the water we swim in. It's not that everyone has a good one or that in hard times everyone can get one, but that for most people, earning a living means having a job. Parents harangue their kids to "get a job" in the summer. Then they tell them how important it is to have "a good job" before you start a family. Americans grow up hearing people with "good jobs" praised or envied or resented, depending on the parent's own circumstances and perspective. But a good job clearly makes you somebody. Even as small children, long before Americans can understand what a job is, they pick up adults' anxieties when their jobs are at risk. They hear the worry as adults talk about neighbors or relatives who lost their jobs, and they may witness at close range the devastation that comes when a parent loses a job.

All of this is simply to say that contemporary Americans, both rich and poor, are programmed to view jobs as the natural building blocks in society and the very core of a stable life. An old joke tells of two factory workers speculating about how hard times might affect them:

First worker: "Is your job in jeopardy?"

Second worker: "No. My job is very secure. It's me they can do without."

People come and go; jobs stay. Well, no, not quite. Jobs come and go too, but only specific jobs—jobs in this industry and that. Jobs-as-a-concept stay. They form the bedrock of our economic planet.

Jobs in the Preindustrial World

But jobs are not a part of nature. They are historical products. Nothing makes that fact clearer than the changing meaning of the word itself: *job*. The words we use are living things with histories of their own, and when their meanings change over time we can be sure that changes have taken place in the social and psychological realities as well. I have used *job* almost one hundred times in the book so far. There aren't, it turns out, any simple synonyms for the way most people today get their money, their status, and many of their friends—in addition to their sense of belonging, their feeling of being productive, and their hopes for a better future.

The word job is an old one, going back before the year 1400.

But until 1800 it meant something different from what it does today. In the beginning, the word may have been a variant of *gob*, for it meant "a small compact portion of some substance; a piece, lump, a mouthful." (Both *job* and *gob* may in fact have originally come from a Celtic word *gob* or *gop* meaning "mouth.") Starting by meaning a "little piece" of stuff, the word began to expand its meaning to include "large piles" of stuff—like piles of hay or stable litter. (The idea that this original *job* might be a "pile of dung" sounds very modern to some workers.) Around the time the Pilgrims were arriving at Plymouth, the word took another step in meaning by shifting from the "large pile" itself to the act of transporting it in a cart. From there, it was only a short step to using *job* to refer to "any task which was a single piece of work."

We still use the word that way, when we praise someone by saying "Good job!" or "A job well done!" We also use this premodern meaning when we say, "I have a couple of jobs to do around the house this weekend." We talk about the "many jobs" there are to do on a farm and how it's good to have an "odd-jobs man" to do them. Churchill used this meaning when he spoke in favor of America's planned lend-lease of weapons to England at the start of World War II. "Give us the tools," he said, "and we'll do the job."

Various lines of meaning diverged from this basic meaning of job-as-task. One offshoot led to job-as-piece-of-business, as in "We decided to give the job to the printer on the corner." Another offshoot led to job-as-unit-of-work, as in "I get paid by the job." Still another, as in "I had a hard job finding it" or "She did a bad job of hiding her feelings," came to refer to almost any undertaking or effort.

Before 1800—and long afterward in many cases—*job* always referred to some particular task or undertaking, never to a role or a position in an organization. A job-wagon was one hired for a single occasion. Job-broking (or "brokering") was acting as a go-between to set up a piece of work or to act as a middleman who buys a "job-lot" (we still sometimes use that term) and resells it for profit. Between 1700 and 1890, The *Oxford English Dictionary* finds many uses of terms like *job-coachman, job-doctor,* and *job-*

gardener—all referring to people hired on a one-time basis. *Job-work* (another frequent term) was occasional work, not regular employment. There was even a verb *to job*, which meant "to do odd jobs, or to work by the piece." To modern ears it is ironic that *to job* was to do temporary work.

Language reflects social reality, and the reality of the pre–nineteenth-century world was that people did not "have" jobs in the fixed and unitary sense; they "did" jobs in the form of a constantly changing string of tasks. Their jobs were not provided by an organization, but by the demands of their life situation, the requirements of an employer, and the things that needed to be done in that time and place. Some of the jobs around a farm or homestead were minor everyday tasks and some were huge and laborious undertakings. Some were jobs done for oneself, and some were jobs done for hire. But in the preindustrial world, jobs were essentially activities, not positions.

The forerunners of today's jobs were already starting to take shape in this world of the village, however. They grew out of the weaving, the metalworking, and the shoemaking that craftspeople were doing in addition to their farming or shepherding. These craft activities were still job-work, in the old sense of the term. Yet as the common lands on which these people had kept gardens or grazed sheep began to be enclosed by their nominal owners, and as work in the new factories provided an alternative to household work, more and more people left the old-style job-work and did something radically different: they *got a job* in the new meaning of that word.

The First Great Job Shift

This transition into modern jobs was gradual, happening faster in some places than others. It is worth a quick review of what happened because it parallels and illuminates today's transition away from jobs. The same kinds of economic forces were at work, the same kinds of distress were generated, and people—then as today—polarized into those who were excited by the possibilities and those who were appalled by the costs.

In England the shift to jobs started around 1780 (in America it was half a century later). People were deeply traumatized. The old way of life had had a stability and coherence that was very hard to give up. The enclosure of the common lands, while legal in a technical sense, was an utter violation of centuries of unquestioned usage. English people had always had a "right" to use these lands under the common law, and it was only as the concept of property changed with the new ideas of capitalism that that right was swept aside.

The preindustrial values ran deep. As late as 1795, the Lord Chief Justice delivered an opinion that held that "engrossing" was still a punishable offense. This word referred to increasing the price of goods in the market by buying them cheaply in large lots and selling them for a profit in small quantities. (Under the name of wholesaling, engrossing would become an essential part of modern commerce, of course, and the word itself survives with no moral connotations in our word *grocery* store.) Like any people who see their whole way of life disintegrating, the village householders struck back at engrossers and other forerunners of the new order whenever they could, burning their flour mills, as well as confiscating and distributing foodstuffs believed to be priced too high.

In England the old rules (village customs and the common law) and the new rules (industrial practices and statute law) overlapped for a tumultuous half century between 1780 and 1830. The former represented order in a world that was disappearing, and the latter provided the ordering principles for a world that was taking shape. Working for wages was a precarious existence, and it created in the cities a kind of poverty that had never been known in the village. People protested and fought back. There were riots, arson, and killings. On the other side, the authorities handed out harsh punishments to anyone even suspected of those acts.

Many of the most sensitive writers and artists of that period denounced the factories and the cities that sprawled out around them. William Blake denounced "the dark satanic mills." Charles Dickens portrayed a long line of harsh and heartless employers who cared more for the job than the person who filled it. In *A Christmas Carol*, Bob Cratchit had a *job*, and (Christmas or no) it had to be done! Wordsworth wrote that "getting and spending, we lay waste our powers." (Note that he denounces "getting and spending" and not labor itself.) Thomas Carlyle cried out that it is "not the external and physical alone [that] is now managed by machinery, but the internal and spiritual also. . . . Men are grown mechanical in head and heart, as well as in hand."

In these reactions, we can see the beginning of a great divide in modern thinking between those who follow the line of socioeconomic development and those who take a more humanistic path. As with *job,* we can see what is happening in the changing meanings given to words, particularly in the way *industry* and *art* developed. At the time of the American Revolution, both words referred to human qualities rather than to areas of economic and vocational activity. *Industry* referred to the attributes of diligence, perseverance, and hard work, the qualities that we think of when we call someone industrious. It was Adam Smith, interestingly, who first used *industry* to refer to manufacturing and other productive activities. *Industrial* was spawned as an adjective to refer to such economic areas or institutions, while *industrious* kept the old meaning alive.

Art veered off in a different direction. It, too, originally referred to an attribute rather than an activity. In this case, it was "skill" or "ability" of a technical or practical sort. As a matter of fact, a person who had the "art" of some kind of work and the habit of "industry" would have made a good living in the pre-job world. But at the time that "industrial" activity was relocated into the factory, "art" was sent off to the painter's studio and the poet's garret. It likewise became a special activity (e.g., "the art of sculpture") or even (in "the arts") a special area of human effort. And ever since that time, there has been a kind of natural antagonism between the two, the industrialist seeing what the artist did as mere decoration, and the artist seeing the industrialist as corrupt and destructive.

The Transition to the New World of Jobs

The antagonism was fed on both sides by the distress that almost everyone felt during this changeover from the old world of the village to the new world of the factory. The partisans of the factory were embittered by the refusal of people to see the handwriting on the economic wall: The machine was changing everything, and those who resisted the new work conditions were standing in the way of progress. Industrial goods, they argued, could now be made available to all instead of the few. England could seize control of international commerce and accumulate wealth that would cascade down through the whole society to give everyone a better life.

On their side, the partisans of the village were embittered by what they saw as the destruction of England, its people, and its culture. The new world of jobs was destroying the old interpersonal relations that defined social rights and obligations; it was making obsolete the traditional crafts that had produced all of the household objects that everyone knew; and it was undermining the time-honored ways of interweaving home life and work life. On the one side the new industrialists emerged as a potent rival to the old power of the landed aristocracy; on the other side the Chartists and other radical groups emerged to challenge all power that was not populist. This polarization of the opinion-makers of the society fed the vehemence with which each side of the argument pursued its campaign and made the discovery of any common ground almost impossible. Each side had an important half-truth in hand. It *was* a threshold period in history and societies that succeeded in crossing the threshold into the machine age *would* have an enormous advantage over those that did not; and in time the new wealth *would* trickle down through most of the layers of society and bring comforts and little luxuries to almost everyone. At the same time, the conditions created by the early stages of industrialism *were* atrocious, and the society *was* being dragged into an only vaguely understood future at an enormous cost.

Even those who more or less successfully made the transition from the old world to the new had a terrible time of it. It is difficult for us today to appreciate how new and different the world of "holding a job" was for village-born people. They could no longer move about among a variety of tasks, in a variety of locations, on a schedule set by the sunlight and the weather and the particular demands of the season. There were no longer seasonal periods of slack and recovery to offset the periods of feverish activity. No longer could they intensify and speed up their efforts to complete a particularly urgent task and then drop everything to quit for the day or for the respite provided by a holiday. The demands of work in the factory never varied. They were uniform and all-encompassing. From dawn to dark, and much longer in the winter months, people worked in one place, doing one thing. That was their new *job*, and the word changed its meaning to reflect that new reality.

It was difficult to give up the old ways. Writing of early industrial workers in America, Herbert Guttman has noted that even after the Civil War, "despite the profound economic changes, . . . artisans did not easily shed stubborn and time-honoured work habits." By way of illustration, he refers to spontaneous partying that closed down work completely on occasion, as well as the chronic habit of "Blue Monday" (the hangover-extended Sunday holiday), which some groups of workers seemed to regard as their natural right.

It was hard to learn the job-based rules too. At the time, many did not believe that ordinary people could ever make the change because, as historian E. P. Thompson has written, it "entailed a severe restructuring of working habits—new disciplines, new incentives, and a new human nature upon which these incentives could bite effectively." Developing a "new human nature"! What an immense undertaking!

Take the matter of wages. People had always provided as much of their own food and clothing as they could and worked at (old-style) jobs for money to meet their extra or special needs. Once those needs were met, preindustrial people slipped back into subsistence until new needs arose. The idea of working constantly for wages and then using that money to purchase everything one needed; and the idea of continuing to work, even after essentials were provided for, to accumulate savings that could be used to buy a house, start a business, or provide for one's old age—these were totally new concepts and behaviors. "There was more to overcome," writes economic historian Sidney Pollard, "than the change of employment or the new rhythm of work; there was a whole new culture to be absorbed and an old one to be traduced and spurned."

Writers like Dr. Andrew Ure were self-selected guides on this journey. In his influential *Philosophy of Manufactures* (1835), Ure proved himself a forerunner to today's management gurus by laying out a total plan for creating the new habits, attitudes, and values that were required to do the new-style job effectively. These new jobholders required what Ure called an "education in 'methodical' habits, punctilious attention to instructions, fulfillment of contracts to time, and in the sinfulness of embezzling materials."

The relatively new institution of the Sunday school was pressed into service to teach these new workers, many of whom were only children, the proper new habits. Dr. Ure pressed the case for moral training hard on his audience: "It is, therefore, excessively the interest of every mill-owner to organize his moral machinery on equally sound principles with his mechanical, for otherwise he will never command the steady hands, watchful eyes, and prompt cooperation, essential to excellence of product."

Summing up the influence of such "education," E. P. Thompson writes that "it is clear that between 1780 and 1830 important changes took place. The 'average' English working man became more disciplined, more subject to the productive tempo of 'the clock,' more reserved and methodical, less violent and less spontaneous." He notes that contemporary observers complained that the traditional village sports of quoits, wrestling, football, "prison-bars," and archery were becoming obsolete by the end of that period and that passive hobbies and innocuous pastimes were taking their place. From the vantage point of an age where most people are couchbound and watch their sports on TV, nineteenth-century hobbies and pastimes look relatively active; but compared to those that characterized village life, they were not.

The transition from *doing jobs* to *having a job* came later in the United States than in England (after 1840), and the trauma was somewhat buffered by the fact that people were not being forced off the land here as often as they had been there. The transition was, nonetheless, difficult enough. And it was recapitulated in a concentrated and painful form with each new wave of "village folk" from Ireland, Germany, Italy, Poland, and Russia that landed on American shores. This continous flow of immigration extended the duration of the transition from the old ways of working to the new ones. Long after the sons and daughters of New Hampshire farms were settled solidly into the new world of jobs in Boston or New York, boatload after boatload of village people from southern and eastern Europe were being faced with a crash course in the skills and disciplines necessary to manage the demands of a job.

Today's World: The Second Great Job Shift

You cannot read about the coming of industrialism, first in England and then in America, without thinking of the present. For once again we have come to a turning point at which the assumptions about living and working that people had grown comfortable with are being challenged. And once again we are polarizing between those who don't acknowledge the cost of moving ahead and those who can't see the cost of staying in place. This time we are grouping into those, on the one hand, who are dazzled by the promise of the electronic age and impatient with people who have misgivings about change and those, on the other, who are alarmed by the growing gap between haves and have-nots and the impact we are having on the environment. This time it is not Dr. Ure vs. the Chartists, but Tom Peters vs. the UAW, or *The Wall Street Journal* vs. The Sierra Club.

You get a snapshot of the new polarization if you compare the *Time* magazine article by Lance Morrow called "The Temping of America" with Tom Peters' response to that article. Morrow writes of "the great corporate clearances of the '90s, the ruthless restructuring efficiencies." He says that "millions of Americans are being evicted from the working worlds that have sustained them." He talks of the sense of "betrayal" among American workers, comparing it to that felt by our troops in Vietnam.

Peters belittles Morrow's article and responds to its "hand-wringing" with a rebuttal full of upbeat talk about the exciting possibilities created by an entrepreneurial workforce. Near the end he admits that the transformation of today's employees into "business people" will be "utterly wrenching" and that it will take "decades." But the whole tone of his piece conveys clearly the message that anyone who is worried about today's transition is a "hand-wringer."

Peters' lack of empathy echoes an even harsher assessment of the situation, which is quoted in a lead *Wall Street Journal* article on reengineering. This is the article, cited earlier, that contained the estimate that reengineering could ultimately cost 25 million Americans their jobs. It notes that the question of where so many new jobs will come from is a perplexing one, but it concludes with a statement by Princeton economist Orly Ashenfelter, "'Just let the market take care of it,' advises Ashenfelter, who is critical of recent hand-wringing about a lack of 'good' jobs. 'I think what that means is a job that pays more than you are worth.'" Dickens's Ebenezer Scrooge couldn't have said it better. Bah, hand-wringing!

As was the case a century ago, each side of this argument is articulating an important half-truth. The organizational experts and the economists are right when they say that these changes are coming, whether we want them or not. And they are right in pointing out that there are real opportunities. It is also worth saying, as some of them do, that these changes once again put a premium on the distinctively American values of self-reliance and individualism.

But it is equally true that this shift undermines something on which most people built their sense of security and that it takes away the core of many people's identity. When people lose things of such magnitude, they easily lose hope too. It is not enough to let the market take care of the problem, for there is simply too much "social breakage" in such a policy. We will address the question of how to handle the transition to a job-free career in Chapter 6. Here we will confine ourselves to the question of what will take the place of the job, for without a clearer picture than most people have of other possibilities, the future is going to look even darker than it needs to.

What Do People Do without Jobs?

Some of the alternatives to jobs are obvious: you can start a business of your own; you can become an artist; you can become a consultant; you can do freelance work, or part-time work, or piecework in your home. And under the pressure of the dejobbing in American organizations, more people than ever before are doing all of these things. But there is also another answer, which is harder to articulate (and impossible to measure) because it does not fall within the familiar outlines of "part time" and "self-employment." That answer is that you can do what more and more people are doing: working within organizations as full-time employees but under arrangements too fluid and idiosyncratic to be called jobs.

"You won't last at Microsoft if your job is just a job." That is how Teresa Stowell, a software design engineer, describes what it is like to work at the Seattle software powerhouse. To begin with, there are no regular hours; buildings are open to workers twenty-four hours a day. People work anytime and all the time, with no one keeping track of their hours, but with everyone watching their output. They are accountable not to conventional managers but to the project teams of which they are a part. Those teams, in turn, are likely to be subsets of some larger group, and in a very big project like the development of the Windows operating system for PCs, there may be many project-within-larger-project groupings.

Within each team, individuals are always given a little more than they can accomplish on their own, so there is constant collaboration among team members. New employees, given important responsibilities from day one, are assigned a "buddy/mentor" to help them learn the ropes. In the words of a reporter who interviewed people throughout the company, Microsoft "trusts them to do what they already know how to do, turns them loose to solve problems and helps them when they get stuck."

Workers make regular reports to their team on how their work

is going. If an individual is not getting his or her share of the
common project done, the team is going to suffer. According to
software developer Tom Corbett, "It doesn't take long to
straighten out a team member who isn't pulling his weight. The
next team meeting, in which a developer stands before the group
to explain what he has contributed to the project lately, becomes
a strong incentive to have the work done, and done right." As we
shall see in a moment, the pressures generated in this way can
become very intense.

When a project ends, Microsoft employees move on to a new
one, taking with them the reputation they earned at the last project. There are no standardized career routes, and in the words of
human resources manager Mike Canizales:

> If people want to change functions or they want to go get
> different experiences, that's not frowned on at all. There's a
> lot of movement internally and laterally. . . . Employees
> drive their own development, and we need to design all of
> our management and our training programs to support,
> augment and facilitate that development. . . . [You] start
> from the person's goals—the long-term goals—and then fit
> in your short-term tactical methods for augmenting those
> [goals].

Lest you think that the dejobbed world of Microsoft is pure
paradise, there is another side. The dejobbed system lacks the
normal kinds of "edges" that tell workers when they have done a
normal, satisfactory job. Since they are expected to do *anything
necessary* to accomplish the expected results, they are no longer
protected by the boundaries of a job. *Normal* and *satisfactory* come
to be synonyms for *substandard*. Microsoft employees, like those
at many other dejobbed companies, are expected to work beyond
the limits that any job could set for them.

Many projects include round-the-clock periods of work. The
recently released Windows NT program is a case in point. Two
hundred code writers, broken down into teams, entered the project as if it were some underground cavern. That is, they disappeared. Driven by David Cutler, the Windows NT leader who, in
the words of a *Wall Street Journal* writer, "shares some character

traits with Captains Ahab and Bligh," they worked incredibly
hard and struggled with one another constantly. Toward the end,
as they pushed (and were pushed by Cutler) to have a finished
"kit" ready for a software developers' conference in July 1992,
the project turned into what some of them called The Death
March. "The workload increased, the briefings and builds [pro-
gressively more complete integrations of the various program
pieces] were extended to Saturdays and Sundays, dinners were
brought in, and a fair number began sleeping at work—under
desks, in lounges and on the floor." One programmer's marriage
broke up. ("I didn't even try to save [it]," she reflected afterward.) Another programmer's son told him as he dropped the
little boy off at a soccer game on his way to work on a Saturday
morning, "I would throw away all my toys if you would be here
after the game." (He decided to forgo work that day.) And a few
simply quit.

But the kit was delivered on time. In the words of a developer
who attended the conference, "It was a turning point. It moved
NT from being all talk to being a viable product." Was it worth it?

[The workers] are divided in their feelings about the future.
Many eagerly anticipate working on the next version of NT,
while others sense that a chapter in their lives has ended.
Some are tired, almost to the breaking point. . . . Says
Charles Whitmer, a graphics programmer: "A lot of people
are angry, tired and burned out."

The same freedom from job limits that unleashes enormous effort also encourages people to overextend themselves.

This is not an unusual outcome at the end of one of these
immense dejobbed projects. Ex–Apple CEO John Sculley once
estimated that at Apple a third of the people on a new-product
development team quit the company for six months or more
("weary and burned out") after the product has been launched.
Most of them eventually return to the company, however. We will
discuss the psychological costs of the dejobbed work life in a later
chapter. Here we simply want to note how different this way of
working is from the job-based 9 to 5.

Not coincidentally, the pattern described by Sculley is reminiscent of how historian E. P. Thompson characterized work patterns among English artisans who had not yet given in to the demands of an industrial job: "alternate bouts of intense labour and of idleness." Consider also this nineteenth-century description of a cabinetmaker's shop in preindustrialized America: "Frequently . . . after several weeks of real hard work . . . a simultaneous cessation from work took place. As if . . . by tacit agreement, every hand contributed loose change, and an apprentice left the place and speedily returned laden with wine, brandy, biscuits, and cheese." That is nothing less than the forerunner of the Friday-afternoon beer busts that were common in the early histories of Silicon Valley electronics companies.

Other Examples of Dejobbed Organizations

IDEO Product Development, a 130-employee developer of high-tech products located in Palo Alto, California, is the largest industrial-design firm in the United States. *Inc.* magazine featured the company in its second annual survey of "The Best Small Companies to Work For In America." In its description of the company, the magazine noted: "At IDEO, no one has a title, or a boss, for that matter. Designers form teams around specific projects; each of those teams has a leader whose authority lasts only as long as the project, so today's manager may be tomorrow's subordinate."

In such an environment it is much harder to track the reporting relationships that used to be the glue in the world of jobs. After describing an overlapping set of groups that was working together to design and implement a complex project for a major client, the then-president of Union Pacific Railroad, Mike Walsh, said simply, "Everyone reports to each other."

Or consider Chiat & Day, the advertising firm that created the famous Apple Super Bowl ad, which showed corporate types, looking like something from Orwell's *1984*, marching in lockstep over the edge of a cliff—only to be "liberated" from their bondage by a female figure representing the creativity offered by Apple. How do people get their work done at Chiat & Day? Account executive Sean Hardwick said, "I've been here two years and I've never seen a job description."

That these organizations, some large and some small, function differently from traditional organizations is not really news—although just how they function is not widely understood. But what is news is that they do what they do without conventional jobs. It is as though the San Francisco 49ers or the Miami Dolphins were discovered to have done away with positions, playing a given player sometimes in the defensive line and sometimes at running back. But that metaphor is inadequate, because football is too position-driven a game. Listen to how Lori Sweningson, the CEO of Minneapolis-based Job Boss Software (another of the *Inc.* magazine "best companies to work for"), describes the way her people interact as a team: "I think of the company as a volleyball team. It takes three hits to get the ball over the net, and it doesn't matter who hits it." What a different game we are in!

Companies are still trying to find how best to describe these new work arrangements for people. One electronics company acknowledges that job descriptions make no sense any longer and that they provide employees no guidance once they get caught up in organizational activity, but it still uses them for hiring and setting initial salary levels. (Not surprisingly, the human resources vice president at this company is a little nervous that some new hire will sue it for misrepresenting the terms of employment.)

■ At the Grass Valley Group, a California maker of television broadcast equipment, they use "flexible job profiles," which (as the name suggests) change frequently. They describe the outcomes for which the individual is accountable.

■ At Intel Corporation, Marile Robinson, the redeployment manager, says, "We no longer look at a job as a function or a certain kind of work. Instead, we see it as a set of skills and competencies." Intel, like many other companies, uses this "skill set" as the basis for training and evaluation.

■ In many parts of Hewlett-Packard, managers are using "ranking" as a way of evaluating people. To do this, they take everyone in a particular group and put them into a numbered list according to their "value" to the group. Such a value, needless to say, has little to do with their job, for it measures total contribution and cuts across all job categories.

Each of these approaches has its pitfalls, and no one I've talked to feels very confident about having found the answer. But the significance of these examples is that people are searching for alternatives to jobs and job descriptions.

Don't be misled by the fact that some of the foregoing examples have been taken from small firms. Big companies are beginning to work without jobs too. A senior executive from a large Canadian corporation described to Gareth Morgan the way in which what used to be distinctly different jobs are blending together. "Secretaries are becoming managers and many managers are becoming secretaries! As the new technology is introduced, conventional roles, patterns of decision making, and general relations change." Under such conditions what used to be fixed jobs become flexible roles, which cannot be described in terms of "duties" (which are established) but only by relationships to other parts of the system (which are likely to change). That is the way it is at the huge and wholly project-driven computer services firm EDS, where one of the linchpin elements in the system is the "sub-project team leader." Tom Peters, who studied how such a figure actually worked, concluded that the function was "a role more than a detailed job title."

Jobs (and the "job-mindedness" that they create) make it difficult for any size organization in any field to respond quickly to a rapidly changing market. At Condé Nast Publications, former executive Véronique Vienne complained that "employees who try to keep a tight hold on their job miss the point and fail to comprehend the reason why they were hired in the first place: to contribute to the molecular activity at the magazine. . . . " The variable is not the size of the organization or the economic sector it operates in. The variable is how rapidly its environment forces it to change how it works.

The New Focus: The Work That Needs to Be Done

What Lori Sweningson is doing with her volleyball metaphor is breaking down the attitude and habit pattern that Véronique

Vienne found so damaging at Condé Nast. Let's call it the TIM-J syndrome: "That Isn't My Job. It's his or hers or I-don't-know-whose, but it's not my job!" David Glines, the head of employee development at the San Diego Zoo, tells a story that illustrates the point. (That was the zoo, you remember, where they reengineered work processes and reorganized their organization into cross-functional teams that run Gorilla Tropics, Tiger River, and half a dozen other bioclimatic-zone exhibits.) Glines had started working at the zoo as a groundsman. His job had been to keep the zoo's paths and public areas free of trash. When there was a lot to do or when he was tired, "sometimes I'd sweep a cigarette butt under a bush. Then it was the gardener's problem, not mine." In a job-based organization, work doesn't get done. It gets "passed around," to get rid of it (if no one wants it) or to find its proper home (if everyone wants it).

Leaders and managers who are trying to speed up the pace of change in their organizations will find themselves pitted against job-mindedness. Robert Frey, the CEO of Cin-Made, a manufacturer of specialized cans and containers, was trying to turn around that rapidly declining, old-style company:

My role was to make sure that people [at Cin-Made] changed at a faster pace than they would ever have chosen for themselves. . . . I made people meet with me, then instead of *telling* them what to do, I *asked* them. They resisted.

"How can we cut the waste on this run?" I'd say, or, "How are we going to allocate the overtime on this order?"

"That's not my job," they'd say.

"Why not?" I'd say.

"Well, it just isn't," they'd say.

"But I need your input," I'd say. "How in the world can we have participative management if you won't participate?"

"I don't know," they'd say. "Because that's not my job either. That's *your* job."

Where the business of an organization is all parceled out into jobs, it isn't going to be easy to change how it is done or to get it done faster.

So What Should We Do?

The common answer—which is good, as far as it goes—is to educate people about the larger outcomes that the organization is trying to achieve and show them where their "piece of the work" fits in the larger pattern. But such efforts are maddeningly slow, and the results are often disappointing. We say that the workers "just don't get it" and are "only concerned with themselves." What we fail to see is that we are encouraging those limited outlooks by keeping them in *jobs*, organizing them into clusters of *jobs*, evaluating them as to how well they do their *jobs*, and paying them according to a *job*-based pay system.

"We are trained to be loyal to our jobs—so much so that we confuse them with our own identities." That statement, by Peter Senge, suggests why jobs have such a powerful hold on our thinking. We'll return to this point in Chapter 6, when we discuss how to deal with the deep and pervasive psychological impacts of dejobbing. In the present context, the point is that Senge makes his statement in a chapter called "Does Your Organization Have a Learning Disability?" He lists seven "disabilities" that keep organizations from learning what they need to know to survive in a rapidly changing environment.

Disability #1 is "I Am My Position." Senge describes how American automotive design engineers used three different kinds of bolts (which required different wrenches) in an engine block, while their Japanese counterparts used one. Why? Because the American engineers were simply "doing their jobs"—that is, their three, separate tasks. The other side of the TIM-J coin is IJDM-J: "I'm Just Doing My Job." The job world encourages people to do things that don't really contribute to a good outcome by telling them to "just do your job."

Focusing on the Team Task

You can illustrate the shift from the prejob world, to the world of jobs, to a world that is being dejobbed by comparing how tasks get done on the dominant modes of long-range transportation in those three worlds. The prejob world used sailing ships. Sailing requires an enormous amount of activity, but the sailors were

loosely grouped into task units rather than given narrowly defined jobs. When the sails had to come down, everyone pitched
in. When the boat had to be unloaded, everyone pitched in. The
twenty-four hours of a day were divided into "watches," but otherwise people did not have fixed hours of work. You worked long
but variable hours every day, taking time off only when the boat
reached port. (Then sailors could celebrate in true artisan fashion.) The boat itself was an autonomous floating world, with few
levels of command. The captain, though subordinate to the
boat's owner, was given total autonomy over operations. TIM-J
had no place on the sailing ship. It was a crew operation.

Then came the railroad. The train itself was much more closely
tied to the larger organization. Policies and time schedules were
set, not by someone on board but by someone "at headquarters,"
someone at a higher level of command. People had firm jobs. The
fireman shoveled coal; the engineer drove the train; the conduc-
tor took tickets and supervised the passenger areas; the porters
took care of passenger needs; the dining-car steward and the
waiters handled meals. Everyone had a job. Running on time and
providing good service resulted from people doing their separate
jobs well. Conductors didn't shovel coal, engineers didn't carry
luggage, waiters didn't drive the train. We talk of this as "division
of labor," but that is a fancy name for a system in which everyone
has a job and does it. TIM-J was not only common on trains, it
was expected behavior.

Then the airliner came along. At first, it was jobs all over again.
And there are still pretty clear task responsibilities. But contemporary airlines are starting to move away from traditional jobs
and toward CRM, or crew resource management. As practiced by
most airlines, CRM "focuses on communication, team building,
work-load management, situation awareness, decision making,
and a host of other safety related topics." Southwest Airlines,
however, has taken it a step further: Their version of "CRM
training treats the crew, rather than the individual, as the job
performer." Pilots are not given the familiar military job of
"commander" or the industrial jobs of "boss," or even "manager." Instead, according to Captain Pete Wolfe, the chair of

Southwest's CRM Steering Committee, "We see pilots as team leaders." It isn't coincidental that Southwest is currently the only airline of any size that is making money—or that it is consistently at the top of the on-time listings, and at the bottom of the number-of-complaints listings.

Finally, there is the NASA flight crew. They have specialties. Indeed, they must be just about the most individually specialized operating team in any transportation system. But their special knowledge and skill are team resources to be drawn upon in special situations, not the basis of and rationale for distinct and exclusive roles. Their specialties do not limit their function in the joint endeavor. Most of the time, they are operating together as a cross-trained, tightly knit unit that is collectively responsible for the success of the mission. Just as the sailing ship belonged to a world before jobs, the space ship belongs to a world after jobs.

The "New Rules" of Employment

We are much farther down the path toward the dejobbed organization than most people think. Already people are starting to go back to the old meaning of the word *job*, talking about the "jobs" they have to get done today at the factory or the "job" they promised to do for a coworker at the office. At the totally project-organized Oticon, a very successful Danish hearing-aid manufacturer, an employee told Tom Peters that she "used to say I was a secretary, but now I suppose I'm more like an 'octopus' " (a slang term in Danish for somebody who does a little of this and a little of that).

> I take care of more things. . . . Now I work for a project leader in the legal department, for example. That can be exciting. I do investigative *jobs* for him, not just typing. . . . [He and other project leaders] tell me when they need the *job* done and I tell them whether I can manage it. It's my obligation to keep the *jobs* organized, and get done what I promised on time. [Italics added]

We're back to doing jobs, not having them. Or rather, not back but forward into the dejobbed organization of tomorrow.

Such an organization operates according to wholly new rules. Yesterday's organizations, built on the job paradigm,

■ "located" the employee at a particular level of a vertical hierarchy, responsible to the person above and responsible for the people (if any) below;

■ "located" the employee horizontally, as well, in a department or functional unit that was responsible for some particular kind of work, for example, engineering, accounting, or sales;

■ gave each employee a well-defined area of responsibility, which was formalized in a job description;

■ laid out before ambitious employees "career paths" that they could aspire to follow upward through the hierarchy and the salary structures of the company—a stepping-stone path of jobs toward greater power and financial reward.

The intersection of the vertical and horizontal axes, bounded by the job description, was the employee's place in the organization: his or her *job*. The rules were that if you did this job well, you could look forward to upward promotion through the ranks and a long (in many places, lifelong) career. You had job security. You would have to move when the organization said to, of course, and you might have to submit to other things you didn't like. But the organizational beatitudes made it clear that the jobholders were blessed and would get the rewards.

The old rules are gone. Finished. Disappeared and left no forwarding address. Although organizations are remarkably uncomfortable in articulating them, some new rules have been slowly coming into focus, and the sooner today's workers understand them, the better off they will be. The new rules are these:

■ Everyone is a *contingent* worker, not just the part-time and contract workers. Everyone's employment, that is, is contingent on the results that the organization can achieve.

■ Recognizing the turbulence in the business environment, workers need to regard themselves as people whose value to the organization must be demonstrated in each successive situation they find themselves in.

■ In the light of their "contingency," workers need to develop a mindset, an approach to their work, and a way of managing their own careers that is more like that of an external vendor than that of a traditional employee. Workers will be wise to think that they are "in business for themselves" and that their tasks have, in effect, been outsourced to them by the organization.

■ In its own interests, the wise company will work with these new-style workers collaboratively to make the relation as beneficial to them as possible, but the "benefits" of this new work arrangement will be different from the old ones. They will likely inhere in the nature of the work itself rather than being add-ons, like sick leave, guaranteed pensions, and free health care.

■ Workers must, therefore, also act like people in business for themselves by maintaining a plan for career-long self-development, by taking primary responsibility for investing in health insurance and retirement funds, and by renegotiating their compensation arrangements with the organization when and if organizational needs change.

■ Because more and more of the organization's efforts are likely to be undertaken by project teams made up of individuals from different functional backgrounds, workers must be able to switch their focus rapidly from one task to another, to work with people with very different vocational training and mindsets, to work in situations where the group is the responsible party and the manager is only a coordinator, to work without clear job descriptions, and to work on several projects at the same time.

■ Just as workers will need to be ready to shift from project to project within the same organization, they should expect that much more frequently than in the past they will have to move from one organization to another. Long-term employment is, for most workers, a thing of the past. The organization will try to minimize these shifts, recognizing that they are difficult and disruptive to the effectiveness of both the organization and the worker. But both parties will have to make their long-term plans with the likelihood of such shifts in mind.

■ Recognizing that these are new and difficult demands, the

organization will do its part in providing information, training, and counsel to people who are making this difficult transition from the old rules to the new rules; but ultimately it is the workers, individually, who must manage this transition in their careers and their lives.

These new rules are still evolving and are becoming operative in some parts of the economy more quickly than in others. Nowhere would there be complete agreement with them as they have been stated here, but everywhere companies are either openly or covertly moving toward them. At Sun Microsystems, Apple Computer, Intel, and a hundred smaller high-tech companies, these rules are already obvious—though seldom spelled out so explicitly.

There is, in fact, considerable nervousness about saying these things in so many words. The human resources staff at one successful Silicon Valley company wrote out a draft version of the "new employment conditions," and one member of the group started circulating it among senior managers with a request for their comments. The human resources vice president was immediately called by another vice president, who said, "Do you know what [your subordinate] is doing? Stop him. Don't let that paper get into circulation!" He went on to say that such a statement would "give people ideas" and that it would make employment at the company seem "insecure" (my, my!). Besides, since Company X (their major competitor) did not talk about employment this way, people might jump ship, thinking that "jobs" at Company X were more secure.

If articulating the new realities can still be controversial in high-tech companies, it is completely unacceptable in slower-moving industries; in the traditional professions of education, medicine, and law; and in government service, where job security has been highly prized. But even in those organizations, we see layoffs, early retirements (which, whatever the terminology, are often not voluntary), reorganizations that lead to de facto demotions, cancellations or radical trimming of benefit packages, and forced relocations and functional reassignments. All of these actions say clearly that the rules have changed.

These new rules spell the end of jobs as we have known them. They define an approach to work and a career path that few of today's employees understand. Unless we can begin soon to re-educate our workforce in these new expectations and the economic realities that have shaped them, we are in for decades of economic chaos that will damage our organizations and devastate several generations of workers. Without such reeducation, our workers will be like the eighteenth-century British redcoats who marched into battle shoulder to shoulder in the traditional way, only to get mowed down by fighters from the New World, who operated singly and in little teams, moving quickly from place to place, using the natural terrain to their advantage, and operating under new rules.

Armies, it has been said, are always trying to fight the last war, not the present one. They, like nonmilitary organizations, are essentially conservative. (Even startup companies try to replicate the history of the previous generation of startups.) And the more successful they have been in the past, the more difficult it is for them to pick up the clues that signal a sea change in how work is going to be done in the future. It was so in the America of 150 years ago, when industrialism transformed work into jobs. It is so today, when jobs are being transformed into something else.

You may not notice the change in the rules until you leave your present situation, for until then your assumptions and expectations may be protected by the refusal of everyone around you to deal with the new realities. Such a situation reminds one of the story of Balmung, the magic sword belonging to the Germanic hero Siegfried. Balmung was so sharp that it could slice an armored warrior in two, from the top of his helmet to the soles of his iron boots. But the cut was so fine that the wounded man could not even feel it. Until he moved. And then he fell into two pieces. Today's jobholders may likewise feel that nothing has happened. But just wait until they leave their jobs!

A Career Guide for the Twenty-first-Century Worker

I was used to working in the corporate environment and giving my total loyalty to the company. I feel like Rip van Winkle. You wake up and the world is all changed. The message from industry is, "We don't want your loyalty. We want your work." What happened to the [American] dream?

—Former Chicago advertising executive,
now working as a temp for $10 an hour

Our employees look at change and learning as job security.
—Harry Quadracci, CEO of Quad/Graphics

What percentage of the workforce is "temporary"? Estimates vary from article to article, but the real point of what we have discussed in the last two chapters is that the estimates are all too low. The real figure is 100 percent. *All* jobs in today's economy are temporary—for two reasons.

1. As we have been arguing, the work arrangement itself ("the job") is a social artifact on the wane, along with the conditions that created it; and so it is only temporarily a significant part of the economic scene.

2. The work arrangements that are taking its place, whatever their details, are themselves temporary in the sense that they are created to meet the productivity needs in an immediate but changing situation.

Thus, even the full-time employment of a general manager or a vice president, with a place at the top of the organizational chart, is contingent on a continuing need for what he or she does. And needs change overnight, as many executives and senior managers have found to their dismay in the past several years. That's why AT&T, until recently a job-based outfit if there ever was one, has stopped referring to *any* of its positions as permanent ones.

Employment security is going through one of those fundamental redefinitions that marks a societal turning point. Now security resides in the person rather than the position, and to a cluster of qualities that have nothing to do with the organization's policies or practices. From now on, you will have a harder and harder time finding security in a job. In the future your security will depend on your developing three characteristics as a worker and as a person:

1. **Employability:** Your security will come first and foremost from being an attractive prospect to employers, and that attractiveness involves having the abilities and attitudes that an employer needs at the moment. Ironically, the employer's need is likely to be created by the very changes that destroyed traditional job security.

2. **Vendor-mindedness:** Being a traditional, loyal employee is no longer an asset. It has, in fact, turned into a liability. So stop thinking like an employee and start thinking like an external vendor who has been hired to accomplish a specific task.

3. **Resiliency:** Organizations today operate in such a turbulent environment that no arrangement serves them for very long. What you will need (both for the organization's sake and for your own) is the ability to bend and not break, to let go readily of the outdated and learn the new, to bounce back quickly from disappointment, to live with high levels of uncertainty, and to find your security from within rather than from outside.

These abilities and attitudes will provide you with the only kind of security that exists today, because they will fit you for what is going to be the work world of the foreseeable future: the project, and an organization built around a changing mix of projects. A quarter of a century ago, Melvin Anshen wrote a prophetic article in the *Harvard Business Review* in which he argued that the "accelerating dynamics of technologies, markets, information systems, and social expectations of business performance" were beginning to undermine any kind of organizational design that encouraged a built-in bias in favor of the status quo:

> The single organization pattern that is free from this built-in bias, is the project cluster. Project-oriented structures offer the important advantages of tailor-made design to fit unique tasks, flexible resource commitments, defined termination points, and an absence of enduring commitment that encourages resistance to innovation.

Although the average American organization has not yet abandoned traditional vertical hierarchies in favor of project clusters, time has only served to underscore the logic of Anshen's insight. In fields where rapidly changing technology, fashion, or work demands (e.g., CNN, where "the business" changes hourly), projects have already become the norm. Where that has happened, the terms of work have been reframed: away from positions and toward assignments or even gigs. People move from one organization to another (or even out of employment completely, for periods of recuperation or self-employment) more frequently than people do in traditional organizations. Such a situation creates a gravitational pull toward contractual arrangements and a corresponding push away from employment in the traditional sense.

In the light of the changing history of the word *job*, it is worth noting that *employment* too has shifted its meaning. Its original meaning had nothing to do with work. It meant simply being "applied to some specific purpose." The employment of a person or thing was its "use." By Shakespeare's time, it had picked up a work-related connotation, but (like job) it meant work that was occasional and temporary. Oliver Goldsmith wrote in 1760, "I went from town to town, working when I could get employment." As more and more people were employed in modern, full-time jobs, however, *employment* lost its meaning of engagement on a time-limited basis for some particular purpose.

But today we need to go back to the original meanings of *employment*, just as we find that people are already beginning to return to the earlier meanings of *job*. Employment is becoming temporary and situational again, and categories are losing their boundaries. Today, when working sixty or seventy hours a week is common, a "half-time" worker can easily put in thirty hours a week. At the same time, Wal-Mart touts its employment growth but defines full-time work as twenty-eight hours or more.

The line between the self-employed condition and working for an "employer" has likewise become unclear: Communications technology and flex-work arrangements allow official, full-time employees to telecommute and to do their forty hours a week without leaving home. At the same time, self-employed people may get contracts that not only require them to perform the tasks that used to be done by a jobholder, but also give them an in-house office, membership on a task force within the organization, and even a discount at the employee store.

If you are like most people, you don't have a very good idea how to dance to this music. But thousands and thousands of people, just as puzzled and discouraged by their situation as you are, have learned to do well in it. And you can too.

When you read that, you may feel like starting to argue why these techniques won't work in your case. It may even make you suspicious and angry to hear someone say that there is a way out of your bind. And I grant that you have evidence. You might claim:

- The situation is impossible. Look at the numbers.
- Maybe a few individuals can work out ways to live without jobs, but this is a big social problem. We need a solution that millions can follow!
- You tried to start a new career once. It didn't work.
- That fancy career-rebuilding stuff is for the well-educated people. You just want a job.

If you catch yourself making such excuses to yourself or others, watch out. Such excuses will immobilize you.

Besides, you don't have to make excuses, as though you had something to be ashamed of. It isn't your fault that you were brought up on a diet of Get-a-Good-Job-and-You're-All-Set. Of course you bought into it. Everyone did. It would have been almost un-American to do otherwise. It isn't your fault that you were born just in time to get swept up in The Second Great Job Shift. Everyone is in the same boat today.

As to the argument that your career-rebuilding project is only an individual solution to a very widespread social problem, there are a couple of answers. The first is that we are going to tackle "societal remedies" in Chapter 8, and you'll see that there are, indeed, things that the government can and must do to deal with dejobbing. The second answer is that social action in America is a painfully slow process, and if you wait for it you'll be making a big mistake. You can't put your life on hold while politicians and special-interest groups fight it out. You need to put together a personal strategy, at least for the short term.

As far as your past efforts that didn't work, they probably weren't as well motivated as this one will be. It's one thing when your job goes away, but it is much more serious when jobs in general start to vanish. Remember, we're dealing with an irreversible change here. The job hugger is going to be left clutching an empty sack. A few minor changes and a resolve to work harder aren't going to do it this time. You need a fresh strategy for a new day that is distinctly different from yesterday, and the time is growing short.

Finally, as to the argument that this career-redesign stuff is just for the talented and the well educated (those aren't the same, incidentally), you're still working inside the old job paradigm. In that system, things *were* rigged in favor of the haves. Education? That takes money. Experience? Sure, but yours is in an old industry, not one of the new upscale ones. Skills? You're too old to learn new ones. But listen: formal education, experience, and skills are not what tomorrow's career-building will depend on.

Instead, reinventing your work life depends on four new strategies, each of which requires some abilities and attitudes that old-style career development did not. A Ph.D. from M.I.T. or an M.B.A. from Stanford does not develop these attributes, nor do ten years of good job evaluations at DuPont or Hewlett-Packard.

We'll devote this section of the book to showing how to develop and practice these abilities and attitudes, but here they are in brief.

1. Learn to see every potential work situation, inside an organization as well as outside it, as a market. Even people who are currently out of work will find, ironically, that many of their best prospects for future work situations are in the organization that recently laid them off or talked them into taking an early retirement.

2. Survey your D.A.T.A. (that is, your Desires, Abilities, Temperament, and Assets) and recycle them into a different and more viable "product." Every market is full of people who are looking for products, even when no jobs are being advertised. You just have to know how to turn your resources into what they are looking for.

3. Take the results of #2, build a business (let's call it You & Co.) around it, and learn to run it. In the years ahead, you are going to get less mileage out of a career plan in the old-fashioned sense than out of a "business plan" for your own personal enterprise. Whether or not you are employed in what we used to call a job, you are henceforth in business for yourself.

4. Learn about the psychological impacts of life in this new work world, and put together a plan for handling them successfully. It isn't going to be enough to know where you're going if you can't stand the stresses of the place once you arrive.

While these strategies will take some time to learn to execute really well, they do not take special skills or unusual levels of intelligence and creativity. In the early stages, their practice may feel strange and somewhat uncomfortable, but think back on your early jobs: you were learning a new way of functioning that initially felt unnatural back then too. You did it once, and you can do it again. The next four chapters will help you put together a career and life plan for the years ahead.

Everything Is a Market

He that will not apply new remedies must expect new evils; for time is the greatest innovator.

—Francis Bacon, "Innovation," *Essays*

We've said that being committed to "jobs" is to be enclosed in a paradigm—that is, to define a piece of the world (the work one does) by establishing boundaries and setting rules for operating inside those boundaries. The job is part of a larger paradigm, as well: the organization.* The jobholder's world is organizational, for there aren't any jobs outside organizations. In the job world, everything (including the job) serves an organizational master. Jobs are an essential element in the same world that contains

---

*I am using *organization* to cover the widest possible range of employers, including big corporations, small firms, educational and health-service institutions, nonprofit associations, and government agencies. You can substitute *hospital, automobile manufacturer, law firm, community college, department store,* or wherever your job is (or was) located each time you see *organization.*

plans, budgets, hierarchy, traditions, salary, supervision, and reporting relationships. Jobs are "boxes of activity" that are bounded by job descriptions. Job descriptions are to the organizational world what property lines are to the homeowner's world: they tell you what is yours and what is his or hers.

In a *market*, however, things are different. In a market, you don't do something because somebody tells you to or because it is listed on page thirty of the strategic plan. A market has no job boundaries. It is a place where things are exchanged. It is a framework within which buyers look for what they need. It is a place where sellers come to meet buyers. Markets shape behavior and attitudes, just as organizations do. Markets define things in terms of their exchange value. The rules of the market define how all parties to the exchange can best meet their needs and achieve their objectives.

One of the most far-reaching changes in the latter part of the twentieth century is that "the market" has become the dominant metaphor for framing an enormously wide range of human activity. It is a metaphor because, to the invisible world of finding a customer, it applies the terminology of the actual marketplace where tangible goods are bought and sold. When we buy tomatoes at the Farmer's Market on Saturday, we are in the literal world; when we try to "market our services" to a new customer, we are in the metaphorical world.

Metaphors have side effects, although sometimes it is difficult to detect them until they have had a considerable influence upon us. One side effect of the market metaphor is that it screens out values that do not have a place in the give-and-take of economic exchange. We will address this problem later, but recognizing the shortcomings of the market metaphor must not blind us to the fact that anyone who wants to thrive (or even survive) in the work situations that are becoming dominant is going to have to learn how to look at those situations as markets.

People are more or less used to doing that with the world outside of organizations. No one is unaware that Sears, IBM, and General Motors have markets—or that their present difficulties came in large part from the way they lost touch with them. We would also agree that Wal-Mart, Compaq, and Toyota read the market more accurately than yesterday's frontrunners did. Some people find it more difficult to think of nonprofit organizations in the same way, and they may even be offended by talk about the market served by a church or college or hospital. But it is undeniable that the most effective institutions of those sorts are very conscious of their markets.

Very few people, however, think of the world inside each of those organizations (or their own) as a market too. It was once not important to see the world inside the organization that way. The internal organizations were so self-contained and the demands they made on their employees had become so codified into widely understood expectations (and even formal rules) that we could afford to forget that the internal affairs of organizations are as much the product of internal "market forces" as are those surrounding the organization.

Today, as more and more organizations decide to focus their resources on exploiting their own distinctive "core competencies" and "unbundle" their other component elements, the old boundary between the self-contained organization and its market "environment" becomes not only irrelevant but dangerously misleading. As organizations increasingly replace many of their support functions (and even parts of their central operations) with services provided by external vendors, they invite market forces into their interior workings. Employees find themselves being evaluated in comparison to (and even bidding against) external suppliers.

Outsourcing has a logic to it, and that logic leads to one conclusion: anyone seeking to work for an organization (as an external vendor or as an employee) must either learn to view the organization as a marketplace or else lose the organization's business to someone else who does. For the organization will not only be deciding between "building or buying" the parts it uses in manufacturing, but between employing or contracting for every single activity it requires in all phases of its business.

The old organizational paradigm encouraged employees to view themselves as the occupants of a box called a job. Jobholders had supervisors or bosses, who also had a job, which was to translate the signals they got from above into orders that they gave out to subordinates. In that way, they could parcel out the common work into individual and team tasks. The traditional employee had two sources of authority: the boss and the job description. If the employee belonged to a union, that entity would protect the employee when authority one (the boss) violated the terms set down by authority two (the job description).

In a *market*, however, people don't have bosses or supervisors, and job descriptions belong to some other universe. There are no orders, no translation of signals from on high, no one sorting out the work into parcels. In a market one has customers, and the relationship between a supplier and a customer is fundamentally nonorganizational, because it is between two independent entities. According to the market paradigm, one's boss is really a major customer rather than an authority in the old sense. (The boss is only *one* of the customers, since the boss's customers had also better be considered customers, as should the organization's traditional customers—those buying or using its products and services.)

An organization's employees—superiors and subordinates alike—are dependent on the organization, for without it they are unemployed. In a market, however, resources can be underemployed, but since there are no jobs to hold, *unemployment* in our sense is a meaningless term. It is no accident that unemployment did not even exist as a concept until the late nineteenth century—just about the time people were realizing that "having a job" had become the dominant economic arrangement for individuals, as well as the social norm.

Identify Your Customers, Inside the Organization and Out

If your work has not already been dejobbed, it soon will be. When it is, you will find that "doing your job" suddenly means very little. It will be a little late to start learning to see your superiors as customers, and to approach them the way an independent supplier would. It will be too late, in short, to start to look at that organization as a market.

What you have to begin doing before that happens is to market your services as self-employed people do. The "good employee" who just takes orders already plays a dysfunctional role within most organizations, although the old behavior still pays off in some places because it meets the ego needs of old-style managers. To be well adapted to the new environment will require you to know what your customer-boss needs and how to provide it effectively. Since your boss, too, has customers, tomorrow's organizations are going to be linked chains of suppliers and customers. Which ones are inside the organization's boundaries and which are outside is a secondary issue and one that will change through time. Inside and out, the rules will be the same.

Inside and outside are connected in another way as well. The internal, organizational market that you are working in is also tied to the external market of the organization itself. Your organization's ultimate survival is as customer based as yours. Tomorrow's vendor-minded worker will be more valuable than yesterday's employee, for the same reason that Wal-Mart is doing better than Sears, and Toyota is healthier than General Motors. In each case, the winners serve their customers better. So you cannot ultimately serve your organization well in your new vendor role unless what you do enhances the organization's ability to meet the needs of its own external market.

As an employee-vendor, your new "position" in the organization may not show up on the organizational chart that depicts who reports to whom. You are probably "positioned" on one of the organization's interfaces (we'll talk about that word in a few minutes) with its market. At that meeting point between the inner and outer, you're going to have to translate the external customer needs into data that the organization can understand— *and at the same time* translate the organization's efforts into service that the external customer can appreciate. You have the unenviable task of serving two masters: an internal customer who pays you and an external customer who supplies the money which makes that pay possible.

The customer-service and quality-improvement movements that have been so prevalent in recent years simply integrate and formalize these trends of the market economy. They are simply two more of the many forces undermining the foundations of the job. We can profitably view them as cue systems for anyone seeking to shift from an employee outlook to vendor-mindedness. Two useful texts can be cited:

■ Jan Carlzon, the CEO of Scandinavian Airlines, coined the term *Moment of Truth* to describe the worker's encounter with an organizational customer and to convey the idea that in that instant, there is an opportunity to convince the customer that the organization is wonderful, ordinary, or terrible. Every such encounter is a Moment of Truth for the organization. Well, every boss's encounter with the vendor-minded worker is a Moment of Truth too, an instant in which the worker's status is either enhanced or degraded. This is no time for TIM-J. Ordinary employee habits will get the worker into trouble, while the vendor-minded worker has a great advantage.

■ TIM-J has no place in the world of quality improvement, either. Quality guru Joseph Juran tells a story about his own early experience at Western Electric, Bell System's manufacturing unit. He discovered how to change the manufacturing of a kind of circuit breaker, so that defects (which had run at 15 percent) all but disappeared. In his own words, here is what happened: "I went to my boss and said, 'I know that problems like this exist throughout the plant. Why don't we search them out and fix every one of them?' [My boss] agreed with me that this would be a wonderful thing to do, but he said that process improvement wasn't our job. 'We're the inspection department,' I remember him saying, 'and our job is to look at these things after they're made and find the bad ones. Making them right in the first place is the job of the production department. They don't want us telling them how to do their job, just as we don't want them telling us how to do ours.' And that's where it ended."

Juran had acted the way a vendor would, someone who was being judged on outcomes, someone who was trying to improve the customer-organization's results.

His boss was a good "employee," staying within the confines of job descriptions and departmental mission statements with all the care that the property owner expends on not building a vegetable garden across the line into the neighbor's backyard.

Looking for Unmet Needs

To serve each of your customers effectively, you must learn to find (a) the needs they have that (b) are not yet being effectively or economically met by other vendors either inside or outside the organizational boundary. Your customers' worlds are changing just as fast as yours is, and yesterday's services are either no longer as useful as they once were, or are so widely available that neither you nor they can profit by concentrating on them. That's the bad news.

But the good news is the flip side of the bad: every change creates new needs. It is important to understand this fact, because the more obvious effect of change is to destroy old opportunities. If the bad news is all that you can see, then change is going to be your enemy. But if you can see that change simply *relocates the opportunity by changing customers' needs and the terms under which success is possible*, then change can be your friend— especially if others are not so quick to recognize this truth. Change creates opportunities in at least four ways, and since you're going to have to hone your skills at spotting such unmet needs, you need to understand them:

1. Change creates unmet needs by opening up gaps between available resources: the "missing piece" phenomenon.

As things change, gaps or niches open up between areas that used to be covered by existing services and products. In the external market, take-out food filled such a gap—between grocery stores and restaurants. Home-delivered medical services filled the gap between care by overworked family members and impossibly expensive care in hospitals. Low-cost tax-preparation services filled the gap between expensive accountants and do-it-yourself incompetence. In each case, change created the gap: a change in the complexity of tax forms, a change in the cost of institutional health care, and a change in the time available for meal preparation in two-career families.

Here is a more specific example. Lechters is a chain of stores specializing in housewares—575 stores in forty-four states at last count, and growing at a rate of more than one new store each week. At a time when many chains are losing money, Lechters is turning a healthy profit. It has a really modern computer system, salespeople that are (as they say) well "incentivized," and a store-opening process that it has down pat. But those things wouldn't have mattered if it hadn't had a strategy to exploit a need created by a change in the retail market. In CEO Donald Jonas's words,

> In 1980 we opened our first *real* Lechters store in Woodbridge, New Jersey, . . . [the concept for which] was inspired partly by the major retailers—Sears, Penney's, etc.— walking away from housewares because the category didn't have the turnover or sales per square foot that apparel had. . . . [They were also discouraged because] housewares required a strong support structure because of its diversity and large number of vendors. . . . For us, this amounted to a great opportunity.

Gaps opened up by change always present "great opportunities," although one can imagine the talk by Sears and J.C. Penney employees in 1980 about how there were no "opportunities" in housewares any longer.

The same gaps exist within any organization.

- New government regulations require someone who can monitor compliance with them.
- Going public creates the need for a shareholders' services coordinator. A new quality-improvement program requires trainers, as does the new initiative to set up self-managed teams.
- Even downsizing creates needs: for people who can do two or three different kinds of activity, for people who can turn out more work than the average employee can, for people who know how to make an unproductive activity pay for itself.

Inside the organization as well as outside it, the more that services and products are differentiated and specialized, the more that gaps between them are created. In other words, "niche-ing" creates still further niches.

The faster products change, the faster they become obsolete, and even obsolescence creates openings. Columbia University business professor Kathryn Rudie Harrigan has made a career out of studying products, businesses, and industries that are dying out. Her maxim is worth remembering: "The last iceman always makes money." In other words, change can destroy the size of a particular market, but that is not the same thing as destroying the market itself. If nearly everyone leaves the market, what remains goes to those who stay.

The question to ask yourself is this: How are the changes currently taking place in my industry, profession, or organization leaving need gaps that are not yet filled by an internally or externally provided service? Or broaden the question a little: How are the changes currently taking place in my *community* and in my *own life* leaving such need gaps? (One of the shortcuts to understanding what others' needs are is to understand your own. You will find that plenty of other people share them.)

2. Change creates unmet needs by creating new interfaces.

By now you know that I believe that words have a story to tell us. The word *interface* is sometimes dismissed as newspeak jargon. On the contrary, I think that *interface* is not only a useful word, but that its creation tells us something important about the nature of the changes going on today. The word is useful because there is no other term to describe the face-off between two organizations, a business and its environment, two patterns of experience and expectation, or two paradigms. "Boundary" is simply a line on a two-dimensional surface; "interface" is its three-dimensional equivalent, and it captures much better the way in which whatever is on the other side is experienced as different, unintelligible, foreign, and threatening. For a number of reasons, ours is an age of many disturbing interfaces.

Today organizations are entering markets where unfamiliar

cultural norms determine what is desirable, where diversity is increasing and being encouraged, and where cross-functionality is becoming the norm. The organizational "unbundling" we mentioned earlier encourages once-integrated organizational components to develop into separate organizations. The old corporate coherence is gone, and consensus is becoming more and more difficult to achieve. Joint ventures proliferate in this globalized, multimedia world, where no organization has the financial or technological resources to go it alone. Needless to say, interfaces abound in such a world.

Technology creates new interfaces too, both between different technologies and between unsophisticated workers and the alien technologies they are asked to use. Only a small percentage of workers are naturally comfortable at such an interface, so under the rubric of user-friendliness, technology companies are trying to build an answer to the problem of interfaces into the technology itself. Even so, the "technology interface" is a notoriously threatening location for most people.

Because interfaces juxtapose value systems, assumptions, needs, and languages, they create unmet needs. They demand workers who are good at brokering, translating, interpreting, training, linking, and servicing. These activities bridge the gap in comprehension and familiarity that the interface creates. The unmet needs created at an interface might require someone to train the ethnic majority about the values and needs of a new group of employees belonging to an ethnic minority; or a technical writer to explain an arcane new technology to the organization's traditionally minded customers; or a lobbyist to guard an organization's interests as a new patent law is being written; or a specialist to market to a particular demographic group, when the organization is trying to expand its customer base to include that group.

Traditional employees, immersed in the organizational culture, are not likely to have the objectivity or the empathy with the new and different to play these roles effectively. So it is no accident that such forms of assistance are often sought from external consultants, who are, by the nature of their external status, more likely to be vendor-minded. There is, however, no reason why they cannot be provided by a vendor-minded worker who is on the organizational payroll.

3. Change creates unmet needs by introducing new technological or economic possibilities waiting to be capitalized on.

The widespread use of electronic databases, available for public access over telephone lines, was impossible until computer modems and electronic networks were fully operational. But once those things became readily available, it was just a matter of time until someone supplied the economic and organizational tools to link them together and make public electronic databases available. When they became available, yesterday's way of doing almost any kind of work became an anachronism.

The Swedish furniture chain IKEA has capitalized upon the new possibilities opened up by electronic technology. On the surface, it looks like just another chain of huge stores selling low-cost products that require purchaser assembly. But IKEA is actually a pattern of technological and economic possibilities that have been capitalized on to answer an unmet need for inexpensive, high-value furniture. The company produces 45 million catalogs (in ten different languages) every year, each of which features a different mix (roughly a third) of the company's 10,000 products—and a short introduction to the "new rules" that IKEA operates under: customers do some of the assembly, the company provides good instructions and excellent quality at very low cost.

The company keeps its prices low by outsourcing all manufacturing to locations where the raw materials and craftsmanship are readily available, integrating its 1,800 suppliers in more than fifty countries with the help of a computer network; product components are handled by fourteen huge warehouses around the world, each of which is computer-linked to cash registers in its region's IKEA stores. The customer sees a huge store and boxes full of fine, low-cost furniture components, but the deeper reality is a network of electronic information and a sophisticated structure of decentralized operations that have been capitalized on to fill an unmet need.

You won't be likely to capitalize on technological or economic possibilities on anything like IKEA's grand scale, but every day that you stay home to write a report and then fax it in to the office, you're doing the same kind of thing, because you are using technology to redefine the outlines of your work life. Such unrealized potentials exist everywhere, waiting for someone to capitalize on them. Take the case of Drew Melton, who started working for Prospect Associates, Ltd., a Maryland health-communications-policy consulting firm, as a copy-machine operator. Within two weeks, he had met with the company president and explained how he could produce better documents faster. The president gave him a green light, and in the next three years he re-created his role at the company completely. Now he runs a highly complex printing operation, partners with Prospect's consultants to prepare more effective and professional-looking proposals, and earns almost half again as much as he did when he began.

Then there is Brian Hulsey, who was hired by Destec Operating Company, which sets up and operates cogeneration plants, to do technical maintenance on its gas turbines. In the words of Oren Harari,

> while doing his official job, [Brian] began to circulate through every nook and cranny of the organization asking people, "How can I help?" "Is there anything else that I can participate in?" . . . Gradually people began to invite Brian to brainstorming sessions and project meetings, and began asking him for assistance on complicated problems. . . . On his own initiative, he started an internal project that formerly had been farmed out to an outside vendor, with less than satisfactory results.

Hulsey's activities at Destec continue to grow, as do his responsibilities. He has long since outgrown his "job," but no new fixed position has been found for him. Instead he works on a number of projects, "reporting to" a senior vice president in one location and the manager of advanced technology in another. "It's all very ambiguous. I just do my own thing."

4. Change creates unmet needs by rendering obsolete—and thus needing replacement—existing technical, economic, or organizational arrangements.

I got a call recently from a man who had been hired by a large pharmaceutical company to help it deal more effectively with the huge changes taking place today throughout the health-care industry. One of the most far-reaching of these changes is the collection of formerly independent physicians into groups of health-care providers (HMOs, PPOs, and the like). Such groups, rather than the individual doctors themselves, are going to be deciding which drugs to prescribe for which ailments, for standardized prescription policies can lead to much larger purchases of fewer drugs and to much lower drug prices.

My friend explained that he was leaving his position in frustration because he couldn't get the company sales force to recognize the implications of the change. They had always called on individual doctors. They were organized into regional groupings to call on individual doctors. They were paid a commission based on the drugs prescribed by individual doctors. Their *job* was to sell to individual doctors! Were they about to change, now that the new economic realities of health care had changed where decisions would be made? No, they weren't. So my friend quit the employee world altogether and became a consultant. He finds that he is now in a better position to help customer companies get ready for this change in the health-care industry.

The employee-vendor's relation to his or her customers is something like professional/client relationships in the past, but the difference lies in the pace of change. Traditional professional/client relationships were not change-driven. They developed slowly over time, and they settled into mutually satisfying patterns of complementary activity and reward. Today, however, change occurs so quickly and so constantly that customers, both inside and outside the organization, always need something that they don't have.

Entrepreneurs have traditionally been those best positioned to capitalize on that fact in the external marketplace. They regularly launch ventures to satisfy the emerging needs of their chosen customer group: two-career families require take-out food;

offices full of PCs require networking; new environmental regulations require cleaner fuels or even electric cars. But the same
thing happens in the market within your own organization as
well. Your customer ("boss" in the old style) is part of a management team that has been given a new strategy, so he or she has
some as-yet-unmet needs. This customer may need some help figuring out what to do, organizing resources to get it done, monitoring the process to see that promises are acted upon. As a
vendor-minded worker, you must develop the habit of asking,
"How can I meet those needs?"

This customer-serving orientation is not a one-way street. As
we will see in Chapter 7, the style of "management" that is most
appropriate to the dejobbed organization in a fast-moving environment requires that the manager view his or her "subordinates" as customers too. The manager of dejobbed people needs
to ask, "What assistance, resources, information, support, or reward do they need in order to provide our organization's customers what they are seeking in the Moments of Truth when they
encounter us?"

The traditional jobholder's mindset does not lead to asking
that question very often. Jobholders do not see the organization
as a shifting pattern of needs. The only "opportunities" they recognize are the jobs that are currently posted on bulletin boards
down at Personnel. And they grumble about how damned few of
those there are, failing to note all the while the expanding range
of unmet needs all over the organization.

The first of today's new career-development strategies can be
summarized as follows, and as you go through it, think of how
you would put it into practice.

1. **Your environment, on both sides of the organizational
   boundary, is a *market*.** Try looking at your organization (or
   another organization, if you have your eye set on something
   new) as a market. What do you see inside the organization?
   Who's selling what to whom? What customers are *not* finding what they need in that market?

2. **Markets (inside the organization as well as outside) are
   made up of individuals who are best understood as**

customers. Forget your job description and forget who reports to whom. Scan your environment for people with needs. Those are potential customers, for they are in the market for services. Then look at your managers and colleagues. They are customers too.

3. **Your relation to them must be based on *need*-satisfaction.** What are their needs, their real needs, not the demands they make or their wishes? Whatever it would take to satisfy those needs will have more staying power within the organization than your job does.

4. **Today, all markets are *changing* very rapidly.** What are the changes that are currently reshaping your organization? Good changes, bad changes, little changes, big changes—it doesn't matter. Stay current on the change situation, because change is your ally when you are thinking in these terms.

5. **Change, by its very nature, creates *new* needs constantly.** This is a place to do some brainstorming: Take all the changes and imagine all the needs that they have created somewhere in the organization. Then look at your list and see what ideas pop out at you.

6. **The vendor-minded employee must develop an eye for unmet needs.** This isn't a one-time effort. Future changes will create future needs, so you'll have to do it periodically. But more than that, these need-spotting habits must be ingrained in your everyday outlook.

So where *are* the unmet needs in and around your own organization? In your industry? In your community? In your own life? That would be a good topic for a page or two of notes and ideas. That page could start a work notebook you ought to be keeping.

This notebook is part journal, part idea book, part scrapbook, and part to-do list. It is a place to jot down ideas that occur to you in reading this book or in running through the morning paper. It is a place to put articles that you want to reread later. It is a place to record your thinking as it takes shape or your decisions as you make them. Hunt up a notebook of some sort before you begin the next chapter, because there is a lot in it that will require pencil and paper.

Survey and Recycle Your D.A.T.A.

> *When a large American steel company began closing plants in the early 1980's, it offered to train the displaced steelworkers for new jobs. But the training never "took"; the workers drifted into unemployment and odd jobs instead. Psychologists came in to find out why, and found the steelworkers suffering from acute identity crises. "How could I do anything else?" asked the workers. "I am a lathe operator."*
>
> —Peter Senge, *The Fifth Discipline*

When I left teaching (and my last job) twenty years ago, I found myself trying to figure out what to do next. The bind that I was in ran something like this: what I wanted to do was to leave teaching, and what I knew how to do was teach. If you have had your own version of that experience, you know how all roads out seem to lead back to where you began. It's very frustrating, and it is one of the main reasons that people find it so difficult to break out of the job mindset.

To get yourself out of this bind and to maintain your freedom thereafter, you need to get off the merry-go-round of wanting to do something new but only knowing how to do the old thing. To get off that merry-go-round, you need to ask four questions:

1. What do I really want at this point in my life?
   The answers to that are your *Desires*.
2. What am I really good at?
   Those are your *Abilities*.
3. What kind of a person am I and in what kinds of situations am I most productive and satisfied?
   That is your *Temperament*.
4. What advantages do I happen to have . . . or what aspects of my life history or life situation could I turn to my own advantage?
   These are your *Assets*.

Together, your Desires, Abilities, Temperament, and Assets represent important and reliable D.A.T.A. (get the acronym?), a new core that you can rebuild your work life around. This new work life will not only provide you with an alternative to traditional employment, it will also fit you much better than the old one did. Since modern work lives are extremely taxing, it will also be more psychologically sustainable, since it will less often violate who you really are and what you really want out of your life.

The First Source of D.A.T.A.: Your Desires

"What *do* you really want at this point in your life?"

Too many of us have grown up with a prejudice against our desires.

■ It started with parental training: "I don't care what you *want* to do. It's what you *have* to do that matters! (And, incidentally, I'll be the one to tell you what you have to do!)"

■ Then the spokespeople for your religious heritage entered the picture: "Desires are selfish. You mustn't keep talking about what *you* want. Think of others."

■ Then it progressed to peer pressure: "You like *that*? That's dumb. This is much better. (Don't be such a jerk!)"

■ Our teachers chimed in: "I'm sure you don't *want* to do four hours of homework a day, but if you are going to go to college

. . . What? You want to drop out of school? You *don't want* to
drop out of school! You just *think* you want to drop out!"
■ And then our employer entered the scene: "You *have* to get
this done before you leave on vacation. The vacation is when
you can do what you *want* to. We don't *do what we want* to on
company time!"

Finally, just to add the final stroke, you spend your weekend doing all the loathsome things you have been accumulating, leaving
no time to do what you *want*—just the way that you used to get so
full on regular food that you had no room left for dessert.

Don't you ever get to do what you want to? Well, not at work—
at least, that is what most people would say. But that is changing.
I would like to think that the Puritan streak in American life is
finally dying out, but it is more likely that our need to be more
productive is forcing us to reconsider what really motivates a person to do his or her best. The motivation issue is all part of the
larger organizational shift that we are studying in this book. Specifically, we are finding that the most successful organizations are
made up of people doing what they like to do and believe in
doing, rather than of people doing what they are "supposed to"
do. We sometimes say that this represents the shift from *compliance*-based organizations to *commitment*-based organizations. We
could as well say that it represents a shift from *requirements* to
desires.

Given our histories, it is not surprising that we don't quite
believe it: "Sure, sure," we say, "but you can't *really* do what you
want with your life . . . can you?" In fact, when you are trying to
decide what you are going to do next in your life, what you *really
desire* is the only valid place to begin. All work situations are difficult enough these days without trying to do good work in a situation that conflicts with what you really desire. Or turn that
around: the only way to do the kind of first-rate work that is going
to make you indispensable to an organization is to be doing the
kind of thing you really want to be doing. *Desire* is the first and
most important ingredient of powerful motivation, and powerful
motivation is essential to success. Anything else is driving with the
brake on.

What *Do* You Want?

I mean *really* want. Desires must be deep-seated if they are to motivate you effectively, not just "wishes." (I wish I were younger, I wish I weighed less, I wish I weren't so lazy, I wish I had a million dollars.) Wishes are itches. They lead to fantasy, which is like scratching in that it feels good for a little while but very soon leads to more serious discomfort. Wishes have a make-believe quality about them: the Good Fairy, after all, grants wishes, not desires. We respond to wishing with a fantasy in which we magically become whatever it is that we are not, and make everyone sorry that they weren't nicer to us before.

With desires, however, there is no magic. You simply want something so much that you knock yourself out to get it. People who desire something work long hours; they make sacrifices, they swallow their pride and forget how others might perceive them; they discover talents they never knew they had; they argue their case so persuasively (because they believe in it) that they gain allies; and they solve problems that in any other setting they would have considered insoluble. Desire is one of the immense advantages that the underdog often has: simply wanting to win more than the top dog does.

So, what do you really want? Such a big question! Let's break it up into more manageable questions, like these:

1. If you were to write down your first twenty-five answers to the question "What Do You Want?" what would they be? That's something that you ought to set aside a couple of hours sometime soon and do. (Use that notebook you started at the end of the last chapter.) When you do it, you'll find that the answers are all over the lot. Some are just wishes. ("I want more time in the day . . . want to become less selfish . . . want to become more creative.") Others are more reality-based. ("I want to get more exercise . . . want to save some money to take care of myself in the future.") Some are materialistic. ("I want a nice, new stereo . . . want to take a long, hot bath tonight.") Others are more idealistic. ("I want to contribute something, make the world a little bit better . . . want to spend more time with the people I love.")

Set aside the wishes for a later look, and take the rest of your desires one at a time. Write each one on a separate page in the notebook. Look at them one at a time, and as you do, jot down your thoughts. What do the desires say to you? What do they mean? What do you mean by them? You say that you want more money, but does that mean that you want some new clothes (if so, why?), or that you want to send your daughter to a private school (again, why?), or that you want to save to buy a home (and again, why?)?

In this way, take a detailed look at what you say that you *desire*. What questions do the words ask you to reflect on? You ought to pause on each of these questions and turn it over in your mind. Write down whatever you think when you do that. And then write whatever you think when you read what you have written. This is meant to be done with as little mental monitoring as possible. Just think-and-write, feel-and-write. And when you have finished with one of your twenty-five answers, turn to another page and repeat the process with the next one.

When you have done it with all of them, set your notebook aside for a day or two and don't think about the topic any more. Return to what you have written with as fresh a mind as you can and look over these pages as though they had been written by someone else. Imagine you were asked what you thought the writer was trying to say. Under the surface, what were the writer's most significant desires?

After you have finished doing all that, look at the *wishes* you didn't go back over in this way. Sure, you wish you could win the lottery and be a country-and-western singer and own a beautiful house on an island—but not in quite the same motivated way that you desired those other things. Yet these wishes aren't insignificant. They say something about you and what you really (really) want at this point in your life. That lottery: maybe it's an end to all this worry about money; maybe it's a way to do some nice things for the people you love; or maybe it's a chance to take a breather from working so damned hard! And the country-and-western thing: Is it to have people in the palm of your hand, the way a singer has an audience? Or is it to express yourself, let your feelings out? Or is it to create something like a well-sung song? Or is it to have some fun, not be so straight and reliable all the time, dress in a metallic outfit, and have a hairdo as big as a bushel basket?

In other words, look at your wishes as though they were clues, notes left behind by someone who hasn't been seen in some time. What do they say to you? What do they say about you? Don't get psychoanalytic about it. Just let your imagination run and try to pick up the underlying message.

2. Another important question to ask yourself: Where do you want to live? You can (as before) write out your answer—or, more likely, the many answers that come into your mind when you begin to take that question seriously. You can also talk out the answer with someone else, asking him or her first to help you explore the question. (You can also do it reciprocally, in dialogue with someone else who is important to you. This can be a very meaningful conversation, although it can also throw you off your own mark if you begin to worry about the other person's reaction.) Alone or together, try to get under the surface of your own answers. Is it the apartment in New York City or the house with the big backyard in Bozeman, Montana, per se, or is it the excitement of a metropolis or the quiet friendliness of a small community that you are looking for?

The reason that location is an important issue is that it matters so much to some (though not all) people, and that too many job searches treat it as a secondary issue. Another reason that location deserves some careful reflection is that relocation often does increase your chances of finding good work today, and so you need to know where you want to live. Maybe your unwillingness to move has less to do with loving where you live than it has to do with the investment you have in your house or your desire to let your daughter graduate from high school with her friends. In the latter case, everything may be different in a year; in the former case, maybe you can get a renter to pick up your mortgage payments on the place and free yourself to move without selling it.

3. A third question (and one where a clear answer may change your whole view of your life and career) is this: What do you want to be doing and how do you want to be living in ten

years? If that seems too unreal, what do you want to be doing in five or even three years? (Again, write this down or talk it out with someone.) You can answer the question either by describing in general the kind of activities and circumstances that you want to be engaged in then, or by describing an imaginary day in the life that you would like to be leading in that future time. In the latter case, start out with getting up in the morning: at what time? in what kind of a room? in what location? Imagine what you do before the day really gets rolling: What do you have for breakfast? Do you exercise, bathe, meditate? Who, if anyone, is living there with you? Then imagine how you will spend your day, breaking the hours down into chunks so that you do not overlook anything that might give you a clue to what it is that you are currently desiring from your life. End with going to bed and reviewing the day in your mind—another chance to highlight important elements to capture for later thought and, perhaps, for final incorporation into a real plan for the future.

4. When all is said and done, you have just one irreplaceable resource: this particular, unique, unrepeatable lifetime of yours. What were you meant to *do* with it? What were you meant to *accomplish* during it? What were you meant to *be* in it? Although you may find the idea of various literal incarnations hard to swallow, play with the idea of "this lifetime" (as though there might be others) for the sake of its evocative power. This particular journey: What is its destination and its purpose? Why are you traveling this way? These questions are meant to steer you away from the standardized answers ("to help my fellow man," "to use my talents") and toward specific, personal, meaning-rich ones.

Again, write or talk this out. You will probably find that this question, more than the others, leads to an introspective state of mind. The key to exploring that state of mind lies in not steering yourself and in not judging yourself. Let your sentences pull one another out, like train cars coming out of a tunnel. If you are talking to someone else, you may find yourself embarrassed by statements that seem a bit grand. Choose your audience with that possibility in mind.

The point of all these questions is to clarify your desires so that you can use them to launch you on your new career. Desire is a motive force, an attractive force. With it, anything is possible. Against it, everything is a struggle. The point is not—as some New Age gurus would have us believe—that "you can do anything that you want to" or that "affirmations create their own reality." If that were true, we'd have been flapping our arms (affirming our desire to fly) and rising into the air long ago. And we'd need no more than self-flattery ("you are lovable . . . you deserve love") to make ourselves as lovable as we wish we were. No, the point of these questions is to activate and focus the powerful field that real desire always creates. People have crossed oceans and survived prisons and built huge corporations and developed their unique talents for the most profound and reliable of motivations: because they really, really, really wanted to.

The Second Source of D.A.T.A.: Your Abilities

"What are you really good at?"

Isn't there some test, somewhere, that tells you what you ought to be when, and if, you ever grow up? I used to think so in high school and wonder why the counselors never let me take it. I listened intently to any teacher who would say, "You ought to be a [something-or-other]," in hopes that she or he had seen down into the murky water of my being and spotted some gleam of useful talent. The things that I was good at (understanding an essay, planning a school event, or making a wise-guy comment when the teacher was out of earshot) were trivial. Anybody could do them. The things that I wanted to be able to do—like busting through the line for a touchdown or making the head of the pep squad fall in love with me—I seemed to lack any skill in.

As I went through school, I picked up a few skills. Typing, which I fought against with all my might (it was for girls!), is about the only one that has really made much of a positive difference in my life. But along the way, I got good grades, was a manager on the high-school track team, sold things to raise money for groups I belonged to and causes I believed in, held school offices, acted in plays, wrote funny letters to friends, and worried and worried because I lacked any skills that would prepare me for a career or even for life as an adult. I was mesmerized, I think, by those few classmates who had known from the time that they were eight that they wanted to be doctors, physicists, or homemakers, or who had such clear talent—the artists, athletes, and wheeler-dealers, especially—that they seemed to have emerged from the shell ready for an adult career. Compared to them, I was without skill, a vocational basket case.

I got into teaching "because it interested me very much." That is a phrase that really means, "because my father and mother had both been teachers, because two aunts were teachers, and because one grandmother and two great aunts were teachers." It was the family business. But I thought that "it interested me." Twenty years later, teaching interested me less. But whenever I sat down to do a résumé, I could only make myself look like a . . . uh . . . teacher.

- Education: there were the liberal arts courses and the major in English Literature. You couldn't very well talk yourself into a job at IBM or Chase Manhattan with those, I thought.
- Experience: teaching here, teaching there . . . and then teaching at the other place too. Another dead end.
- Recommendations: fellow teachers, former professors, a couple of college presidents.

"Hmm," I imagined the résumé reader saying, "have you ever thought of . . . uh, teaching?"

What I was painfully slow to learn was that ever since childhood my activities had been shaped by a cluster of basic "abilities." They weren't fancy and visible like this classmate's dancing talent or like that one's mathematical genius. My abilities were more general: I was pretty good at sensing people's motives; I could see the relations within a cluster of ideas; I was by nature pretty focused and hard working; I was good at getting others to see things from new perspectives; I was a quick study, learning my way around new subject areas fast; I was good at explaining things. These things didn't show up on my résumé, but they were largely responsible for anything noteworthy that did.

I use my own case because I know it best. I also know how

much time I lost by not understanding sooner what my real *abilities* were and how important it was to understand them. In fairness to myself, people weren't talking much about such abilities back in the mid-fifties when I was agonizing over my future. By the seventies, when I was trying to reinvent my career, Bernard Haldane was talking about "dependable strengths" and Richard Bolles was starting to talk about "transferable skills," but I struggled along without their help. (Oh yes, another "ability" of mine: doing everything myself, even when there is help available. My wife can speak with some exasperation about that one.)

What I was learning the hard way is what people are still learning the hard way: that is, that you can do a lot of things very well that you "don't have the qualifications for," and that if you know how to market yourself you can get paid well for doing them. This discovery is especially important during a time, like ours, when the nature of the work needing to be done changes constantly. It is important when jobs that once defined our competence are collapsing around us like the Three Little Pigs' House of Straw. In such situations, we need to be able to get under the descriptive surface of the jobs we held and find what we had to be able to do in order to do those jobs well. When we have done that, we can begin to put these abilities into a new frame that fits a new work situation.

Terri Stynes did that. She had managed the seventy-five employees at Bank of America's credit-card division's late-debt collection unit in its San Francisco headquarters. By any standard, she had a good job. But then, along came change. Bank of America announced that her group's task was being relocated to Phoenix and asked her to go. Having decided that she wanted to stay in San Francisco (remember "Where Do You Want to Live?" above), Stynes looked for new work that Bank of America needed doing in the Bay Area. She found that the bank needed an "employee assistance consultant." Let *Fortune* writer Ronald Henkoff describe what followed:

> The squib demanded at least five years' experience in human resources. Stynes had none, but she applied anyway— and got the job. How? By persuading her future boss that her years as a manager had given her the techniques

necessary to communicate one-on-one with employees. Outspoken and energetic, Stynes now arranges counseling for workers with personal problems, especially drug and alcohol abuse. She offers this advice to uprooted managers: "Be creative. Don't limit yourselves to a small sense of who you are and what you can do. Skills are more transferable than most people think." Dealing with substance abusers, she has discovered, is not all that different from her previous experiences dealing with the deadbeats—or with bill-collectors, for that matter.

What Stynes did—taking her abilities and reconfiguring them to be relevant to a new kind of work—is really what American organizations are doing today. Like them, she is cutting back to what in today's lingo is called "core competencies"—those things that one does well and that were the source of one's past accomplishments. She can then recycle them for new uses. An individual's abilities (or an organization's competencies) are far more widely useful than their possessor might guess.

Obviously the place to start is to decide what your own abilities are. Think about what you've accomplished in your life—going back, as I did, to what you accomplished in school (or at your church, or at home, or in sports or hobbies) before you ever joined the world of regular work. Think about what you've done successfully in the string of jobs you've held as an adult. Think about what you've accomplished within your family or your community in recent years. Then ask yourself: What did I know how to do that helped me accomplish those things?

We're not talking formal "skills," remember.

■ Forget the Art of Microwave Cookery. Think instead of learning to operate unfamiliar appliances and machines quickly—or being able to take data from several different sources (in this case, recipes) and combine them into new and interesting combinations.

■ Forget Knowing the Ins and Outs of the MegaBank Policy Manual: Think instead of understanding how bureaucrats think, how the financial world prefers to make decisions, how executives protect themselves from criticism with "policy."

- **Forget Operating Spreadsheet Programs.** Think instead of deciphering complex instructions, remembering a large number of apparently arbitrary steps, and finding it easy to think in numerical terms.
- **Forget Speaking French and Understanding Gallic Business Practices.** Think instead of learning foreign languages easily and picking up readily the cues from others as to what the "rules" are in any new situation.

In each case, you will note, it is a facility with general process rather than a knowledge of a particular procedure that characterizes the ability. (It is not coincidental that today's reengineering projects involve a similar shift in focus from functional procedures to work processes.)

You will probably notice that many of your abilities have to do with one or another kind of learning. That is significant. Whenever things are changing fast, what people already know becomes obsolete quickly. Only the ability to learn lasts. Now, don't worry if your grades weren't that great in school—they have little to do with your ability to learn, except to learn through formal courses of instruction in a school setting. (In a fast-changing world, such courses are themselves quickly obsolete and ought to be treated as a resource of last resort.) Everyone has an ability to learn. It's just a case of finding out how you learn best, and that takes us to the next part of your D.A.T.A.

The Third Source of D.A.T.A.: Your Temperament

"What kind of a person are you, and in what kinds of situations are you most productive and satisfied?"

There is a kind of vocational folklore which says that bankers, carpenters, social workers, chefs, doctors, and art teachers each have a basic "personality type." We say, "What do you expect? He's a lawyer." But in fact lawyers vary all over the lot in their personality characteristics. There are friendly, people-person lawyers, and there are distant, cold lawyers who make you feel like a crook when they ask you a question. There are flamboyant, expressive art teachers, and there are quiet, "have-you-ever-tried-charcoal?'' art teachers. So different temperaments have their place within any particular field. But each temperament carries with it some implications for the particular roles or situations where the person is likely to work well and be happy.

The Myers-Briggs Type Inventory (MBTI) is one of the most useful and well-researched instruments for determining temperaments (there are four) and the more detailed "types" (there are sixteen). In the space available to us here, I would rather not make glib but misleading generalizations, but instead recommend that you look further into the MBTI and what its results can help you to learn about your temperament. You will find that it helps you to better understand and appreciate your temperamental strengths and to more quickly spot situations where your weaknesses may get you into difficulty.

Instead, let's take a simpler and more common-sense approach to the question of temperament. Ask yourself these questions, and use your answers to take a further step in your D.A.T.A. collection process.

- Do you learn best through trial-and-error experiments or by following detailed instructions? You can usually get some of each in any situation, but one or the other is likely to be the dominant and expected learning mode. The question is, Which fits you best temperamentally?

- Do you learn best through working with others and engaging in the give-and-take of discussion, or do you learn best when you are left alone with a problem?

- Do you learn best when you hear explanations from a person or when you read explanations that are written out?

- Do you learn best when you start with the "big picture" of the whole process or when you start with the step-by-step procedures?

- Do you learn best when you are allowed to adapt the outcome to your own distinctive style of doing things or when there is one clear "right way" to follow?

- Do you learn best when you are turned on by a flash of insight or when you work methodically to add new information to what you already know, one piece at a time?

■ Do you learn best in organized events like courses, or in the natural setting of a particular situation?

You can learn a lot about your temperament if you will simply reflect on this question: What was the last new subject that you learned a significant amount about? What were the circumstances that led to that learning? What did you do to learn what you needed or wanted to know?

If all this talk about what you are going to have to learn is a little discouraging, remember this: your need to learn is not a sign of ignorance. Even the most knowledgeable people alive today don't yet know much of what they will need to know to succeed in tomorrow's dejobbed companies, institutions, firms, and agencies. Once you have accepted that, you need to do two things: first, decide what knowledge and skill you need in order to move into the future with more confidence; and second, design a learning project adapted to your own temperamentally based learning style. One of the casualties of dejobbing may be that the company has abandoned most of its standardized training programs. You're on your own now, and if you don't have a learning project going at the moment, you're missing an opportunity.

Temperament and Work Situations

Some people work best alone, while others do their best when they are part of a closely knit team. Some people feel at sea until they see "the numbers," while others agree with the English statesman Benjamin Disraeli, who said, "There are three kinds of lies: lies, damned lies, and statistics." Some people want their organization's expectations of them spelled out in great detail, while others prefer to agree on goals and priorities and then be left free to figure out the specifics. Some people like to tackle insoluble problems, while others want to come onto the scene after others have worked most of the kinks out of the system.

When asked to visualize themselves in their ideal work setting, some people picture themselves bent over a cluttered laboratory counter; others see themselves talking animatedly with an interested customer; others see themselves working at a machine of some kind; others see themselves standing up in front of a group of learners; others see themselves doing something with their hands in a shop or studio; and still others see themselves hunched over a laptop on which they are writing something.

How do you see yourself? Try it. Think of yourself as you would look in your ideal work situation?

- What are you doing?
- Are you alone or with others?
- If with others, are you face-to-face or side-by-side?
- Are you talking or silent?
- What is the setting?
    - Indoors or out?
    - An urban or a rural one, suburban or wilderness?
    - A huge room or a tiny one—or are you outdoors under a tree?

The usefulness of this kind of a visualization—and again, I suggest that you take the time to do it for yourself soon—is that it so readily expresses your temperamental preferences. Don't be too literal in your interpretations of what you end up visualizing. If you see yourself hiking cross-country in the wilderness, it may not mean that becoming a park ranger is the only thing that will make you happy. It may simply suggest that you're feeling drawn to situations where you are on your own exploring new possibilities or living by your wits, rather than following established paths.

Temperament and Activity

People react in temperamentally different ways to the challenges posed by change. There are no ways that are inherently good or bad. But each way has its natural disadvantages, and a person can be severely handicapped by not understanding and being able to compensate for his or her own temperamentally natural activity patterns. Each activity pattern also brings with it certain natural strengths, and a person needs to understand those in order to capitalize on them. There are essentially four of these activity patterns: inactivity, reactivity, proactivity, and coactivity.

Inactivity is an important part of the activity cycle, and anyone who cannot enjoy periods of inactivity is likely to burn out. At the very least, it is necessary for a good night's sleep. It is also a natural part of recuperation after heavy exertion or stress. Most people can feel the appeal of just sitting and doing nothing for a while. People who must deal with fast and frequent change need to be inactive periodically and may actually have to work to develop their capacity to do that.

Inactivity is also sometimes the counsel of wisdom. Asian religions and philosophies have extolled for millennia the benefits of letting-be, of attentive passivity, and of being and not doing. Christians were asked to consider the lilies of the field, which did not do anything, but still dressed exquisitely. Modern psychologists talk about staying very busy as a "manic defense" against anxiety and suggest that many people use it to run away from themselves and from their real problems. So inactivity has a good deal going for it.

But it also has some serious drawbacks, especially during times of far-reaching change. For inactivity can also be the product of denial, and denial is the way that we keep ourselves from taking a good look at the handwriting on the wall and acting before it is too late. If inactivity is your natural activity pattern, you probably rehearse inwardly all the reasons not to do anything rash; you urge yourself to wait until all this blows over; you think that you will just wait and see . . . and then wait and see some more. You may look back sadly or bitterly at all the chances you missed, but you are likely to have a kind of fatalistic view about such possibilities: they probably wouldn't have worked anyway!

To adapt John Milton's words, inactive people are those who "also serve by standing and waiting," but they are also people who show up on the layoff lists with disturbing regularity. And when they do, they have no plan of action; they don't want to act hastily, they want to see what others are going to do about it, they want to think it over, they don't want to rock the boat. Inactivity makes it almost impossible to seize any of the change-created opportunities we talked about earlier. Inactivity turns desires into idle fantasies. Inactivity renders abilities powerless to help you. Inactivity, when it is chronic rather than periodic, is a dangerous habit pattern in today's rapidly changing work world.

Reactivity: Watching people who have been immobilized by some announced change or some unforeseen event, I've often wished that they would *react*. Do something, don't just stand there! Here comes the train, jump! Fire, fire, run for your life! The person who cannot react (and react quickly) to a threat is in trouble. And for most people the dejobbing of America is a distinct threat. The changed conditions that have redefined employment security (being employable, being resilient, etc.) pose threats for anyone—which is most of us—who has not been thinking in those terms. I hope that this book will cause you to *react* and give you some guidance in how best to react to a work life that very few of us grew up expecting.

But reaction too has its price. The ball is always in your opponent's court. When you are reacting, you are simply coping with situations created by somebody else, playing by rules set by somebody else, solving problems defined by somebody else. When you are reacting, you are dashing to wherever the action is. When you are reacting, you are putting out fires.

Now, fires need to be put out, and as long as they are burning, fire fighting had better be well up there near the top of the agenda. But for most people a work life shaped wholly by reaction is always going to be both unsatisfying and unsatisfactory. If you are an emergency medical technician or (the organizational counterpart of that) a turnaround specialist, you may make a go of it. But unless disaster containment is your idea of a good time, you're going to have to initiate the action yourself, at least some of the time. And that brings us to proactivity.

Proactivity is activity that grows out of you and is not undertaken in reaction to some external signal. In times of change, the new beatitudes suggest that it is the proactive who shall inherit at least a good piece of the earth. These are the folks who singlehandedly launch startup companies. They are the people who hear about a great piece of property for sale, come up with the down payment over lunch, and have financing arranged by dinner. These are the individuals who, just before layoffs are announced by their company, talk their way onto the company-wide task force on new business opportunities and get themselves removed from the List of Excess Workers. Such people have what used to be called Get Up and Go. They have initiative, which a recent study of "star performers" at the Bell Labs identified as their most important quality.

It is impossible to overemphasize the advantages of proaction over reaction in a rapidly changing internal or external market. "The best way to be ready for the future," said notoriously proactive John Sculley, "is to invent it." And he is right. But proactivity, like the other patterns of activity, has its price. Proactivity isn't a team sport. Since the output is only as good as the input and since the individual person has only a limited amount of input to draw on, proactivity is always going to be limited to what the initiator understands and can imagine. The proactive person is playing a solo, and the soloist has to give up on many of music's most exciting possibilities. That's why coactivity is so important.

Coactivity is collaborative proactivity. That does not mean that it is group activity in which the individual is submerged and within which the individual's desires are relinquished. It is joint action for mutual benefit. It is you and me working together to get both of our needs met. Its value to its individual participants is that it enlarges the pool of creativity, skills, information, contacts, and past experience from which each one can benefit. To be coactive is to act together, not as a mass but as a collection of individuals. In a time of wrenching change, coactive patterns of action are less likely than other kinds of activity to disregard dangers and more likely to capitalize on all the opportunities in a situation. The rationale of the joint venture is based on the logic of coaction. Japanese management is designed to harness the power of coaction.

The logic of coaction underlies the redefinition of marketing that is going on today. As articulated by people like Regis McKenna, "marketing is not a function; it is a way of doing business." The contemporary way to market is "to integrate the customer into the design of the product and to design a systematic process for interaction that will create substance in that relationship." An example of such marketing is taking place in Xerox Corporation's so-called Express Project, where one of its customers (Syntex Pharmaceuticals) has some of its employees working on teams with Xerox researchers, engineers, and marketers to help "coproduce" (their term) new products that will benefit both the customer and the producer.

But even coaction has its pitfalls. It takes a lot of time, and so it may not be appropriate where opportunities are fleeting or threats are close at hand. It also requires trade-offs and compromises, just as any collective action does. Under the pressure of numbers, coactivity can also turn into groupthink, with no one feeling in control of the situation any longer and everyone plunging ahead with less concern for the destination and more fear of being trampled. If that happens, a good, strong *reaction* to what may be a threat created by the group itself would be appropriate. You may decide that it is wise to split from the group—*proactively*. And before you refocus your energy and head off in a more profitable direction, you will probably need to step back for a period of *inaction* and stocktaking.

Having temperamental tendencies inherently, you will find it easy to do one or two of these things and much harder to do the rest. Just don't get locked into any of them. Try to be aware of all the possibilities and choose what would serve you best in your rapidly changing situation.

The Fourth Source of D.A.T.A.: Your Assets

"What advantages do you happen to have . . . or what aspects of your life history or life situation could you turn to your own advantage?"

What "assets" do you have that you might build in to your career plans? Some of these are literal assets, like the equity you have in a house or an insurance policy that you can borrow against. If you were to decide that your best next move was starting a business of your own, you could use these assets to raise money for startup costs or to support you until your business began to turn a profit. You could use the literal assets of savings or investments to provide you with living expenses while you took the time you need to find exactly the work you want. Toward the end of your working life, you might use the literal assets of pension payments to supplement part-time earnings in such a way that a different and more appealing work life would be possible for you.

But assets need not be so literal. If you have a reputation in your field, it is an asset that you may be able to "cash in on" when you are setting yourself up as a consultant. If you have a good network of contacts, you have a valuable asset. Such assets are, like your house or your savings, the result of past "investments" of time and effort. Like any investments, they can be enhanced, even at a late date, by further contributions of time and effort. There is no doubt that such investments can pay off today. Just as you ought to have a learning project going, you ought to have an "investment project" under way to enhance the value of your assets in reputation and contacts.

If you have an advanced degree (regardless of the field or the institution it came from), it may be an asset. Its value will depend on what you decide to do at this point in your career, so when you come to finalize your career plans you may want to move toward areas where your educational assets mean more. Don't overlook a major (or even a minor) in some subject, even though your work has taken you in very different directions and you've never utilized your asset before.

Let's say you majored in Spanish and then went to business school. You sold stocks and bonds after that, and your Spanish major faded into invisibility, along with the clarinet and the Twist. Then, let's say that you decide to go into international investments. You have an idea that there is an unmet need for somebody to travel through Latin America to study companies, talk to financial writers, visit mines and agricultural projects, shop at local retailers, and send back independent, firsthand intelligence to investors. Suddenly your Spanish major, regardless of your present facility with the language, is part of your credibility when you approach a newspaper, a newsletter, or an investment firm with your proposal. The same thing could be done with an art major or many of the other majors that people put away on the upper shelf when they get out into the work world.

Educational assets, like financial ones, can be enhanced. I am not talking here about the substantive learning project that we already discussed. I am speaking here about the way we defined an asset above: it is an "aspect of your life history or life situation you could turn to your own advantage." A nearly finished degree might be worth finishing, just as an asset. Undergraduate premedical study might be remodeled into an asset with some current updating through reading. An old summer job selling shoes or teaching handicapped children to swim might be turned into an asset, as could your uncle's having roomed with the governor's brother, or your aunt's having taught in a Montessori school, or your cousin's knowing how to play the piano wonderfully.

Now just *how* (i.e., under what conditions) each of these things would prove to be an asset, I don't know. Being six-foot nine might be an asset if you were trying to get a history-teaching job at a school that was also looking for a basketball coach, though it would certainly be a liability if you were looking for work that involved a lot of coach-class airplane travel. Even things that have been handicaps at other points in your life can be turned into assets now. That happened for Jerry Lopez, the CEO of Technautics, a one-time defense contractor in Arlington, Virginia. Faced with recent funding cutbacks, Lopez went after a National Institutes of Health contract to survey career opportunities for minorities in biomedical research. Suddenly the fact that Lopez was Hispanic became an asset. Assets are your wild cards. They can change the whole hand, though they tend not to be worth very much in and of themselves.

"Recycling" These D.A.T.A.

In relatively stable societies, people carry their futures around with them. A particular education will be considered to be the natural path toward some vocational goal. Careers in any particular field will have a good deal of sameness to them, and whatever place one occupies in the present carries along with it a logical future. In such a situation, career planning and career development hardly deserve the titles. They involve little more than getting on a good train at the start of the trip and riding it through to the end of the line.

But during times like our own, everything gets confused. Career tracks disappear. Nobody is on a scheduled trip; everybody is making things up as she or he goes along. Career development starts turning into something more like cross-country hiking. It becomes, to change the metaphor, a kind of vocational collage-making: a piece from here, another (trim it a little and it will fit better) from there, and how about this leaf and that stick and . . . Voilà!

We're all going to be recycling our D.A.T.A. more frequently into new work specialties and work situations than people ever have before. It is getting common to put some figure on how many times we'll do this during our work lives. I've read, variously, that new workers will have five, seven, and nine such career changes ahead of them. I have no idea why it is always an odd number. In fact, no one has any idea how often you or anyone else will have to change careers. But we do know that the number is still rising.

Career mobility has always been a characteristic of the American worker, so we actually have something of a tradition to build on here. An Englishman named Frederick Marryat wrote a book about his visit to America in the 1830s. "There is one very remarkable point in the American character," he wrote,

which is that they constantly change their professions. . . . An American will set up as a lawyer, quit and go to sea for a year or two; come back and set up [running] a steamboat, merely because he wishes to travel; then apply himself to something else and begin to amass money.

Compared with Europe, we have always considered career development to be an off-road sport. The difference between then and now is that today we lack the expanding economy that made it easy to find a track.

As the economic growth slows and we become less and less likely to find our next work opportunity easily, we are going to need disciplines that we have never needed before. One of those might be called the ability to clearly define our "product." The logic of the market is based on customers who need something and suppliers who have it to sell. We've talked about the customer's needs above, but what about the supplier? That's you, remember? What do you have to sell? What is your product?

Even people who know all about the products of the company that they have worked for may never have given much thought to their own. But in a rapidly changing career marketplace, you are not going to get very far until you can describe your product very clearly and demonstrate exactly how it meets the as-yet-unmet (or not optimally satisfied) needs of some customer. Describing your product is not the same thing as being able to say "what you do," although it is related to that matter. It is, rather, defining the specific thing that you are trying to sell.

I, for example, sell training programs and advice to organizations and individuals in transition. These seminars and this counsel provide people with the skills and knowledge that they need to plan and manage changes in such a way that they disrupt organizational and personal effectiveness as little as possible. (As before, I use myself as an example for lack of knowing another person's product as well.)

You may find the word *product* distasteful. You have a body of knowledge. You are highly skilled. You are professionally trained. You practice a craft. You have a great deal of business experience. Fine, and so do I. But those aren't what the customers out there are shopping for. They have a need. They are looking for something to meet it. They are looking for a product, just as surely as a shopper at the local mall is.

Actually, let me put that differently. Your customer-shoppers are looking for an experience, a way of feeling about their lives and work situations.

- They feel threatened by all the changes taking place and wish that they felt less at sea and out of control.
- They feel excited by the possibility that the service they or their companies are developing could really take off and put it back into the black again.
- They feel worried that the recent staff cuts have taken away so much talent that it may be impossible to achieve last year's results.

■ They feel puzzled over the contradictory signals they are getting from the market and want a way to make sense out of them.

You may feel that this customer isn't looking for a product, but rather a service. My experience is that framing it as a product forces you to define it much more clearly and enables you to address it much more directly and reliably to the customer's experienced need.

The D.A.T.A. review that you completed in this chapter was only partly for the purpose of constructing something that would "fit" you well. You also did it to deconstruct your own resources into their elements so that you can rebuild them into something new: your product. Going back over your D.A.T.A., what could you use them to build? Remember, it has to be something that someone would pay for, something that satisfies an unmet need that someone has, something that improves the way in which someone experiences his or her own work situation. Forget how you will deliver it—we'll get to that in the next chapter. (Needless to say, don't try to make it into a "job.") Just get clear on what you're selling and why in the world someone (who?) would buy it. Until you do that, you might as well be asking people for contributions. When you've done that, you're ready to go into business for yourself.

Run "You & Co." As a Business

The days of the mammoth corporations are coming to an end. People are going to have to create their own lives, their own careers and their own successes. Some people may go kicking and screaming into the new world, but there is only one message there: You're now in business for yourself.

—Robert Schaen, former controller of Ameritech, currently a publisher of children's books

One idea that has been around for a long time (but that keeps getting rediscovered) is the self-managed career: "You've got to look after your own career prospects; nobody else is going to." But today that idea is being taken a step further. You had better be not only taking care of your own future, but also looking at yourself as if you were self-employed. Outplacement executive William Morin, whose firm has worked with tens of thousands of out-of-work people, puts it bluntly: "You have to see yourself as a business."

Every industry, business, and profession is full of people who have done just that. They found themselves, often unwillingly, outside the organizational boundary, and they capitalized upon that fact. Take the case of Paul Farrow, the former executive vice president of Groundwater Technology, a

Massachusetts environmental-services firm. He lost his job in one of those reorganizations that rate barely half a dozen lines on the local business page.

Reflecting on his own *temperament* and the changes in the organizational world, he decided not to look for another job. "Working in corporate America is no longer a loyalty game," he reasoned. "That has made it harder for me to go back and do it again, because I'm one of these people who gets so invested in what I do." He thought through what his *desires* were. "I wanted [to start] a business that would be healthful and related to outdoor exercise. I wanted it to be environmentally responsible and get people out into the environment and make them more sensitive to it." One of his *assets* was his long experience in manufacturing, and so he decided that his business should "make something—as opposed to just being a service." Another of his assets: "He had some money saved up after 20 years in the work force, and he was able to take that equity and borrow against it."

Farrow drew on his *abilities* too. One of the people that he brought into his venture was a specialty plastics molder named Joe Strzegowski, who says that he got involved in Paul's undertaking because Paul's *abilities* impressed him: "Paul understands, he listens. He's a sponge for information. . . . Paul's background is in finance, so he set his company up from there. I saw that as one of his strong points." Another of his joint-venturers is a designer named Jeff Allott, who said later, "I feel real good about his marketing skills. Paul did a bunch of formal and informal surveys, and every time he met with us he had another piece of information that was valid."

After Farrow lost his job, he took his family to Maine for a vacation on a lake. His two young sons rented a little kayak there, and although it was a poorly made piece of plastic, the kids loved it. When he inquired how much the boat cost, he found that the price was about $400. Drawing on his manufacturing background, he figured the raw materials cost less than $15. Hmm. The wheels started turning in his head. Farrow recognized that he was looking at a gap in the market and had mentally created the

"missing piece" that would fill it. In the words of the *Inc.* magazine writer who profiled him,

> Farrow returned from Maine in early September [and]
> delved deep into the kayak market. . . . The kayak market is
> almost entirely given over to the enthusiast, making the
> sport intimidating to the uninitiated. . . . Kayak prices
> range from $400 to $2,500 and you've got to spend at least
> $600 for any kind of quality. . . . Farrow wanted to design
> some ability to perform into a kayak that would retail for
> $390 . . . and could be paddled by a middle-aged person on
> a languid pond. What's more, he believed that a kayak built
> from recycled plastic would have clear appeal in the water-
> sport market, in which environmental awareness is a core
> value. . . . All the available research told Farrow a lot more
> people would participate in the sport if they felt less intimi-
> dated by the cost and the technology. . . . Coming in at the
> low end of the market with a high-performance boat, Far-
> row has kept one basic objective in mind: "I'm not selling
> kayaks. I'm selling access [to the experience of kayaking]."

One of the most interesting parts of Farrow's business (which
is now called Walden Paddlers and is located in Acton, Massachusetts) is that it is a one-person operation. That is to say, he inten-
tionally chose to create a "virtual corporation"—that is, an
organization which is really an assemblage of independent suppliers, linked together only by the product, a business strategy, and
a communications system. That is why he brought in a designer
and a plastics molder as subcontractors. To lower his upfront
costs, he gave each of them a percentage of the sale price of each
boat in addition to an initial fee for services.

Here's another example. Michael Bressler lost his job (vice
president of marketing, sales, and customer service) when the
Virginia-based printing company that he worked for went belly-
up. He found one of the interfaces we discussed earlier, this one
between a confusing array of printing services on one side and a
group of often inexperienced small-business customers on the
other side. He set up a company called Affiliated Graphics, whose
product is not the services themselves—that is the printers' prod-

uct—but the lower costs, the improved quality, and the better service that he can ensure for his client.

Or what about Virginia Snyder, who (at age fifty-five) was fired from her job as an investigative reporter on a small Florida newspaper? In a brilliant piece of what we've been calling recycling, she went back to school, got a private investigator's license, and went into business as a private detective. She thought of her *abilities* in the way we have been urging: "There is really not all that much difference between reporting and investigative work," she commented. "The same principles apply: accuracy, detail. Dig, dig, dig. Being able to get people's confidence, treating people with respect and dignity, no matter what background they come from." In the next seventeen years—she is still active at seventy-two—she worked on all sorts of cases, including fifteen for death-row inmates. Her batting average there: five stays of execution, one commuted to life in prison, and two men freed completely. She has also appeared on the "Today" show and "Late Night with David Letterman."

Farrow, Bressler, and Snyder became businesses more literally than you may wish to. In that case, consider Dick Ferrington, a former human resources director at Crocker Bank in San Francisco. At a casual glance, he looks as though he simply moved on to another executive job: he currently has the title of vice president for human resources at a biotechnology company called Scios Nova. But he doesn't have a "real job," because he's just freelancing there while the company looks for a replacement for the previous VP who left the company suddenly a few weeks earlier. Ferrington is definitely in business for himself: in between assignments, he works out of a home office, flanked by the PC, fax board, and printer that he bought himself when he went into his new business.

Or consider John Taylor, an "information designer" based in Oakland, California. Originally trained as a literature professor, he went through a variety of jobs (including mailman and machinist) before he took a job as a technical writer for Hewlett-Packard. There he learned that as a jobholder he lacked the power to do what needed to be done to create high-quality publications. Only an independent vendor had such power, so after seven years, he decided to leave the world of jobs and find a better way to do the work that he saw that companies needed done. Since then, he has worked as an external vendor for a variety of high-tech companies, sometimes from his own home office and sometimes in a fully equipped workspace on his client's site. He has taken some assignments on his own, but on other occasions he has been the integrator of many contributors to a project.

Using conventional terminology, we'd probably say that Farrow started a manufacturing company—though it is strange that he is the only employee. We'd say that Bressler launched a service company, or an information-brokering outfit, or a project-management firm, depending on how you see it. Snyder went into business for herself as an independent professional. Ferrington is a freelance executive, self-employed as a provider of temporary expertise. And Taylor is a contract professional, "doing jobs" in the old-fashioned (and newly fashionable) sense. Using the terms that more accurately refer to the present career realities, these people have all turned themselves into businesses.

Converting Yourself into a Business

All right. But how do you become a business? We've already talked about the first step in that process: getting yourself a clearly defined product and doing some effective market research. We drew many of our examples of filling unmet needs from businesses that did that. Now that you're going to be a business yourself, you can follow their lead.

To do that, you must see yourself as a self-contained economic entity, not as a component part looking for a whole within which you can function. That is why it is so important to see yourself as surrounded by a market, even when you are on the payroll of an organization. That is why I've been urging you to think like an external supplier of services and to be "vendor-minded," rather than to think like an employee. That is why—although I didn't put it this way at the time—I urged you to identify and find new ways to exploit your individual "core competencies," just the way your organization is.

It's a case of joining 'em when it's too hard to beat 'em. In this case, joining in their new strategy of outsourcing much of their work; using contract workers to do much that used to be done by regular, full-time employees; and depending on "coaction" to extend their reach beyond their own, solo capabilities. In an earlier day this idea of "being in business for yourself" while still drawing a paycheck would have been viewed as the height of disloyalty. Today it provides the organization with useful and highly motivated assistance, which is what the organization needs today far more than it needs the kind of old-fashioned loyalty that is really the dependency that grows from an inability to be self-sufficient.

The Outsourcing Exercise

Here's a practical way to try out what I'm recommending.* Be sure that you have at least an hour of free time before you proceed any further with these instructions, so set the book aside until later if you do not have the hour now. Whenever you are ready, imagine yourself in the following situation:

■   ■   ■   ◪

You go to a meeting where your boss's boss is talking about all the changes your organization is going through. She announces that a decision has been made to trim the workforce to those people doing the most essential "core" work and to put the rest of the work out to bid by independent, external contractors. (You can hear a pin drop.) Some of this work will be awarded to individuals and some will be awarded to small subcontracting firms. Because your organization is "grateful for our employees' contributions and loyalty" (there is a rude sound from some members of the audience here), it has been agreed to award as much of the work as possible to the organization's own alumni. They are, however, going to be competing against independent firms

---

*The way this exercise is written presumes that you are currently employed. If you are not, go back mentally to a time when you were; read and carry out the instructions from that point of view.

with a lot of experience doing such work as vendors. So competition will be tough.

The next month at the organization is going to be spent reframing the organizational work into assignments, tasks, and projects that can be put out to bid. You will assist in that process. But at the same time, you will be putting together a business plan on your own for the one-person company that is going to bid back on some of your group's old work as an external supplier.

To get a first indication of how this process might go, the next hour is to be spent writing a preliminary proposal—not a full-scale business plan, but a brief prospectus that covers these topics:

■ *What product you are offering to your organization.*

■ *What organizational needs your product will fill.*

■ *How that product will be made and delivered.*

■ *Why you think that you and your product are better qualified to meet the organization's needs than other vendors and vendor products would be.*

You can also add anything else that the organization ought to consider in thinking of you as an external vendor. Oh yes, and since all the "jobs" in your area are disappearing, your proposal can cut across what used to be job boundaries. In fact, in the light of the process improvements that the organization is currently attempting to make, proposals that suggest better ways of getting work done (with your assistance) will be given preferential treatment.

OK, there. Take your notebook (and an hour) and write out your preliminary business prospectus. Go ahead.

■　■　■　■

Well, what *does* it take to create a little solo business? We've already talked about having a clear product—and a clear idea of why the customer needs that product. Oh, by the way, just who is your customer? What relation does your product have to the customer's customers or to the organization's customers out there in the external market? Don't just copy your old job. Do something that the organization really needs. So think carefully before you say what you'll do for the organization.

Oh, yes, how do you know what the organization needs? Has your little business—let's call it You & Co.—done any market research? No? (Where *is* that marketing VP when you need him?! Oh, yeah. It's you. Right.) Well how is your business going to assure itself that it has a good solid grasp of market needs? (Set that aside for later . . . on a notebook page titled "Marketing: How Will I . . . ?") And oh yes, don't forget that marketing includes studying the competition and differentiating yourself effectively from it, so that it's clear Who You Are and What You Do. (Maybe that product description needs a little more work over the weekend, now that you think of it.)

Then there's product quality. They said that there'll be competition from independents. Maybe you ought to do some benchmarking. Why don't you get some information on real external vendors and how they work? One thing that you'll see is that they pay a lot of attention to customer service and that the best of them work constantly at improving their products. (They benchmark against their best competitors, so you'd better do that too.) They include product evaluation cards with the product, and appreciate complaints as ways to pinpoint product weaknesses. They're big on Moments of Truth. How are you doing on those? They have quality programs that focus on giving their customers (who *were* your customers again?) the experience that they are seeking. They aim not at getting their job done but at Knocking the Customer's Socks Off. How could you do that?

With technology improving all the time and competition increasing, they are constantly working to improve product design, to spin off new generations of product application, and to develop whole new products to fill new needs. They have a research and development team. You're a little small for a separate R&D building, but that doesn't mean that you shouldn't be working to enhance your product. You ought to be viewing your product as a startup company might view whatever it was offering in a rapidly changing market. Such a company would be busy developing the next generation of products and services, even as it sold its current crop. Money, personnel, time, space—the startup company would devote its resources to enhancing what it was offering.

You & Co. will have to do the same thing. Without a clear development strategy, you will be a business without much of a future, for you won't be able to provide continually upgraded and redesigned services to meet the customer/client's emerging needs. Such updating and enhancement will be up to you, although your client organization in its own interests may decide to foot some of the bill, and the government, also in its own self-interest, needs to help out people like you. So updating and evolving your services/products will be an ongoing process that you yourself are going to have to take charge of.

Of course, You & Co. could do all of this good stuff and still go out of business fast if you don't have the ability to sell your product. People who see themselves as employees, even in sales, don't pay much attention to "selling" their own services. Selling is an essentially quid-pro-quo transaction in which you give something and get something.

When I went into business for myself twenty years ago, one of my great shocks was that, although I could talk persuasively about how important my ideas were, I had no idea how to sell them. I learned, but in a slow, groping fashion. My learning was retarded by the idea that "selling" my services was, somehow, demeaning. I had, of course, been paid in the jobs I had held, but salary was seldom negotiated in the teaching world of the '60s and '70s. One job would pay better than another, and everybody understood if you took the better-paying one, but you didn't think in terms of setting fees for the services you delivered. To do so would be to debase them by turning them into commodities.

Since I left that world, I've found a surprising number of people in other fields (even more worldly ones than teaching) have similar problems setting a price on their services. That is why I like so much a passage from *An Unknown Woman* by Alice Koller. Her subject is the winter that she spent living alone in a rented house in a nearly deserted summer community. In this particular passage she is discussing what she learned about her lifelong difficulty with "getting what you want," whether tangible or intangible. In my mind, her discovery has become The Koller Principle.

This is how you get something you want. First, you figure out who has it; then you figure out what its possessor needs and whether you have *that*. Then you're in a bargaining position. How plainly simple! Not the getting, but the thinking about getting. Yet before, I thought that the only way to get what I wanted was to ask for it, or to let it be known that I wanted it. And that I'd get it if the person liked me; otherwise not. It never occurred to me to consider that something was expected of me in return. . . . I wince at the parade of people who must have been baffled by their dealings with me.

I, too, wince at how confusing (and manipulative) my behavior must often have been, as I tried to get people to give me what I wanted without any quid-pro-quo transaction taking place.

Since getting hired to "do a job" involves just this kind of transaction, it is useful to think of the fee you are seeking not as "getting paid" but as exchanging what-you-have-and-someone-else-wants for what-someone-else-has-and-you-want. This kind of an exchange is just how nature works: symbionts in an environment do it, ice cubes do it with the glass of water surrounding them, the earth's waters and the sky do it, and you'll do it when you turn yourself into a business.

Managing You & Co.

Right up there at the top of the list of learning projects for anyone preparing to succeed in a dejobbing environment is "learning to manage your own business." How are you going to do that? (Remember that there are many different temperamentally based learning styles, so there is no single answer to that question.) Take a couple of extension courses on starting a business, spend a week with your neighbor who runs a store, read a book on running a business, hire a small-business consultant, apprentice yourself at a particularly well-run business, buy and start using some interactive small-business software: all of these things may be helpful.

So will some little actions, like getting yourself a business telephone in your home office; having business cards and stationery printed with a professional identification and a logo that captures what your product is and does; joining an appropriate business or professional group and meeting with them on a regular basis. Using one of the business software programs, convert your Rolodex into an electronic database on which you capture useful information about potential clients, contacts and leads, resource experts, and members of your support system. You also ought to put together a business plan, imagining as you do so that you are describing your business to a potential investor.

Some very simple practical actions are also useful.

- Set aside a space somewhere as your "office."
- Gather there all the office supplies and equipment that you will need.
- Make it a place where you will not be disturbed by competing demands.
- Create a calendar, and convert your business plan into a planning chart, with checkpoints and deadlines (make them realistic) that you will hold yourself to.
- Get yourself some simple bookkeeping material or software, and start to chart the flow of business expense and income.
- You may even want to explore the possibility of partnering with someone else. That would make your undertaking less lonely, although it would also make it more complex. (Use The Koller Principle to settle on the right partner: What do you need? Does that person have it? And what will he or she need from you to complete the transaction?)

Don't decide too quickly that starting a formal business is necessarily the answer. Remember that "You Are a Business" is a metaphorical statement first; it's literally true second, if at all. What you are really launching is a new way to think about yourself and to fit into the work world. At an even more fundamental level, it is a new way of seeing the work world. It does not even require that you leave your present job if you don't wish to or have to. It just requires that on that job, you take the market-based approach that we have been describing.

But a word of warning: The longer and more successfully that you use this approach to do your work, the more dissatisfied you are likely to become with the world of jobs.

What about Benefits?

If and when you leave the world of jobs, you're going to have to rethink the financial basis of your life. Your friends who've quit or lost their jobs will have told you all about what it is like to "lose your benefits," and the results can indeed be scary. You are going to have to do what self-employed people have always done: budget health insurance, retirement contributions, and other traditional job benefits into your business plan.

Before you get overwhelmed by the prospect of doing all of these things for yourself, consider the strong possibility that you are only doing proactively what many employees today (and most employees will tomorrow) have to do reactively. For tomorrow's work world—even for most of those who still hold jobs—is going to be a world without many company-funded pensions and health plans. Fully half of the compensation and benefits directors of three hundred large corporations queried by the consulting firm William M. Mercer believe that under the financial conditions currently taking shape, "today's average salaried manager won't be able to afford to retire [on a company pension plan] at 65." As for health care, more companies scale back the corporate contribution or the levels of coverage every year. Layoffs are taking place at those companies that had good coverage and contribution, and hiring is generally occurring at those companies that don't. So before you decide that setting up your work life as though you were self-employed is too taxing and frightening, consider what is going on. You're not so much taking a risky chance as you are simply getting ahead of the crowd.

It will help you to consider what the founder of a very successful dejobbed organization says about this kind of work. Valerie Skonie is the founder of The Skonie Corporation, a Sausalito, California, company that provides trainers and customer-service personnel to medical-equipment companies. She says that, first for herself and then for the contractors who worked for her, she learned to redefine what a benefit really is. She came to see benefits as "the ways that you benefit" from working in a certain way. Jobs have certain benefits, and other kinds of working have other kinds of benefits. You are not so much losing benefits as you are trading certain financial benefits for emotional benefits: greater freedom, increased contact with the results of your work, more chance to express your ideas, and the opportunity to do new and challenging things. It is very beneficial to work for yourself, but there are trade-offs. You just have to design a "benefits package" that fits with your temperament, your assets, and (above all) the realities of tomorrow's work world.

Managing the Composite Career

As you move in these new directions, you are likely to find that you are more and more often doing several things at the same time. Not only will you have a full To Do list, but you will probably split your time between different roles, locations, clients, teams, schedules—whole different work worlds.

The positive side of the old job world was that, however overworked you might have felt, at least TIM-J let you slough off activities that didn't fit your job description. But work within a dejobbed organization is repackaged into projects and assignments, and you are likely to be doing several at once. This composite work life forces you to manage your own time and effort in the way a self-employed person with several different clients does.

Consider the differences over the long term: The job-based career was like a chain, with each successive job serving as a link, where there was a single focus of activity. The demise of jobs is going to remove that point of focus for you. As you become a business, you will find that you now have a composite career, which is more like a woven cable, made up of multiple twisted strands of wire. The strands are assignments and projects, often for different organizations and sometimes involving wholly different personal products.

The job-chain career provided strength, but it was only as strong as each individual link. These days, the job links break far too easily. The strands of the composite career, however, begin and end at various points and weave a more flexible kind of strength out of their multiplicity. Any one strand can break without destroying the career cable. The job-chain career is like a single-product company, with far too much riding on the continued success of some one thing. Or, to change the analogy, the composite career depends on the logic behind diversified investing: during times of unpredictable change, it is unwise to have all your economic eggs in one basket. The vocational investment in the composite career's multiple activities and sources of income is like a financial investment (e.g., a mutual fund or a portfolio of stocks, bonds, cash, and real estate) that spreads the risk around.

Something over 6 percent of the workforce currently reports holding more than one job, although that figure is undoubtedly too low. Some people don't want their primary employer to know that they have another one; other people don't want the IRS to know; and a few may not want the police to know. Beyond the ambivalence people feel about saying that they have more than one job is the fact that, like just about all our work statistics, this one only measures "employment" that is packaged in the form of "jobs." It does not include the incredible variety of freelancing and interesting sideline activities that do not qualify as conventional jobs in the statistics.

Clearly, a composite career is often just a way to make ends meet. Especially at its lower end of the pay scale, the job world does not reward people adequately. Among some groups, like nursing-home employees and restaurant workers, it has become the norm to moonlight. Dominic Bozzotto, president of Boston's hotel and restaurant workers union, reflects that the two-career family was "the good old days. [Now] we've got four-job families." When people talk about how important jobs are and how impossible it would be to abandon them, they conveniently forget how badly the job world serves its less advantaged citizens.

But the motive for following a composite career is often not purely financial. Sometimes the composite career is a way to express those parts of oneself that are excluded from the narrow world of the job. Barbara McGraw is a corporate attorney at the big Los Angeles firm Skadden, Arps, Slate, Meagher & Flom. Her clients there may know that she was on the law review at USC, but few of them realize that in the evening she often trades in her legal briefs and dark suit for a strapless gown and a mike at a local nightclub, where she sings an hour-long program of rock, pop, and Broadway songs. "I want to be a success at life," she says. But "instead of giving 100 percent to any one thing, I want to give a lesser percentage to a number of things, so that I have a taste of everything." John McBride, the director of information for Kansas City–based Livestock Marketing Association, feels the same way. Outside job hours, he pursues a second vocation as a joke writer. His one-liners bring $10 to $50 each from people like Jay Leno, Joan Rivers, and Roseanne Arnold. But he says, "I'd do it even if they didn't pay me."

Lyn Snow, a successful watercolorist and printmaker in Owls Head, Maine, reverses things, making creativity the vocation and her trained "profession" a sideline. She leaves her studio two mornings a week to drive in to the office in Rockland where she sees psychotherapy patients. A licensed therapist, she kept her practice going while she made the transition to her artwork. Now that her art sells well, she keeps the practice going "to give me a change of pace. I'd actually do a third kind of work if I had one and had the time," she says. "I love the variety."

For some people, a composite career can serve as a bridge from one work life to another. Charlie Herrmann was a sales trainer at Jostens, the yearbook and class-ring company, when he decided to create a business out of his ability as a speaker. Starting with his contacts in education and a few invitations to speak at graduation ceremonies, he parlayed them into a small but rewarding sideline business (called Speeches Unlimited) as a speaker at national conferences and meetings.

In other cases, the composite career develops when someone pursues a hobby far enough to turn it into a business. A physician named Marty Griffin loved wine and bought some property in Sonoma County, California, on which he started raising grapes. You can't raise grapes without trying wine making, so he bought some equipment and started bottling wine for himself and friends. Everyone liked the results, and the Hop Kiln Winery was born. A similar thing happened in the case of Henry A. Lambert, a New York investment executive, who was drawn by his interest in food into starting a little pasta business. In his case, the sideline was so successful that it became a major asset. Ten years after he founded it, Lambert sold Pasta & Cheese to Carnation Co. for more than $20 million.

Not all ventures ever develop significant financial value or even become stand-alone businesses. They may be almost invisible to the people at the organization where the person has a "regular job." A divisional controller in a Silicon Valley electronics company is a tax consultant on the side, although few of his associates know it. The great modernist poet Wallace Stevens supported himself as an executive at a Hartford insurance company. When he died in 1955 and his obituaries listed his Pulitzer Prize, the titles of his nine books, and the praise lavished on his writing by international critics, a fellow insurance executive exclaimed incredulously, "Wallace wrote poetry? Can you beat that!"

Whatever the motivation and the circumstances, the composite career is a significant part of today's work world. Doing all your work for one employer, at a regular place and time, for a single salary, and containing your work life within a single entity called a job—these are ideas that were brand-new in the nineteenth century. Before that, everyone had a composite career, although no one talked about such a commonplace fact. It would be hard to imagine Thomas Jefferson (planter, architect, statesman, writer, inventor) and Benjamin Franklin (printer, postmaster, statesman, humorist, scientist) holding down "jobs."

Even after the job became a dominant work paradigm, upper- and lower-class people kept their composite careers—the latter because they needed them to survive, and the former because their mix of leisure, social responsibility, and wide experience gave them multiple points of concern and influence. Only the middle class gave up the composite career, and today even they are returning to it.

The New Career

George Gendron, the editor of *Inc.* magazine, recently commented that "the traditional admonition of one generation to the next, 'Get a job,' has been replaced with the more complex and bewildering mandate, 'Go out and *create* a job for yourself.'"

Gendron is clearly on the right track, although the work life that today's conditions encourage is both less and more than a job. It is less because it lacks the coherence, the longevity, and the organizational backing of a traditional job. But it is more than a job as well, in that it provides the chance to do a number of different things and thereby gain the security of diversification and the personal rewards of variety.

The people who do well in this new world are not necessarily those who were viewed as "well qualified" in the traditional world of jobs. Women who have run an organization as complex and constantly changing as a household may be specially well adapted to the confusing multiplicity of the dejobbed world. The WASP men who were most at home in the job world are relatively less equipped for those aspects of a life without a job. It is significant that although women have still not progressed very far toward equal opportunity in the job world, thay have been notably successful outside it. Women-owned businesses currently employ more people than the whole of the Fortune 500, and in 1987 there were forty-nine metropolitan areas where the sales at women-owned businesses exceeded $1 billion.

The careers of women like Jane Hirsh and Frances Hesselbein are instructive. Hirsh was a hospital pharmacist who needed to hold down two jobs to save money to start a family. She founded the generic drug maker Copley Pharmaceuticals because an organization of her own "was the only way I could have a crib in my office." She continued to juggle multiple responsibilities, raising six children and building Copley into a huge and successful enterprise. She recently sold 51 percent of the company to Hoechst Celanese for $546 million.

Frances Hesselbein did not even hold a paid job until she was over forty, but she had already demonstrated all the abilities that the composite career demands during the years that she ran a household and did volunteer work. In a remarkably short time, she rose through the organizational ranks to become executive director of The Girl Scouts. Its volunteer staff of 750,000 is even bigger than the Manpower workforce. Hesselbein's "career" did not start or stop with her short sequence of jobs, for today she is both without a job and with plenty of good and rewarding work to do. In that sense hers is typical of the career pattern that will become more and more common in the years ahead.

As with the other key terms in our discourse, we should note that *career* has an interesting history that parallels those of *job* and *employment*. It comes from the Latin word for "road," and it meant "the course over which any person or thing passes." A writer in the seventeenth century spoke of "the Portoguese [finding a] *career* to the East Indies by way of the Cape of Good Hope." It wasn't until the nineteenth century that anyone thought of applying it to the road that a person took through life, and it wasn't until late in that century that it came to mean "a course of professional life or employment, which affords opportunity for progress or advancement in the world."

Now we'll have to go forward and return to the older meaning. Our career will become our "course or progress through life." Hesselbein's career started long before she took her first job and has continued since she left her last. The same is true for you. Career doesn't mean "rising in the world." It is just the word for our individual journey, the path that each of us follows to find meaning in our lives. To paraphrase Gendron: "Go out and create yourself a 'career.'"

But that isn't quite right either, because you have always created yourself a career. But today, instead of creating it by your taking or passing up jobs, you must exercise your creativity across a wider band of possibility. You can no longer afford to limit yourself to jobs. You need to compose your career the way you would write a piece of music or paint a picture. You've been doing the vocational equivalent of those old "painting by the numbers" kits. These last three chapters have tried to show you how to paint on a bare canvas—to paint the picture you want, not the prefabricated one that someone decided a million people ought to paint.

The Psychological Impact of Dejobbing

It's humiliating. . . . It's difficult both in terms of meeting expenses and on an inter-personal level. In our society, the first question people ask is what do you do? You are what you do.
—Christine, former health-care social worker

Since college, I'd always worked at top speed. From a demanding law practice, I'd gone to work in Richard Nixon's White House. Days began at 6 a.m., and I seldom was home before ten at night. Suddenly there was a vacuum in my life. I had nothing productive to do.
—John Ehrlichman, former White House domestic policy coordinator

What Jobs Do for Us

In our society, people need jobs. That statement sounds so obvious as to be trivial, although we have already seen that before the nineteenth-century, people lived productive and meaningful lives without jobs. They still do in many nonindustrialized parts of the world. But giving up jobs after building a whole way of life around them is very different from living a life that has never included jobs. The process of dejobbing our lives and our organizations is going to involve extremely difficult changes. We will have to learn to live with work situations that are not framed by job descriptions and clear reporting relationships. We will have to learn to live with multiple roles, where the role mix changes frequently. And we will have to learn to find the income we need in such unstable and unpredictable conditions.

The financial aspect of a job is so evident that people underestimate its psychological function. But many people who have lost a job would agree with former business executive John Baratti, who said, "The hardest part of being laid off is the mental aspect." In the long run it will probably be the psychological aspect of dejobbing that people find most difficult. Incomes are modular and portable: they can be replaced. Finding new sources of income may require time and effort, but once the income is found, the task is done. Replacing the psychological rewards that jobs have provided is far more difficult. As Terry Cantine, former product marketing manager for a large manufacturing company, put it, "My life was my job, but now I'm finding out how wrong that is."

Although they usually fail to realize it until they become unemployed, most Americans are defined in terms of their jobs, connected to a wider community through their jobs, and provided with structure and purpose by their jobs.

■ A job helps people to tell themselves and others who they are. In village and tribal societies of the past, identity was established by birth. It might have been enhanced or degraded a little by subsequent activities, but for most people Who You Are was one of life's givens. With us, that's not so. No one can say at birth who individuals will turn out to be in our fluid society. People weave their own identities out of the friends they make, the family life they create, the activities they pursue, the schools they attend, the churches they worship in— and the jobs they have. Especially the jobs. When people meet one another for the first time, they usually ask about work, about the other's job.

■ The job provides most people with their core network of relationships. Whether or not their coworkers are their best friends (and that is not uncommon), the job is for most people the ongoing social context in which they live their lives. It is their little tribe, their tiny village. Even if they don't like everyone there, the other people become part of their lives. When one of them disappears for any reason, a hole is left. If an individual loses his or her job, these people all disappear. Life feels flatter, thinner. People without jobs feel alone.

■ The job has a time structure to it, and without it life can feel as vast and empty as outer space. With it, a person has clear boundaries: You come at 8 and leave at 5. You take forty-five minutes for lunch. The phone rings and you have to pick it up by the fourth ring or it rolls over to the message service. The mail comes right after lunch and the parcel pickup is at 3:15. There are eight holidays a year and three weeks off in the summer. The job gives a pattern to the days and weeks and years of people's lives. It makes living—a confusing business at best—more predictable. Without a job, time stretches off toward the edges of doom.

■ A job gives people parts to play and tells them what they need to do to feel good about their contribution. It gives them a way of knowing when they have done enough, and it tells them when their results are satisfactory. Jobs provide people with a place where they need to show up regularly; a list of things they've got to do; a role to play in some larger undertaking; a set of expectations to be measured against. It gives them an everyday sense of purpose. And fulfilling such purpose is a source of self-esteem. For people whose personal lives are not going very well, the job may be the only source of self-esteem. For most people, in short, a job is a primary source of meaning and order in their lives. No wonder that losing a job is so psychologically devastating.

Leaving the world of jobs is going to confront you and everyone else with a psychological problem that has both an acute and a chronic aspect. The acute aspect, which involves the very disruptive transition from the old way of working to the new one, is the subject of Chapter 9. The chronic aspect involves the ongoing strains and dilemmas produced by the new way of working. Managing those is the subject of the present chapter.

In the last three chapters, we have talked about dejobbed work from a practical point of view. Here's some of what we have seen:

■ To do well in this new environment, people need to learn to

view every work situation as a market full of customers whose needs are being changed by a constantly changing environment.
- Every individual's D.A.T.A. represent the only reliable source of the product that she or he can bring into such a market, and these D.A.T.A. must be continually "recycled" into new products to meet customers' changing needs.
- Anyone doing these things will be better off viewing himself or herself as a microbusiness than as a worker or a manager. Better, certainly, than as an employee.

So far, so good. But how do you live in a world like that, a world where today's work is in one place and tomorrow's is in another; where the workload fluctuates wildly with the opportunities of the moment; where you can't say what you will be doing or earning next year; where colleagues come and go like passersby; where you spend as much time hustling for tomorrow's work as you spend doing today's? How can we live with a world that is nonstop change, as far as the eye can see?

Dealing with the Fluidity of the Dejobbed World

Sixty years ago the philosopher Alfred North Whitehead said, "The art of progress is to preserve order amid change and to preserve change amid order." It is important to recognize this reciprocal relationship and to understand that change and stability are not in an either-or relation to one another. Destroying one ends up destroying both. Without order, change has nothing to work on. In a situation of pure disorder—war conditions in what used to be Yugoslavia, for example—you can't really talk about "change" because change presumes an intelligible pattern to change from. The only change that a situation of pure flux can undergo is to stop being in flux. Anything less is not a change but only a continuation of the flux.

But without change, order cannot be maintained through time. Tex Schram was once asked why his Dallas Cowboys fell apart after almost a quarter of a century of football success. He answered, "We didn't react quickly enough to our failures. I think it's too easy to get caught up in your own success. You've got to know when to change. We didn't know when to change."

You can feel this same relation between change and order when you ride a bicycle: you need to keep making little turns, or else you won't travel straight and stay upright for very long. So what the dejobbed worker needs to look for is neither a way to recover some absolute stability or a way to live with utter chaos, but a dynamic kind of order that does not block the flow of change. (Tom Peters notwithstanding, people and organizations can learn to capitalize on chaotic conditions, but not to "thrive on chaos" as a steady diet.) There are, it turns out, a number of sources for such an ordering principle. Here are some of them.

Cut continuous change down to size

Many situations that seem completely random and meaningless are really only situations in which you lack a way to disclose the order inherent in many different change events. It's like those connect-the-dots diagrams in kids' magazines: once you find out how to "connect" the changes, the chaos disappears and an intelligible pattern emerges.

You need to find ways to cluster the changes under a few larger umbrellas of meaning. "The dejobbing of your organization" is one such umbrella, for it covers the reengineering project and the layoff that followed it, as well as the computerization project and the current outsourcing. Similarly, "the composite career" is an umbrella that covers a whole cluster of productive activities. There are many other umbrellas: "getting my act together," "rebuilding my support system," "upgrading my skills," "launching You & Co.," and "reprioritizing my activities."

That last phrase introduces a second approach to the task of bringing order to change: revising the priorities you give to your activities, your responsibilities, and your goals. Most of us had some priorities once, but time has changed our situations and we need to update our thinking on what is important and what isn't. We're either locked into old priority systems, putting energy into things that are no longer very important to our lives; or else we have just kept adding "utterly critical" items to our top-priority list until we have no way to decide any longer what really needs our attention. There are several ways to deal with this problem:

1. If you're already overwhelmed, you will have to clear the slate and start over again. Start by listing the three most important goals you have now. In the short term, at least, you just don't have time to serve more than these three masters. If you think you have a lot more than three, go back and do the clustering just described. We're looking for the big, comprehensive goals here, not the many little ones.

   Then, decide what intermediate objectives (no more than three) each of your three goals requires you to reach in the near future. Your to-do list comes from these nine objectives, but nine is too many. Prioritize them. Which three need to be done pronto? Which three could wait until next week? Which three simply have to be done sometime pretty soon? Now, take the "prontos": What immediate, first step does each one of them demand? Write them down. Those are the actions you are going to take this week.

   Make sure that your action items are really actions. For example, "Find out when our department is going to be reorganized" is not an action. That is, it doesn't specify what you are going to do and when you are going to do it. But "In the next department meeting, ask the director when the re-organization will take place" *is* an action. (A backup action would be "If she says that hasn't been decided, ask who is making that decision and when it will be made.")

2. After any big change in your life, you are going to have to reprioritize again, because any big change changes the value you put on everything in your life. When you change priorities, however, do so consciously and explicitly. Otherwise, you will just keep adding top-priority items to your list and falling further and further behind. (It's also important to keep others up to date on what your priorities are, since any change is going to affect other people too. The minute you start considering others, you will find that priority-setting isn't a game of solitaire. It probably calls for what we earlier termed "coactivity.")

3. Keeping your priorities in order is easier if you are not being swamped by sudden and unexpected changes. For that

reason, it is important to improve your capacity to see disruptive changes coming. You cannot avoid an accident, of course, and there are always a lot of things going on behind the scenes that you cannot be aware of. But most of what we call unexpected changes don't actually fall into those categories. Rather, they come from shifts in the environment that have already taken place but have not yet been fully recognized by the people who will be affected by them.

The demise of jobs is such a shift: people are still calling it a temporary phenomenon. There are dozens of other shifts-that-have-already-taken-place in today's work world, and it is sad to see people fighting rear-guard actions in the belief that the change can be avoided. The closure of military bases, the massive restructuring of the health-care industry, the loss of lending business by banks and S&Ls, the end of American dominance in world markets: all of these things are "done deals," but they are still regarded by many people as things that could be reversed.

What economic, technological, demographic, or cultural changes in your own work environment fall into this category? The sooner you know the answer, the readier you will be for the effects of these changes—which are, of course, changes in themselves. As Peter Drucker so cogently argues, "Entrepreneurs are mistakenly assumed to have the ability to foresee change. All that the entrepreneur does is to understand better than others the implications of changes that have already taken place. Then the entrepreneur seizes on a product or a service to capitalize on such a change."

Improve your ability to manage change

It has always been astounding to me how seldom organizations and individuals take a hard look at their capacity to manage change, and how little time and effort they put into improving that ability. If there is one thing that today's environment guarantees to organizations and individuals alike, it is a steady diet of change. The shift to a continuously changing environment is one of those "changes-that-have-already-happened," but too many of us are seeing the trees and missing the forest. We are coping with this change and that, but failing to enhance our capacity to manage change in general. We are focusing our strategic effort on attempts to capitalize on particular changes, and missing the enormous opportunity offered to any individual or organization that can capitalize on the fact that it is no longer possible to gain lasting strategic advantage by profiting from any specific change, no matter how large it may be. The only lasting strategic advantage tomorrow will come from dealing with today's challenge, which is to manage change better than your competitors do. This is just as true for you as an individual as it is for an organization, and that is why pegging your strategy to finding a job or succeeding at a job is so self-defeating.

So how do you enhance your capacity to deal effectively with continuous change? You conduct an "audit," an evaluation of your characteristics and situation, as they affect your ability to handle constant change. What is hindering you? What is helping you? Ask those questions in relation to each of the following categories.

1. **Expectations.** Do you have expectations that are continually being violated by the next change—expectations like these:

   ■ After this change, things will settle down.

   ■ If you are employed by a large organization, you will be insulated from the ravages of constant change.

   ■ If you "do a good job" for your employer, you'll remain on the payroll.

   ■ A human being will always be able to do your job better than a machine will.

   ■ The government will step in if the competition from overseas gets too intense.

   ■ Some positions in an organization are, by their very nature, secure.

   ■ Long service to an organization will be viewed as a plus.

2. **Habits.** It is critical for you stay up to date on the social, technical, and economic changes that are likely to have an impact on the kind of work you do. To enhance your ability to do that, decide what periodicals you would read regularly

and what professional or trade meetings you would attend if you were an independent professional in your field. And, instead of counting on single lines of action, regularly sketch out possible alternative scenarios to help you be readier for the challenges that you face.

3. **Contacts.** Are you ready to launch a personal business-development effort tomorrow by contacting the first two or three of the several dozen people who could help you move in whatever direction you decided was appropriate? These would be people who, themselves, have contacts; or who know a lot about something you'll need to understand; or who might be partners in a joint venture; or who have resources that you might be able to use; or who would be able to attest to your potentials and accomplishments. With typical extravagance, Harvey Mackay (the swimmer-with-sharks) underlines the importance of contacts by asking business audiences to name the most important work-related word in the English language. After people have tried *effort, creativity, strategy, cost, selling,* and *teamwork,* he gives his answer: "Rolodex."

4. **Personal "Rules."** Most of us are still playing under the old rules. While we have already talked about the new rules, it is important to talk about some of the old ones so that you can keep an eye out for them in your self-audit and replace them when you find them:

■ *Don't leave a job when good jobs are so hard to get.* Remember the point of this book's first two chapters: the same thing that makes jobs scarce "out there" makes your present job only a temporary expedient. It too is going to disappear. This is no argument to make ill-considered moves. It's just meant to challenge the rule that you are depending on. That rule is dangerous.

■ *The best jobs go to the people with the best qualifications.* The unspoken part of this rule is " . . . and my qualifications aren't very good." This rule is a half-truth, because it fails to acknowledge that the whole idea of "qualification" is changing. The old qualifications included degrees (or other formal certification), length of experience in a similar job, and recommendations.

Today, however, most recommendations are known to be hot air and tail-covering platitudes. Experience is more likely to produce a repetition of the past than the kind of new approaches that today's conditions demand. And there often isn't any degree or certification in the activity that today's organization needs. The new "qualification" is that you really want to do the work ("desire"), that you are good at what the work requires ("ability"), that you fit that kind of a situation ("temperament"), and that you have whatever other resources the work requires ("assets"). Those D.A.T.A. are the only qualifications that matter in a rapidly changing work world!

■ *Don't try to change careers after forty.* There is lots of age discrimination in the world of jobs. But that's the world you are leaving. There is far less age discrimination in the world of You & Co. Vendors get paid what they can show they are worth. Those age-related bugaboos health insurance and pension contributions are things that you are going to take care of yourself, so they aren't a factor the way they were when you were looking for a job. If you choose a new career on the basis of your D.A.T.A. and an understanding of the unmet needs in your market, go for it! Use whatever elements of the status quo best serve you as temporary expedients to ease the changeover process, but don't make a career out of them.

■ *Getting into the "right business" assures a secure future.* The Dustin Hoffman character in *The Graduate* was told "to get into plastics." Today it might be computers or biotechnology. But designating any field would be bad advice because although there are indeed parts of the economy that are destined to expand, no part of the economy is immune from dejobbing. It is far safer to get a need-satisfying product and build a viable You & Co. around it than it is to "get into" any particular field, as though it were a sheltered harbor in which to ride out the storm.

■ *It doesn't matter what you want. It's what "they" want that counts.* Most of us were raised on this one. Maturity was a matter of tempering our wants and of conforming to what someone with more influence or resources (like IBM or the state department of education) wanted of us. But today it doesn't matter nearly as much what an organization wants as it used to. The power has moved elsewhere; the only "they" that matters much any more is customers. Since what you want is an important part of your D.A.T.A.—that is, of your qualifications—you'd better pay attention to it.

■ *You have to be a salesman to get ahead today.* This is another half-truth that is also half false. The old-style salesman, who "could sell anything," is as much at risk as any other jobholder today. Far better off is the person with a clear product that she or he believes in. The truth element in the idea is that people are going to need the ability to conduct the quid-pro-quo transactions that we talked about in the last chapter. These involve not the old-line salesman's gift of gab, but a clear understanding of why someone needs what one has and does and the ability to make that case effectively. Many people who do that well have no experience or interest in sales as a field.

■ *If you have "responsibilities" (i.e., people dependent upon you for support), you can't leave the world of jobs.* This rule misidentifies the risk. If you have responsibilities, it is *more* important for you to look ahead and develop the kind of career that has a life expectancy beyond the end of the year. *Risky* and *responsible* have been redefined: the good job, which was once the definition of *responsibility,* is now a very risky business. And the old kind of freelance activity that was once risky is now in tune with the future and is becoming the choice of many people who want to act responsibly.

Rules like these are holdovers from yesterday's world—some of them from the day-before-yesterday's world of your youth— and they are doubly dangerous. First, they are misguided and are likely to get you into trouble. Second, following them gives you a dangerous sense of being on the right track, and so they slow down your discovery of a better path.

It is the rules you follow, the contacts you have, the habits you develop, and the expectations you carry around with you that either help you to deal with the psychological impacts of dejobbing or hinder you. Because these things are so close to you as to be largely invisible, it will take some effort to identify them. The best way to do so is by means of an explicit audit of your attitudes and assumptions.

Contain the changes within new, unchanging frames of meaning

The quotation cited earlier from Alfred North Whitehead talked about maintaining order amidst change, but most sources of order are the very things that are disappearing in the reorganizations, layoffs, and other organizational changes that happen so frequently today. So what continuities can be maintained throughout such turmoil? They must be portable, and so they must be dynamic rather than static. They must be "frames" within which a changing content is normalized and made consistent.

We have already discussed one such frame: the composite career. This frame transforms a continually changing series of projects and undertakings into a career with continuity, just as *kaizen*, or continous improvement, gives continuity to a sequence of process-enhancing changes in an organization. These principles and models are valuable because they contribute to a new mindset or cognitive structure within which change is far less disruptive than it would otherwise be. There are many other such frames; here is a list of some of them.

The frame of integrity/identity

The *integrity* I am talking about is psychological rather than ethical. It means "wholeness," and its opposite is *disintegration* and not *dishonesty*. With so much change and fragmentation in the new career world, you need a solid core of self. You have to be true to who you are—to your identity. (*Identity* means "sameness" and refers to the thread of being-the-same-person that runs through all the actions and relationships and statements of an integrated person.) The integrity/identity frame is capable both of maintaining continuity and containing change.

The market world is one where prices are much clearer than values, so the You & Co. approach that is appropriate to it could degenerate into trying to turn yourself into whatever some prospective customer wants you to become. This is why the frame of integrity/identity is so important, for it represents a boundary to the possibilities that one will entertain. Or to change the analogy, it represents a tether post at the center of one's activity that defines the area in which one can "be oneself." Other possibilities, admittedly, exist. And other people may be able to explore them with integrity. But being the-one-that-you-are, you cannot. To do so destroys the very basis of an authentic career.

The frame of integrity/identity is only incidentally a boundary beyond which you do not go, however. It is more fundamentally a way to define the area you *do* explore: this is who you are and what you do, this is the field of your calling. It is (to shift the metaphor) the thread of sameness on which differing activities can be strung. Each activity draws upon the resources of your D.A.T.A., recycling them into something new to meet an unmet need. If you do one thing today and another tomorrow, if you inhabit completely different work worlds in two different settings, if you serve totally different customers at different times, you are still the same person. This is quite different from the universe of jobs, where most people find that in time they become whatever they do—not just to others, but to themselves as well.

The frame of the life journey

"Progress" and the other traditional ideas that used to cushion people against the sharp edges of change have become harder and harder to believe in, but you can still create your own cushion. What these concepts did was to bring together changes into a meaningful pattern, which is important because people can handle large quantities of change if it hangs together and makes sense. Just because a world dominated by events in Yugoslavia, Somalia, and Haiti (not to mention racial violence and sexual abuse in our own country) makes it difficult to believe that we are "progressing" as a species, that does not mean that there are no life-affirming patterns. It just means that the patterns must be individually, not collectively, based.

One of the oldest life patterns, which turns up in all societies and all ages, is the picture of the individual's life as a journey. In that image, life events are stepping-stones or crossroads. We instinctively turn to this metaphor whenever we talk about "the path we followed" to some situation or event. We use it when we talk about life's "beginnings" or its "turning points," when we muse on our "roads not taken," when we say that we are at a "dead end," and when we talk about "where we are going" and "where we have been" in our lives. There are two different ways of seeing the life journeys that people take. Both offer ways of patterning and giving meaning to the changes that we journeyers encounter.

The first is a journey toward some external goal: influence and power, a happy family, salvation, or self-actualization. The characteristic of this journey is that it has a recognizable destination that is so desirable that we are willing to put up with the hardships along the way. Those hardships are just hurdles or barriers to be overcome. We may even see barriers as "filters" that keep the impure, the undeveloped, or the basely motivated from reaching the valuable goal. We may also view them as filters that screen out those elements in ourselves, in which case we say that the journey made us better people.

The second kind of journey is toward becoming the person that you really are. It was this journey that the Jewish wise man Rabbi Zusya had in mind when he said, shortly before he died, "In the world to come I shall not be asked, 'Why were you not Moses?' I shall be asked, 'Why were you not Zusya?' " This journey turns up in many spiritual traditions. Jesus obviously had it in mind when he urged us to become *perfect* the way that God is perfect, because the word he used means (in the original Greek of the New Testament manuscripts) "ripe, mature, developed" rather than "flawless." In terms of this journey, most of us are less like damaged goods than we are like green, hard, underripe fruit.

On this second journey, we are trying to become the people we are meant to be. We're "ugly ducklings" who don't know that we are really swans. We keep imagining that there is some better way to be, some better person to be. We fail to see that most of what the "great people" of the world have accomplished was not done because they were different but because they were not busy trying to be somebody else. Most of what has been worth doing since the beginning of time was accomplished by people who were (like you and me, most of the time) tired, self-doubting, ambivalent, and more than a bit discouraged.

This second journey frames the difficulties along the way not so much as hurdles to be cleared as signals to be attended to, or even lessons to be learned. It does not necessarily presume that "someone out there" has a message for us. Rather, it means that in the process of looking at our experience as if it were full of messages, we can discover meaning that would be otherwise missed. When someone on this journey says that "there are no accidents," that does not mean that we are living according to some great computer program in the sky, but simply that those times when "the wrong thing happens" are simply the times when we are looking at the world through the filters formed by our outgrown expectations. It means that if we could see the accidental as if it were part of a lesson plan, we would be in a relation to it that is creative—much as when an artist takes a found object or a naturally occurring pattern and incorporates it in a work of art.

Over and over again, we discover (and even sometimes admit) that if we had known what our path was really like, we might not have taken it—but that we are glad that we did. We probably even felt that way about being born, but it is hard to remember. Many of us certainly felt that way about getting a new sibling, who was going to be fun to play with but turned out to be an awful pain in the neck. We entered school with no idea about what a drag the multiplication tables were. Most of us started a sexual life, went off to college, got a job, had a child, moved to a new city, and accepted a promotion with motives and hopes that we only partly understood and that we would later call "naive."

This lack of understanding is not caused by our stupidity. The mismatch of intent and actuality is just how life works. Our original goals and expectations are little more than the "bait" that lured us into whatever is the next leg of our journey. Anyone who has come to appreciate these things and can see how often the life journey includes or even depends upon events and situations that we didn't really want to happen can appreciate the definition of the journey offered by an anonymous sage: "A *journey* is a *trip* after you've lost your luggage."

Such an understanding will also make it clear that finding a guide for your journey isn't a question of finding a special person. It is a question of becoming a special person: a traveler, a pilgrim, a person on a journey. When you have done that, the whole world turns out to be full of guides. Events themselves become the guideposts that tell us whether we are still on our path or not. The changes that befall us along the way are just the various experiences that we encounter on our journey. As the novelist Eudora Welty put it, "The events in our lives happen in a sequence in time, but in their significance to ourselves they find their own order . . . the continuous thread of revelation."

The dream as a frame

Closely related to the journey toward a destination (the first kind of journey, as just described) is the dream that draws us forward toward some imagined goal. Martin Luther King, Jr., spoke of one such dream, and it has been shared by many social activists before and after him. There are many other dreams that serve, similarly, to frame the diverse experiences one encounters in life. Some, like dreams of providing a great service, are altruistic. Others, like dreams of fame or wealth, are egocentric. But all of them provide continuities in a time of great change.

Dreams are dangerous frames, though, because under the right circumstances they can be realized. This happens when the revolutionary seizes power, when the poor girl becomes a rich woman, and when the artist completes the masterpiece. In such cases, all the meaning and continuity that the dream provided disappears. Although we may celebrate our "victory," there is a crisis in our inner world and we almost inevitably say to ourselves, "This is *it*? I thought that it was going to be better than *this!*" A realized dream is no longer a frame to give meaning and continuity to experience, which is why from an individual point of view the best dreams are those that can never fully be realized.

The craft as a frame

As people get tossed around in the changes that are constantly happening in today's organizations, they lose their loyalty to organizations and increase their loyalty to the kind of work they do. The result—engineers who are less loyal to the company and more loyal to their profession, or marketing professionals who are more dedicated to their work than to the company where it is done—is often noted as a sign that "loyalty is a dying value." But it is better understood as a shift in the continuity-producing frame. The organization can no longer perform that task, since the individual's connection with it is too easily broken. Only something portable can, so the profession, the vocation, or the work becomes the frame. As in many of the changes that coincide with dejobbing, this loyalty to one's craft takes us back to the preindustrial world.

In another version of the same process, "professional growth" becomes the frame. Here the work and the journey metaphor are blended, as the changes that the person encounters are translated into chances to learn more about one's vocation. That old idea, originally a religious one (a "calling") but long ago secularized to cover any valued kind of work, is very appealing to many people today. The journey of increasing expertise and the journey toward mastery become personally meaningful frames, for they contain and give meaning to not only to one's achievements but to even very serious work-related failures and disappointments.

The frame of "reality"

The journey, for all the turnings and backtrackings that it can endow with meaning, is still an essentially linear image: point A to point B. For many people, that metaphor for life smacks of the outdated reality of Newton and Euclid. For others it feels too "masculine" and intentional. Such people often see their lives more effectively framed by the reality metaphors that modern quantum physics and chaos theory provide.

Quantum physics has taught us to think of energy fields rather than of solid matter and has shown us how change occurs not gradually or piecemeal as ordinary experience would suggest, but in "quantum leaps" wherein a pattern of energy moves suddenly from one state or level to another. Life sometimes has that quality. (We wake up one morning and "everything has changed.") The everyday reality that we live with, which looks as substantial as the coffee table, periodically dissolves into nothingness. The career that looked fine yesterday is today trivial and worthless. The relationship that was very important to us yesterday suddenly isn't.

Maybe our lives are energy fields whose patterning occurs under the subtle magnetism of some idea or dream, as metal filings on a paper do when a magnet moves underneath them. Maybe organizations are just fields of magnetic force in the filings, looking significant and substantial, but falling suddenly into nothing when the magnet disappears. Maybe what we are calling "dejobbing" is just such a demagnetizing: suddenly, the jobs aren't there anymore; just filings, just work that needs to be done in some new way.

Or perhaps chaos theory provides a more effective meaning-making metaphor. If the organization is not like a set of children's building blocks, all horizontals and verticals on the organizational chart, perhaps the organization is more like flowing water (today, it is very fast flowing water) and management is more like kayaking than like getting from point A to point B. "Points" are unreal. It's all flux. The patterns are like weather systems, only predictable in the very short term—yet undeniably ordered by some principle beyond randomness.

Contemporary chaos theory talks about so-called strange attractors, which are the ordering principles within such apparently random patterns. They are found in water flows, in the seasons, in the rise and fall of animal populations, in the behavior of financial markets. Perhaps we can find a similar order in our lives. Such a frame—though *frame* is clearly too rigid a term—has the feel of life, its messiness-without-meaninglessness, its constant change and continuous transformation. Many modern readers have come away from a book like Meg Wheatley's *Leadership and the New Science*, which explores such theories, with the sense that their life has just been spread out before them.

Every "reality" has its metaphorical correspondences to life. The eighteenth-century universe was produced and guided by a watchmaker God. Everything fitted together like so many gears and levers. It was all rational and fully comprehensible. It corresponded metaphorically to a view of life that was similarly rationalistic and intelligible. Ben Franklin, writing in his autobiography, spoke of his misdeeds and his failures as "errors"— he was a printer, so he called them his "errata." He planned out his life logically, the way you'd lay out a printed text. To have an occasional "erratum" was like an occasional misprint. Just human.

Franklin experienced many changes and used an absolutely rationalistic frame to make sense of them. Others have seen their lives as quests for great treasures, as purgatories on the way to salvation, as tests of their courage, as trials of their faith, as the Tao, as ways to get out of the ghetto, or as the road to riches. Metaphors all, and every one of them has worked for someone. All of them have served to frame life events that would otherwise have been too hard to understand or too difficult to bear.

Each age has an affinity for some frames and an aversion to others. Progress was, for many people who are still alive, a workable frame at one time. So was success—success in the sense of "getting to the top." But those frames have largely had their day. Something else is needed, something that fits better with the profound changes we are going through. Perhaps there is no single frame that will work for everyone or even for many people any longer. Perhaps we must each find our own frame.

Be that as it may, all of us need order. Without it even change is in peril. Talking to people whose lives are full of change and yet not out of control, I've found as many answers as there are individuals. And I have come to think that the search for the right answer is misplaced. Each of us has to find a personal way to find order in the chaos, to cluster the changes, to frame them, to thread them on strands of continuity. But one thing is certain: To live meaningfully in a dejobbed world, we'll all need to balance the surrounding changes with new sources of order.

Create "islands of order"

Climbers scaling a rock face can move a hand or a foot if (and only if) they keep their other three limbs in place. It might sound like a time savings to move both feet and both hands at the same time, but the results would be disastrous. One of the ways to manage a life of constant change is to maintain stability in some areas of your life by not letting change into them. Many people with utterly chaotic work lives have very stable home lives. (Contrarily, some people whose private lives are full of change keep a very clear professional focus.) Some people whose careers have taken them all over the world have kept a home base somewhere that they return to whenever they need to put the pieces back together again. Many people whose work associates come and go with each project keep a circle of friends that changes very little. Many people who go through professional identities as though they were seasonal clothing maintain a spiritual discipline, or keep up to date in a particular field of intellectual inquiry, or play a sport seriously. These are the solid points of contact that they keep with the rock, which enable them to move safely.

Other islands of order are temporal and periodic: quiet time every weekend, every other weekend, one weekend every month; or a half-hour of meditation or solitary exercise every morning before breakfast; or two or three weeks "away from it all" every summer. Some time-outs are occasional: a break, a totally free and passive period, at the end of every big project. Some are spontaneous: a sudden decision to spend the afternoon at a ball-game or a movie, taking a hike or a swim instead of working.

Other islands of order are spatial. They are places where the person goes to break the pattern of constant change. It may be no more than a little park near work or a church that you stop by during lunch hour. It may be a room (even a corner of a room) in your house or a chair under a tree in the backyard. It may be a cabin in the woods or a motel room that you rent at the beach. It may be a special place where you like to camp out. Whatever and wherever they are, they are places of order. They are places where you take a break from constant input and output.

Still other islands of order are created by favored activities. They may be hobbies as simple as stamp collecting, little worlds of neat rectangularity and readily determined values. Or they may be as complex as playing a musical instrument or a sport, where you lose yourself in the practice of a skill. They can be cooking, splitting firewood, listening to music, taking walks, gardening, doing carpentry, brushing a horse, or training a dog. Again, there are as many possibilities as there are people with fast-moving lives. The only common element is that time slows down, even stands still, when you do them.

Ask yourself: What do I have in my life, what place or time or activity, where the constant rush stops, where changes stop, where I come back to myself again? Once, many people found such a point of stability in their jobs. The chances are that you won't be able to do that much longer. Maybe you have lost that stable point in your life already. What are you going to do about that?

Conclusion

It is a mistake to underestimate the stability that the job world brought into people's lives and how much people are going to miss that stability when it is gone. Everyone is going to miss it, because it has become the air we breathe. If jobs are going away, each of us will have to find new ways to feel at home in the world.

But though the job world has provided continuity, order, and a sense of identity, it has also made many people miserable. Not only were many of us pigeonholed—and in the wrong slots— many of us find repetitive, work-within-the-lines temperamentally difficult. The job world was also an uneven playing field. I, as a well-educated white male, had a favored position. If you are a person of color, a woman, or someone with a physical, mental, or emotional disadvantage, you were not so fortunate.

Sometimes when I have given a talk on these ideas about the dejobbing of the modern world, questioners have objected: "This all sounds fine for the well educated, but what about those who aren't?" In a sense, everything about the world has a way of favoring the favored. So any change will test particularly those who are already close to the edge in their lives. But I think that this change is going to be different in some important ways. I suspect that the people who were best adjusted to the job world are going to have the hardest time leaving it, and many individuals and groups that the job world has discriminated against will have an easier time when jobs vanish. I have already spoken of how women's experience may prepare them better for a life without jobs than men's experience does, but the same point could be made about ethnic minorities, the aged, physically handicapped people, or members of any group that has been poorly served by the world of jobs.

They not only have less to lose, they also often have the different kinds of temperament and ability that made the job world tough going—but that may also make it possible for them to capitalize on some of the opportunities the dejobbed world offers. It isn't, after all, gender, race, or age that gives you powerful desires or endows you with the kinds of abilities that people use to do new and important things. And assets are not just money in the bank. They are also fluency in Spanish or an intimate knowledge of inner-city life. And temperament: that cuts through all groups.

It was the job world that generated those long lists of qualifications that discriminated against people who did not have good educations. In the dejobbed world, the work will be done by the people who have the desire and the ability to do it. That isn't to say that this new world won't be biased in favor of some and against others. It is to say that the advent of that world changes what it takes to do well—and in the process, changes the terms under which one is favored or disfavored. When such a change takes place, those who feel entitled to the benefits that the old system gave them will cry "foul." If the dinosaurs had been endowed with speech, they too would have cried "foul."

It is a costly diversion to debate which groups this new world is good for; what matters is whether this is actually the world that is coming. I think that it is, and only our identification with the world that is disappearing keeps us from recognizing that fact. It is time to break that identification. It is time to stop trying to turn back the clock. It is time to move forward and to create the conditions, inner and outer, that we will need to deal with that world. We have, so far, been discussing the inner conditions. It is now time to turn to a discussion of the outer conditions: those that our organizations and our society will need to provide.

We're All in This Together

A state without the means of some change is without the means of its conservation.

—Edmund Burke, British statesman,
Reflections on the Revolution in France, 1790

We are in a paradoxical situation. We cannot wait for companies and the government to get their acts together; we must act individually in our own behalf. At the same time, our individual efforts will need to be supplemented by collective ones. We are all parts of the same socioeconomic system, and no one is going to be really secure again until the whole system changes. Dejobbed individuals will require dejobbed organizations and vice versa, and neither of them will function effectively until government regulations and resources stop considering the full-time job to be the natural human condition.

Just to list the areas in which change is necessary suggests the scope of the task ahead of us. If jobs are on the way out, we'll need new ways of securing our income and saving for our later years. We'll need to be retrained a number of times during our careers, and we'll have to find sources for that training elsewhere than in the training department of a long-term employer. A job-based health plan doesn't make sense any longer. The post-job world is also going to force labor unions to redefine what they are and what they do. And where jobs disappear, so does conventional full-time employment—and with that goes the very idea of *un*employment. Ultimately we are all in this strange and difficult situation together. So in Chapter 8 we will discuss how our social institutions are going to have to change in response to dejobbing. And with so much change ahead of us, we need to learn what people can do to manage the transition that we will all need to go through, individually and collectively, to get from where we are today to where we're going to be tomorrow. We'll deal with that in Chapter 9.

But first, in Chapter 7, let us turn to our organizations and look at what the dejobbed worker will do to their policies and structure, as well as to how they must be managed. I will discuss a wide range of ways that organizations can help themselves get through the job shift that is taking place, but these ideas aren't meant to constitute a fixed and formal program of organizational development. Every organization has its distinctive character and its own unique situation, so what works well in one place is not such a good idea somewhere else. View the suggestions as different possible points of entry into the large-scale organizational transformation that we'll have to undertake in the years ahead.

Running the Post-Job Organization

Yet when most companies are confronted with problems, they try simply to fix them. They fail to use a problem or a crisis as an opportunity to explore a new way to do business.

—John Sculley

One of the best things that ever happened was that the IRS was so demanding on our contractor arrangements. If they hadn't been, we'd have never worked out the structure, the roles, the training systems, and the compensation that we did. The IRS constraints actually made some of our breakthroughs possible.

—Valerie Skonie, founder of Skonie Corp.

On Trying to Improve the Job-Based Organization

Organizations, like individuals, are going to find it difficult to shift their expectations and their habits to fit into the new post-job world. Some of them will try to get by with job cuts, reducing thereby the number of hands and heads that do the work but leaving in place the old idea that work has to be packaged into jobs. Not surprisingly, such organizations find that removing job-holders leaves holes in the job field and that less work gets done as a result. An American Management Association survey of companies that had made "major staff cuts" between 1987 and 1992 found that, in spite of the reduced labor costs, less than half thereby improved their operating earnings—while one in four actually experienced a decline in earnings. More ominously, "these figures were even worse for companies that undertook a second or third round of downsizing." And unfortunately, many companies that fail to get their expected results with the first round of cuts do repeat the process.

Other companies cut jobs and use temps to fill in the spaces or to build in staffing flexibility. It is clear that tomorrow's organization needs to turn a significant part of its work over to a "contingent" workforce that can grow and shrink and reshape itself as its situation demands. I'll be recommending a template for organizational planning later in this chapter, but even the most creative design begs the question of how unready most organizations are to *manage* effectively this workforce of temps, part-timers, consultants, and contract workers.

There are some big problems here. One large manufacturing corporation, which used office temps extensively, found that (lacking ongoing loyalty to the organization) the temporaries on the clerical staff had leaked the details of the company plan for union negotiations to the union that represented the manufacturing employees. Another company, a condom maker, found that "every time you'd get a big batch of new [temp factory workers], you'd start finding more holes in the condoms."

Other companies couple the job cuts with reorganization. This makes more sense logically, since it recognizes that you can't just take pieces out of a system and expect it to keep working well. But although the endpoint may be more defensible, the process causes so much distress and disruption that the change that was meant to strengthen the company often ends up weakening it. That is because such changes force people to switch jobs, a process that undermines the three qualities that Michael Beer and his Harvard colleagues have identified as the source of competitive advantage: competence, coordination, and commitment. People are moved to unfamiliar jobs (competence declines); they are working in new teams, for new bosses, and with new customers (coordination declines); and they are demoralized by their new insecurity and the loss of coworker friends (commitment declines).

Still other companies seize on one of the cure-alls currently being widely touted and hope that it will do the trick. These efforts include

- Empowerment
- Flattening the organization
- Setting up self-directed teams
- Launching total-quality-management programs
- Reengineering the work
- Using flextime, telecommuting, and job sharing
- Setting up computer networks and using groupware
- Experimenting with "open-book management"
- Establishing a new vision for the organization

And if one of these efforts isn't delivering the expected results quickly enough, the organization is likely to move on to another item on the list. The unfortunate result can be a Change of the Month routine.

Any of these efforts can improve the organization, but all of them are compromised by the fact that everyone *has a job*. For as long as people are expending their energies on *doing their jobs*, they aren't going to focus on the customer, they aren't going to be self-managers, and they aren't going to be empowerable. They aren't, in short, going to be able to capitalize on the enhancement possibilities inherent in empowerment, automation, or anything else.

The Answer: Creating the Post-Job Organization

It is ironic that most organizations need their employees to stop acting like jobholders but that they only know how to hire, pay, communicate with, and manage jobholders. Most organizations also have policies, strategies, training programs, and structures that are meant to enable employees to be more successful in their job activities. In fact, a wave of the kind of job-free workers we have been talking about would wreck most traditional organizations. So, just as individuals need to rethink their assumptions and their strategies, organizations too are going to have to rethink almost everything they do.

Let's look at the characteristics of the post-job organization. The first is that they hire the right people. That sounds obvious,

although it means something very different in an organization
that is no longer job-based than it does where one is hiring to fill
slots. To begin with, you have to find people who can work well
without the cue system of job descriptions. Remember IDEO, the
jobless design firm described back in Chapter 2? The head of
marketing there, Tom Kelly, leaves no doubt about the importance of hiring: "If you hire the right people—if you've got the
right fit—then everything will take care of itself."

OK, fine. But how do you do that? By paying attention to the
same D.A.T.A. that we've been urging individuals to understand
and capitalize on.

- First, you find the people who are really turned on by the
kind of work they will be doing—the people whose *desires* fit.
Cissy Baker, former CNN managing editor, told Tom Peters
that CNN looks for "reporters desperate to tell their stories."
Then she added as almost an afterthought, "We can teach the
technical part." Joe Hauk, the vice president of manufacturing
at Luitink Manufacturing, a successful Wisconsin-based metal-
stamping company, makes the same point: "Once we believed
in hiring people for the skills they had. We now believe we can
take someone with the attitude and the desire to learn and
make that person into the best machine operator there is."

- Next come the *abilities*. Not skills, mind you. Those, as Hauk
and Baker note, can be taught. It is those general, inherent
abilities that matter. At Advanced Network Design, a California telecommunications company, they never hire until they
have identified fifteen to twenty "specific traits" that the position requires. CEO Dave Wiegand illustrates: "Does it require
someone who's detail oriented or who has good time-management skills? If so, we build an interview that probes for those,
and we put candidates through tests designed to assess
whether they have those traits."

- Although they may not use the term *temperament*, companies
that are moving away from jobs say that intangibles like "fitting
in here," "having the right chemistry," and "being comfortable with so much freedom" are make-or-break issues. Cissy
Baker was referring to temperament when she said that CNN

also required people to be "capable of dealing with extraordinary ambiguity." IDEO's Tom Kelly is also referring to temperament when he says, "A lot of people screen themselves out during the interview process" when they realize that the jobless organization is just not for them.

■ *Assets,* as we noted when we discussed it above, is the wild card in the employability hand. It is meaningless out of context. If a trainer or coordinator is going to work with people for whom English is a second language, being fluent in Spanish or Cambodian may be a terrific asset. In other situations, experience with bar-coding or a CAD program can be a big asset. So might a knowledge of how to put together a grant proposal or a request for an SBA loan.

You can see that the organization that hires people to do work rather than to fill jobs is going to have a different definition of what it is to be *qualified.* The job-based organization stresses training and experience. These can be spelled out pretty easily on a résumé, but the new qualifications cannot. That is why post-job companies not only schedule an interview between applicants and the staffing personnel or the prospective boss, but also have applicants talk with a wide variety of the organization's employees. That is why they put applicants into simulated situations and watch how they behave. That's why they ask weird and unexpected questions and study how the applicants deal with them.

The new qualifications mean that the old categories of under- and over-qualified no longer make much sense. The "underqualified" people may lack a degree and they may not have done that specific work before, but if they are fired up by the prospect, have the ability to do the kinds of things the task requires, have the right temperament, and (if appropriate) have valuable assets, they get hired. The "overqualified" people benefit in another way: the whole idea of slots and levels disappears, and with it goes the idea that a person's age, education, previous salary, and experience are "too much" for a particular job. As Randy Berggren, general manager of Eugene (Oregon) Water & Electric Board, puts it: "If you have a long-term, dynamic, fluid view of a transforming organization, there is no such concept as being overqualified."

"Experience" is a two-edged sword when you are hiring for work rather than jobs. On the one hand, it may mean that the person knows how to do the work. On the other hand, it may mean that the person knows how to do the *job*—and expects to do it for you. Too few people recognize the dangers inherent in experience, however. A recent article entitled "Secrets of Superior Customer Service" notes rightly that "one of the biggest obstacles to maintaining outstanding customer service is finding outstanding employees to deliver that service." But then the advice gets dubious: "But there is a way around the problem. Instead of taking on the expense of culling a few good hires from a vast number of job applicants, *recruit* from companies that already hire and train customer-oriented employees." If times weren't changing so fast, the baggage that such employees bring with them wouldn't matter much. But today, it can easily make it difficult for your organization to make the changes needed to keep up with the times.

The better way to find the right person for customer service or any other task is to start by analyzing just what a really superior worker in that area actually does. It matters little whether you are looking for an employee or a vendor, a part-time worker or a full-time one.

- What are the *abilities* that such a person would need to have? Get concrete. Does the role require a person to analyze problems, to talk reassuringly to upset people, or to understand product malfunctions from rather sketchy descriptions from users?

- Does it involve a particular *temperament*? Perhaps the most important thing is to be calm and unflappable, even when a customer is threatening to sue. Maybe the best service comes from people who are able to identify with frustrated and discouraged customers.

- And how about *desire*? Customer service requires someone who really wants to make things right for people. Customer service in today's organization requires the same kind of desire for results that a self-employed person has.

- And *assets*? Do the customer service people have to be computer literate? to have driver's licenses? to have nice telephone voices? to be self-employed business people who are taking care of their own health insurance and retirement planning? Forget the stacks of résumés and depend on an interview in which you ask for evidence of these D.A.T.A. Have the candidates perform a small task that demonstrates their qualifications, or have them describe what they would do in a simulated situation that would require superior customer service. It is better, in short, to figure out precisely what you are looking for and find it than it is to take on the old baggage that comes from adjustment to some other organization that is probably far behind yours in dealing with the end of jobs.

Structuring the Post-Job Organization

Even if you have the right people, your results will be poor if you organize them in the old way. Complex hierarchies need to be flattened, but that is not because flat organizations are currently fashionable. Rather, hierarchy and "vendor-mindedness" mix about as well as oil and water. Post-job employees are going to need a much more flexible organization to work in than they can easily find today. There is no one right way to create such flexibility, but the organizations that are utilizing such workers most effectively are finding a number of approaches effective.

Common to many of their approaches is a reliance on project teams. The project-based organization is not a new idea, for as we noted in Chapter 2, Melvin Anshen was writing about it in the *Harvard Business Review* twenty-five years ago. Even back then it was clear that the project-based organization was the only form that was not implicitly designed to maintain the status quo rather than to respond to the changing demands of the market. It was, he wrote, a "tailor-made design to fit unique tasks, flexible resource commitments, defined termination points, and an absence of enduring commitment that encourages resistance to innovation." Since those words were written, companies like EDS, Intel, and Microsoft have used the project as their essential building block—although *block* is far too fixed and rigid a term to describe the way projects are actually used today.

In a fast-moving organization like Intel, a person is likely to be hired and assigned to a project. The project changes over time, and the person's responsibilities and tasks change with it. Then the person is assigned to another project (well before the first project is finished), and then maybe to still another. These additional projects (which also keep evolving) require working under several team leaders, keeping different schedules, being in various places, and performing a number of different tasks. Hierarchy implodes, not because someone theorizes that it should but because under these conditions it cannot be maintained. Several of the workers on such teams interviewed by Tom Peters used the same phrase: "We report to each other."

In such a situation, people no longer take their cues from a job description or from a supervisor's instructions. The signals come from the changing demands of the work project itself. People learn to focus their individual efforts and their collective resources on "the work that needs doing," changing as that changes. Managers lose their "jobs," too, for their value can be defined only by how they facilitate the work done by the project teams or by how they contribute to them as a regular member. (We will discuss how this changes the idea of management later.)

It is this kind of situation that led to the remark by a Silicon Valley company executive quoted earlier: "We still hire by job categories, but then we forget about them completely." There is no good word for the place in this kind of organization that an individual fills, and once again our language is going to have to catch up with the reality, just as it did a hundred years ago with *job*. *Position* won't do; it sounds too fixed. *Role* sounds too unitary. Once you get it (whatever "it" is), you are likely to be given *assignments,* and that word is getting much commoner in the organizational lexicon. Whatever this "it" is, it is changing and multiple. It is a package of capabilities, which are accessed variously in different project-based situations. Anything that stands in the way of rapid regrouping has to go.

One thing that has to go is the elaborate matrix of horizontal classifications and vertical ranks. The Blacksburg, Virginia, Corning plant that makes ceramic elements for catalytic converters abandoned an earlier effort to increase productivity through a large automation project in favor of what it calls a people system. They replaced ranks and classifications with "only one job classification, with one manager for 60 employees; and [they] trained each employee to handle as many as 15 different jobs." Productivity has risen by 25 percent.

Where critical responsibilities require that an organization keep separate boxes-on-a-chart, companies may nonetheless use them in ways that violate all the rules of the job world. Intel, for example, uses what it calls its Two in a Box system to split a single set of responsibilities between two people: two people share a single title and location on the organizational chart. Subordinates often report to two people, not because they have two different areas of responsibility but because there are two people sitting at the boss's desk. The practice has worked well and has been used throughout the organization, starting at the top, where CEO Andy Grove has at various times shared a box with other executives.

Such arrangements require a very clearly articulated set of expectations on everyone's part, and that is why they often involve the principles of assignment and ownership. Consider the following descriptions of how work gets done at two very successful companies, the Indus Group (a software company) and Cypress Semiconductor:

> . . . the 250 staffers of Indus organize around projects (new product development, customer support) in groups that regularly expand and contract. [CEO Bob] Felton keeps up with their work through electronic mail: each Friday, all 250 people type up one-page summaries of what they worked on that week, what their plans are for the coming week, and what impediments they've run into. The packet is posted on the electronic bulletin board, and Felton himself reads them all, responding to many himself.

> At California's Cypress Semiconductor, all employees live by a system of self-imposed goal-setting, updated weekly. Every Monday all employees provide a computerized list of prioritized projects they will accomplish over the next month and a

half, as well as updates on existing projects. Managers review
the lists every week to sort out conflicts, correct misjudged
priorities, identify slippages in work progress, and determine
where employees may need assistance.

To those who have argued that you need those clear job descriptions and supervisory jobs to get things done, it is worth noting
that accountability is probably more direct and tight in these systems than it is in conventional hierarchies.

Listen to how new hires are brought into the organization at
Advanced Network Design, the California telecommunications
company we mentioned earlier in our discussion of how important hiring is. The day that they first report for work, new hires
get a list of what the company calls key result areas. CEO Dave
Wiegand describes what happens:

> If they have, say, 30 responsibilities, there might be 4 or 5
> that will generate 80% of the results we expect. We identify
> those key areas, explain them, and then we train. Once em-
> ployees have shown they can master a task, we just turn it
> over to them. Then they just report to management on a
> weekly or a monthly basis.

"Sure," you might say, "but those 'key result areas' are just
objectives and those 'responsibilities' are just 'job duties.' It's just
new names for old things." I don't think so. Job duties tell you
what you have to *do*. Responsibilities tell you what you have to
accomplish. Objectives are *targets*. Key result areas (in spite of its
jargonish quality) are areas in which *results* are expected. These
differences are part and parcel of the whole move away from
jobs. The twin brother of TIM-J ("That isn't my job") is IDM-J,
or "I've done my job (so don't expect anything else out of me)!"
You can do your job and fail to achieve the results that your job
was originally meant to serve. It's like the operation that was a
success—although the patient died.

Just as *assignment* is starting to take over some of the functions
of *job* in fast-moving companies, another word is showing up
more and more: *owner*. At Intel's Information Technology
Group, based in Folsom, California, Rich Martin describes what
he is doing currently. "I own our HR efforts in that area," he

says. I ask what that means. He explains that Intel's planning sequence establishes strategies (with objectives), tactics, and projects to realize them. A set of technological strategies and tactics may require some human resource strategies, tactics, and projects if they are to work. Both the primary (technological) and the secondary (HR) efforts need to have *owners*, because there are no job descriptions to justify placing them automatically in someone's hands. But for the same reason, there are no job descriptions to get in the way of people taking *ownership* of something they see that needs to get done. Rich did that and is now spending most of his time on a set of initiatives that did not exist last spring and that will probably be done next spring. Then, like almost all Intel employees, he'll move on to something else.

Most of these examples are taken from high-tech companies, for that is where the forces that are remaking the modern work world have had the greatest impact. But no business or industry or area of public service is immune from these forces. And very few businesses (with the right people, policies, and pay systems) could not benefit if they forgot the whole notion of jobs and moved instead to a system of assignments, owners, and (ugh!) "key result areas."

The Shape of Tomorrow

Tomorrow's organization is going to have to be configured very differently, if it is to profit from this constantly moving mix of assignments and responsibilities. The British management scholar Charles Handy suggests that the three-leafed shamrock should be its emblem.

■ The first leaf is made up of what he calls the professional core. It will consist of the professionals, technicians, and managers who possess the skills that represent the organization's core competence. Their pay is tied to organizational performance, and their relations will be more like those among the partners in a professional firm than those among superiors and subordinates in today's large corporation.

■ The second leaf is made up of external contractors who supply the services that used to be provided by support and staff departments. Some of these work as individuals and some as employees of vendor companies, but in either case they are paid in fees for results rather than in salary for time.

■ The third leaf is the contingent workers (temps and part-timers), who come and go as they are needed. They are paid by the hour or day or week for the time that they work.

Handy speculates that we may have to add a fourth leaf to represent the customers, for in self-service gas stations, ATMs, cafeterias, IKEA furniture stores, and many other organizations the customer is actually doing work that used to be done by an employee.

These categories are very useful, for they provide the kind of alternative to our conventional views that we so badly need if we are to find order in our chaotic environment. But they need to be modified a little to fit the realities that are emerging in the organizations in America. In the first place, Handy attributes more permanence to the professional core than actually exists. I am struck by how much movement there is, not only between one company's core and another's, but between contractors and the core. Just try to keep track of where your friends are working to see how rapidly self-employment can give way to employment by a company that provides services to other companies, and then from that to employment by the company that used those services. And then, of course, back to self-employment again after the next round of downsizing.

Even temp status is far less marginal than it sounds, for there is often a similar journey from being a temp to being hired full-time and then being hired away by one of the subcontractor firms that is working with the company. Handy's description of the temporary leaf does not do justice to the fact that temporaries include executives, software designers, financial professionals, and engineers. They aren't just clerical workers, nor are they nearly as modest in ambition or talent as his description would suggest. Nor is it easy to draw the line between these temps and the contractors who belong in the other leaf, for they too come in to accomplish a particular task or supplement the core workers in a particular project and then leave when their task is finished.

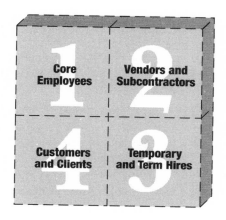

The shamrock might better be seen as a four-square field, with customers being, as he suggested, the fourth element. The boundaries between these quarters of the field are extremely permeable, with individuals moving from one to another or out into another completely different quartered-square. At any given time, the particular work done might be accomplished by an employee or a contractor, might be done on a full-time or part-time basis, might be done for salary, for a fee, for a share of the profit, or for some other form of gain. Whole activities that once were part of the so-called core might be moved over to the vendor quarter, or vendor activities might be brought back to core status. A worker (core, contractor, or temp) with an idea that the company itself did not want to pursue might be funded to do it independently and then return as a contractor to provide the service to the company, as well as to other companies or institutions.

These things are already going on. We have already talked about how many of the activities that were once performed by organizations and institutions in-house are being today outsourced or provided by satellite operations in distant sites. Organizations are also "calving" new organizations, the way a glacier calves an iceberg. Hyatt Hotels has helped employees launch independent businesses in party catering and sporting-equipment rental. Compaq funded Conner Peripherals, and Cypress Semiconductor did the same with Ross Technology. Apple Computer has launched a whole raft of new businesses that supply accessories, software, and networking capability to its Macintosh computers. More companies need to consider encouraging such ventures instead of viewing them as defections, for the result is happy former employees, a network of vendors who really know your needs, and flexible resources that are no longer carried on the company payroll.

Organizations are also starting to "modularize" their operations in such a way that they become essentially clusters of coacting units. Sometimes this involves turning every new project into a semi-independent startup. The Boston-based International Data Group, which has launched almost two hundred magazines and newspapers, gives each new project a chunk of "venture capital," a separate location, and what it calls phantom equity. According to Pat McGovern, the group's chairman, new ventures

> succeed best if they spend most of their time with customers and if they are forced to adjust their product to the needs of the market. Giving new, bootstrapped ventures some autonomy spurs them to do those things; it also forces the people heading the projects to become entrepreneurs themselves, requiring them to understand and accept the discipline of business plans, manage cash flow, keep costs in line, and create a work style that reflects competitive rigor.

Similar things are being done in mature organizations, too, by destructuring them into separate businesses. Inside Chesapeake Packaging Company's Baltimore cardboard-box plant, for example, plant manager Bob Argabright has set up nothing less than eight little "companies." These are not just the old departments with new names, for they hire their own employees, select their own leaders, and design their work processes and organizational structures. They are profit-and-loss centers, responsible to and for their own customers (internal and external)—who can all go elsewhere if they do not like the service they are getting. The plant had been a money-loser in 1988, when it was organized conventionally. Today it is the second most profitable plant in the company. Clearly, dejobbing and modularizing can work as well in traditional industries as in high-tech ones.

Such turnarounds are always thought-provoking, but even more interesting is the fact that such an operation is not so very different from Walden Paddlers, the one-person virtual corporation described back in Chapter 3. True, the kayak company was just one guy in an office, who outsourced design, manufacturing, distribution, and other functions to existing companies located all over the map. But Bob Argabright at the Baltimore cardboard-box plant is just a guy in an office too. Forget the fact that his "companies" used to be departments and that they are located under the same roof. The point is that the organizations most in touch with today's realities are those that are building in the flexibility of modularity and tapping into the productivity and service excellence that comes from developing the vendor mind-set in what may have once been departments full of jobholders.

What is inside and what is outside the organizational boundary, anyway? The "office" full of people that was once inside is now a bunch of people doing forecasting, accounting, or cold-calling out of home offices, or people faxing in orders from their laptops in cars, hotel rooms, and customer locations. When you add that some of these people may not be employees, but rather individual contractors or temps hired to handle a flood of business, you have to conclude that the same forces that are making job descriptions unworkable are also making organizational boundaries so changeable and permeable as to become almost invisible.

Look at what is happening to that champion of the job world, the truck driver. Not only is he (or, increasingly, she) likely to be a self-employed business person driving his or her own rig. Today's driver is also likely to be doing things for a client company that yesterday's truck drivers would never have dreamed of doing. One recent study concluded:

These days, some truckers are more inclined to sport white collars than tank tops. Once (and still) lumped as rednecks and high-school dropouts, they are now fluent with computers, satellites and fax machines—all of which can be found in the cabs of their 18-wheelers. They are being asked to take on tasks never dreamed of: faxing sales invoices;

hounding customers who are slow to pay bills; and training office workers how to use the latest high-tech toy. "The day of the good-old-boy trucker is a thing of the past," says Joseph Coleman, chief executive officer of Volume Transportation Inc., a Lithonia, Ga. trucking company. "Today, they have to be businessmen," adds Robert Fauls Jr., president of Southern Freight Inc. in Atlanta.

The company or industry which imagines that the vendor-minded employee, who breaks loose from the old boundaries of the job, can fit in only at a small startup or a cutting-edge industry is in a state of denial. And that denial is going to be more dangerous with each passing year.

The organizations most in tune with the new realities are not, as Tom Peters would have it, doing crazy things because these are crazy times. They are very deliberately leveraging the technical, political, social, and economic changes going on around us to do new things that make perfectly good sense in fast-moving times. They are re-creating what it means to be "a business," stretching that term to include a one-person operation contracting to do a project for a big company; the group of small companies gathered into a joint business venture; the networked web of far-flung and formerly independent firms; and the large organization that has been destructured into a cluster of little businesses. Businesses all, and all staffed by people who themselves act like little businesses.

Infrastructures for Post-Job Organizations

Some of what it takes to run the post-job organization is part of the environment: the databases and the networking technology, for example, that make it possible for a delocalized operation to function effectively. A sales rep sits in a customer's office and fills out a product order form on her laptop, asking the customer what features he'd like on the product and pricing the order accordingly. When she sends in the order over her built-in modem, it not only goes into the accounting channels of her company but straight into the manufacturing process, where the "desired features" are converted into specifications and into instructions to the automated manufacturing system, which has been designed to customize products on order. Such technology, which is one of the forces transforming organizations and dejobbing the workplace, is part of the emerging organizational infrastructure. It was "out there" waiting to be utilized.

Not so with the socio-cultural infrastructure for this kind of work world. Far less developed, not yet widely embraced, and lagging behind the technical infrastructure, its absence threatens to undermine the new work world. You cannot run a post-job organization the same way you ran the organization when it was job-based. Policies on work hours, for example, won't be the same. Compensation plans will have to change. New training programs will be needed. A different kind of communication (and new paths for it) is essential. Careers have to be reconceptualized, and career development has to be reinvented. New redeployment mechanisms become necessary. And the whole idea and practice of "management" need to be re-created from scratch.

I wish I knew exactly what the territory ahead will look like, but I do not. We will be struggling with these issues for years to come. There will be books written on each of these topics, but we are still feeling our way and learning through trial and error. We can do no more here than raise some of the issues that need be considered. In the remainder of this chapter, I will do that by discussing briefly each element of the new socio-cultural infrastructure that the post-job organization will require.

New Conditions, New Policies

Some organizations have experimented with flextime, job sharing, and telecommuting, but the disappearance of jobs puts all of these matters into a new context. In some ways, we are turning back the clock, for as we saw in Chapter 2, standardized work hours, standardized workplaces, and the equation of one person and one job were products of mass production and the governmental bureaucracies occasioned by it. In the prejob world, dividing labor and standardizing roles would have limited people's productivity.

In the prejob world work was usually shared, under arrangements that varied with the demands of the situation. It was only

when work was divided into little activity packages and distributed one-to-a-person in the form of "jobs" that anyone would
have imagined that anything but talent, proximity, strength, and
availability determined who did what and when they did it. Of
course, once the common task is divided into jobs, then full-time
employment becomes the norm and people have to lobby the
organization to offer work in any other form. Anyone whose
other responsibilities, physical capabilities, or financial needs
make full-time employment unappealing or unworkable may suggest "job sharing." And we treat the suggestion as though it were
some kind of exotic alternative to "real" employment.

But if jobs disappear there is no longer any reason to treat
these eight-hour chunks of effort as building blocks from which
the organizational structure must be assembled. I'm not saying
that "job sharing" will be permitted in the post-job organization—much more than that: I am saying that the issue disappears. Of course work will be shared! People who are working on
more than one project are already dividing their "job" into several pieces. If you spend four hours doing assignment A, two
doing assignment B, and two doing assignment C; if Sally spends
two hours doing A, four doing B, and two doing C; and if Dave
spends two hours doing A, two doing B, and four doing C, then
you are all already "job sharing" anyway. What will the post-job
policy be on job sharing? It will be to put the old policy in the
Policy Museum as an artifact of a bygone age and get on with
doing the work that needs doing.

The same thing is going to happen to policies about flextime
and flex-location, or telecommuting. These matters will be governed partly by the demands of the work itself and partly by other
economic factors, which can include the cost of office space, the
availability of technological linkages between delocalized coworkers, and such idiosyncratic matters as the parties' family responsibilities, their commute conditions, and whether they work better
early in the day or late. Self-employed workers always take all of
these matters into account, and so will post-job workers.

How about policies on leaves of absence, vacations, and retirement? Leaves from what? Vacations from what? Retirement from

what? As we shall see in a moment, the post-job worker is going to be far more likely to be hired for a project or for a fixed length of time than a jobholder is today. Working and leisure are no longer governed by the calculus of constant employment. Without the job, time off from work becomes not something taken out of job time but something sandwiched into the interims between assignments or between project contracts.

And retirement? As more and more people become "businesses-in-themselves," retirement will become an individual matter that has less to do with organizational policy and more to do with individual circumstances and desires. But what about those abstruse pension regulations that hold people in place—until they are vested, or until they cross some threshold that enables them to retire with something like a full pension? As we shall see in a few minutes, the pension is going to have to be disengaged from the job and become the individual's responsibility. The use of 401(k) plans by a growing number of businesses is already a step in that direction, and employees are already far more involved in the investment of their retirement money than yesterday's workers would ever have thought possible. Tomorrow's workers will go even further, and will be managing their own funds. Needless to say, they will retire when they feel able and ready to.

But this new freedom is not an invitation to a life of leisure. If self-employment is any guide, the dejobbed worker is likely to be a stern taskmaster. We've already noted that the dejobbed worker loses, along with the job, a definition of what is enough. Add the fact that the dejobbed worker is going to be scheduling his or her own employment and trying (like any independent professional) to make hay while the sun shines. The result is that post-job workers are going to have to learn to pace themselves. But as far as the organization is concerned, leave policies, vacation policies, and retirement policies are going to be relatively insignificant.

Compensation and Benefits after Jobs Disappear

In our society, the job has provided the salary or the hourly pay that gave us our income. Without an income, we could not survive. But it is more than a question of economics. Hourly pay or a salary is the way that the organization tells us that our work is valuable. A raise is a reward, providing us with more status as well as more money to spend. The end of the job is going to raise very troubling issues, for hourly pay and salaries are going to become less and less common in the future. We are going to see the gradual disappearance of standardized, narrow pay ranges for full-time work within a particular job category and organizational level, as well as the end of the familiar regular increases for longevity and increased responsibility.

Already fast-moving companies are hiring more temporaries and fixed-term employees and fewer regular, full-time employees. The old compensation-and-benefits packages are not available to such workers. And those who are full-timers are likely, as we have already seen, to be "on assignment" to a project rather than carry out ongoing "duties." Compensation is likely to become more closely tied to how those assignments turn out.

Under the realities of the post-job workplace, a fee-for-service arrangement fits the organization's needs as much as it fits the individual worker's, since it ties compensation to the completion of a necessary task and does not commit the organization to pay a person whose services it may no longer need. Time-limited contracts will become commoner. Executives have often been hired with contracts that specify some compensation if the arrangement is terminated sooner than planned, and such clauses will become available to other workers as well. All of us are going to move toward some kind of contract with the organizations that pay for our services.

Two unrelated trends are further undermining the traditional salary. One is the shrinking of simple "pay" and the expansion of shared earnings. The share can take the form of a bonus, stock options, or profit sharing, but in any form it deemphasizes the job and emphasizes the work done and the contribution made. It also blurs the line, which jobs and salaries made very distinct, between the employee and the owner, and it does so with the intention of capturing from the employee the commitment felt only by someone with an ownership stake in a business.

The second trend is that of paying for skills. Milan Moravec and Robert Tucker have noted that we cannot expect to tap into the talents of individual workers or the capabilities of the organization until "we change the way we design, allocate, and talk about work. . . . The focus should be on people's skills and behaviors, not on jobs." Skill clusters, they argue, are much more flexible than jobs and are more closely tied to achieving the outcomes that the organization is seeking.

The authors analyze how the 10,000-person Exploration Division of British Petroleum (where Tucker is the vice president of human resources) has created "skills matrices" to describe the different performance levels for the actual capabilities that different roles in the division require. Levels run from low ("is acquiring basic knowledge and has awareness of the key skills") to high ("conducts and/or supervises complex tasks requiring advanced knowledge of key skills or a thorough working knowledge of a range of key skills"). Capabilities run along the other side of the matrix, and include such things as "technical expertise," "business awareness," "communication and interpersonal," and "decision-making and initiative." In this way, individuals are paid for what they can actually contribute to the organization, not for the job that they happen to hold.

Whether by means of pay for skills, fee for service, share of the earnings, or some still-to-be-discovered form of compensation, the organization of the future is going to find that salaries are as counterproductive as jobs. It is a truism that you get what you pay for, and with organizations needing to get new levels of effort and new degrees of flexibility from their workers, new kinds of compensation are going to become commonplace.

The End of Management

Rosabeth Moss Kanter talks about "The New Managerial Work," making it clear in her definition that many of today's managers would hardly recognize it. In the new-style organization, she says,

the ability of managers to get things done depends more on the number of networks in which they're centrally involved than on their height in the hierarchy. . . . In the emerging

organization, managers add value by deal making, by brokering at interfaces, rather than by presiding over their individual empires. . . . They need to serve as integrators and
facilitators, not as watchdogs and interventionalists. . . .
"We don't even have good words," she says, "to describe the new
relationships" that are created by "the dramatically altered realities of managerial work in these transformed companies."

Others, too, puzzle over what to call the person who used to be
a manager. Peter Drucker tells an interviewer, "I'm not comfortable with the word *manager* any more, because it implies subordinates. I find myself using *executive* more, because it implies
responsibility for an area, not necessarily dominion over people."
Walter Kiechel, in a review of workplace trends, tries to decide
"what to call the people we used to call 'managers.' . . . The best
choice? Probably 'coordinator.' "

The discomfort over names represents the fact that it is still not
quite clear what tomorrow's manager will have to do. Everyone
agrees that tomorrow's worker, untrammeled by the old constraints of hierarchy and job boundaries, is going to be far more
independent and self-directed than today's worker is. The question is, will such a worker even need "managing" in anything like
the accepted sense of the word?

The father of reengineering, Michael Hammer, leaves no
doubt where he stands on the question: "Middle management, as
we currently know it, will simply disappear." Three-quarters of
the middle managers will vanish, he says, many of them returning
to the "real work" they did before they were promoted into management, with the remainder filling a role that "will change almost beyond recognition." He sees the responsibilities of
tomorrow's managers as diverging into two different paths: the
first into coaching and the second into the ownership of some
work or business process (e.g., filling orders or receiving and distributing parts). Gone will be their basic function for the past
century: seeing to it that the workers "did their jobs." We have
indeed come to the point where we need to talk about "The End
of Management."

The reason, of course, is that our so-called manager was cre-

ated only a little more than a century ago to oversee and direct
the work of people who held "jobs." Before that, there were masters and gang bosses and commanders and overseers, but there
were no managers. People were led, but whatever management
existed was self-management. And that is what we are returning
to—though with a crucial difference. The old self-management
was "taking care of yourself" while you followed the leader. The
new self-management is "acting toward the business at hand as if
you had an ownership stake in it."

This means that tomorrow's executive, coordinator, facilitator,
or whatever we choose to call the nonmanager will have to provide people with direct access to the information that was once
the domain of decision makers. Tomorrow's employees (and even
tomorrow's contractors) are going to need to understand the
whys and wherefores of the organization's strategy far more than
today's do; they are going to have to understand the organization's problems, weaknesses, and challenges realistically. The
dejobbed worker is going to need to be much clearer on the organization's vision and values than the job-based worker needed to
be. Drawing on chaos theory, Lisa Marshall distinguishes between that need and the old idea of "vision" as an imagined future destination. "Vision/values is not prediction," she says.

It stems from an understanding of one's province, one's real
value and proper role in the world. In personal terms, your
vision is rooted in your sense of identity—what you bring to
the party, what you contribute. In business terms, it is
rooted in knowing what your value proposition is—why the
world should pay you to exist. . . . In other words, vision/
values is identity and values extended into the future—
choices, possibilities, potential and desire for that individual
or organization.

In a job-based environment, you just do your job. In a dejobbed
environment, you do what needs to be done to honor and realize
the organization's vision/values.

Dejobbed workers must be able to understand how their individual activities affect the organizational balance sheet. Com-
menting on how CNN runs such a successful organization with so

little conventional "management," Tom Peters notes that "everyone at CNN—starting with the V[ideo] J[ournalist]s and other field people—knows what things cost. . . . In large measure, the company is in control financially because each person has a sense of managing the whole, not just his or her bit."

The goal of unmanagement, in the words that John Case used for a recent and very influential article in *Inc.* magazine, is to turn your organization into "A Company of Business People." Case cites the example of LifeUSA, a new and rapidly growing insurance company based in Minneapolis. LifeUSA has no "employees," because the 275 people who work for the company are "owners" who get about 10 percent of their compensation in stock options. The personnel department is called Owner Services. Lest you think that this is so much window dressing, reflect on the fact that LifeUSA has gone from a startup to profits of $10 million on revenues of $146 million in six years. Its CEO comments that this year "we'll write more new business than probably 98% of the companies out there. And we'll do it with fewer people. Because they're owners, they're involved, they run the company."

Or consider the case of Springfield Remanufacturing Corp., a Missouri-based engine rebuilder, which began as a red-ink division of what used to be International Harvester. Today, after ten years of employee ownership, it has $74 million in revenues and $1.5 million in profit. How did that happen? "Employees are trained to understand every detail of the company's financials. Every quarter they get bonuses pegged to goals such as return on assets. In the meantime, they [get] weekly income statements and cash-flow reports, comparing projected figures with the actual. 'What they learn is how to make money, how to make a profit,' says CEO . . . Jack Stack."

There is no mystery about how such companies—and a dozen others that Case cites—get these results:

1. They encourage rank-and-file employees to make the kind of operating decisions that used to be reserved for managers to make.

2. They give people the information that they need to make

such decisions—information that used to be given only to the managers.

3. They give employees lots of training to create the kind of understanding of business and financial issues that no one but an owner or an executive used to be concerned with.

4. They give people a stake in the fruits of their labor, a share of the company profits.

The results speak for themselves.

Training Programs for a Post-Job Workplace

The business and financial training given by the companies just noted does not appear on the training schedules of most traditional companies. Instead, there are all kinds of courses in something or other that one will need to do a particular job. Management training is meant to improve how the manager does his or her job. Computer or machine training gives people the skills that they need to do a clerical or manufacturing job. Sales training? Ditto for sales jobs. "Improving job performance" is the goal of most training.

There is a whole category of training that's getting overlooked here. It is the training that the person-who-is-acting-like-a-business needs. It is training in "reading" a market, in spotting change-generated needs, and in defining one's product in terms that make sense to people that have those needs. It is training in personal benchmarking, so that you know how well other service vendors do what you propose to do—and how they get those results. It is training in being your own sales department, in being your own R&D group, in continuously improving the quality of what you do. It is training in personal time management and personal joint-venturing.

Management training is going to have to become training in coaching and consulting rather than training in oversight and control. Control is getting built into the information-feedback system, just as it is getting built (with the help of embedded computer chips) into the fuel system of a car. Old-style management is going to be as out of place in a post-job organization as a manual choke would be in a contemporary car. Like a choke, the old style of management will not just be unnecessary but will actually undermine the effective working of the new organization.

The future employee-development program is going to be much more like a program for self-employed entrepreneurs than a program for jobholders. Workers won't be dragged into a seminar, the way they often are today. Workers are going to need to know how to do something to get hired for the next project, and getting them to class will be a matter of their push, not someone else's pull. Workers who don't keep up a self-managed program of continuing education will fall behind and will lose out on the opportunities.

That kind of self-directed education is also going to have to be supplemented with organizationally sponsored business-development opportunities, so that someone who sees an unmet need or a problem that needs solving can get funding to tackle it. It will matter less that the person tackles it as an employee or an external vendor than that the person solves it. In fact, it is going to make increasingly good sense for companies to fund "startup businesses" for their employees, businesses that not only serve the organization's needs but provide the service to other organizations as well. Simply to outsource work to existing firms and companies gives the organization no role in the careers of the employees who are going to find themselves without jobs in the next round of downsizing. Rather than send these people packing with a little outplacement help, why not build those who have the capacity into a network of vendors whose goodwill and understanding of the organization will serve you well in the turbulent years ahead?

Finally, training is going to have to become less outcome and more process oriented in the years ahead. We don't know what the precise shape of tomorrow's organization will be, but we do know that it will be different from today's. We don't know just what tomorrow's worker will be doing, but we do know that it will be different from what he or she does today. We don't know what tomorrow's unmet needs will be, but we do know that they will be different from today's. In the light of that, we need to be sure that managing change and facilitating transition are at the core of tomorrow's curriculum.

The New Circulatory System: Redeployment

Most organizations today phase out people when their jobs become superfluous and add new people when new jobs are established. Hiring and layoffs often go on simultaneously, much to the detriment of employee morale, leadership credibility, and budget health. It can, for example, easily cost $10,000 to terminate one hourly worker and hire a new one, and that amount increases rapidly with the salaries of the people involved, the difficulty of finding the right new hire, and the downtime while the new person settles in and comes up to speed. And any cost estimate presumes that the termination goes without a hitch and that the new hire turns out to be the right person. Both are chancy these days.

What is obviously needed is an internal infrastructure for redeploying people that goes beyond the usual job listings on the bulletin board in Personnel and the halfhearted career counsel from one's manager. This redeployment system would include training in how to manage one's own career, opportunities for and encouragement of networking within the organization, and on-line access to "current opportunities" that would be not just traditional openings but emerging needs throughout the organization, even before they become official openings. This training would help people to develop the self-as-a-business tactics we have already described. On-line assistance would also include information on how to tap into career-resource assistance outside the organization: courses, data banks, assessment services, and the like.

In one sense, this redeployment assistance would be an internal version of what outplacement provides people who have been laid off: a kind of "inplacement." But it would go beyond that to include assistance with the practical and psychological challenges that relocation and reassignment bring. Such assistance might

include visits (by the whole family) to a proposed new location
whenever a transfer is contemplated; home-sale and home-
purchase assistance; help with finding employment for a working
spouse; and a program in dealing successfully with personal transition.

Would such assistance be available to the kind of independent
worker that we have been describing? What would keep such a
person from using the move and the training to leave the organization and set up in business independently? And a further issue:
When we talked about the new "vendor-minded" workers who
view themselves as though they were little businesses, we said that
they had to take care of themselves and not look to the organization for the kind of help it used to provide. Are we contradicting
that now by saying that the organization is going to have a redeployment infrastructure that will help this "independent business
person" move?

While understandable, those questions are starting at the
wrong end, because they assume some "normal" kind of employment (full-time job) that is worth investing in and other kinds of
employment that aren't. Turn all of that around: The new reality
is that people are going to come and go with the growth and
decay of projects. So the real question is, how can the organization gain a person's energetic and creative contribution to a project, even though it is not a part of long-term employment?

The answer is twofold: First, such a person is hired the way a
consultant is, with built-in "overhead" to cover ancillary costs—
like temporary or permanent moves. Second, even though the
person him- or herself is ultimately responsible for whatever career moves turn out to be necessary, a good working relationship
between the new-style organization and the new-style worker is
going to be a collaborative effort in which each party acts as
though it had more than half the responsibility for making the
new arrangements work.

The individuals, whether contractors, temps, project hires, or
full-time employees of a more conventional sort, need to let go of
all of their old assumptions about work and careers. Anything less
than that, and they won't be able to shift to the realities of the

post-job world. But the organization too needs to do some big changing: all its old policies and procedures are going to get in its way and make it difficult to capitalize on what the new worker has to offer. The organization needs to reinvent itself to coordinate and profit from the efforts of workers that are more like vendors and consultants than they are like employees. This can be done, and it can be done best in the spirit of a joint venture between independent individuals and the organization.

The organization that wants to move down the path toward the future would do well to start with the little diagram back on page 155. It needs to ask:

- Is the work being done by the right people?

- Are the core tasks, requiring and protecting the special competencies of the organization, being done in-house, and are other tasks being given to vendors or subcontractors, temps or term hires, or to the customers themselves?

- Are the people chosen to do the work in each of those categories hired in such a way that their D.A.T.A. are matched with the actual demands of the task?

- Are such workers compensated in the most appropriate way?

- Is everyone involved—those in all four of the quadrants, not just the core employees—given the business information that they need to understand their part in the larger task? Do they have the understandings needed to "think like business people"?

- And finally, does the way people are organized and managed help them to complete their assignments or does it tie them to outmoded expectations and job-based assumptions?

Too often the new ways of doing things are viewed as add-ons: "If we ever get a spare moment around here, let's flatten the organizational chart!" That's a big mistake, of course. Part of the reason there is so little time is that most of today's organizations are trying to use outmoded and underpowered forms to do tomorrow's work. They insert an empowerment program here and a new profit-sharing plan there and then announce that those things aren't so great after all because the company's profits are still falling! Such organizations won't have better results until they do two things. First, get rid of jobs. Second, redesign the organization to get the best out of a dejobbed worker. A big task.

Sure, but like any evolutionary challenge, it will separate the survivors from the extinct.

What Society Needs to Do about Dejobbing

> *. . . the time has . . . come for a debate about the redistribution of entrepreneurial riches in this country. But the debate should not be about redistributing financial wealth. Rather, politicians and policymakers should be focusing on the need to redistribute basic economic know-how from the few to the many.*
> —George Gendron, editor, *Inc.* magazine

The Challenge

When social institutions are changing in a fundamental way, the first response is always likely to be protective and reactionary. *The changes must be stopped! We must not allow these things to happen! We must restore the old ways!* As Charles Handy says, "We could have passed a law outlawing tractors or requiring every tractor to be accompanied by a man on a horse. We wisely did not." If we had passed such a regulation, we would have paid a very high price, both literally (in uncompetitively expensive food) and figuratively (in failing to free up human and economic resources for the opportunities that lay ahead). We did not do that, and a whole way of life based on farming a piece of land was replaced by a lifeway based on having a job.

At the time that the shift was taking place, what was really happening was not at all clear, and people idealized the life that was being left behind. It is not coincidental that in America the first great jobshift occurred at the same time that the virtues of village life and the family farm were being celebrated in American art and literature. That was the heyday of Currier and Ives prints, showing families traveling to the grandparents' farm for the holidays; it is the age of Stephen Foster's "My Old Kentucky Home," John Greenleaf Whittier's "Snowbound," and Henry Wadsworth Longfellow's "The Village Blacksmith." Americans looked back wistfully to the lost worlds of their childhoods at the very time that they were being plunged forward into the urbanized, commercialized, manufacturing-centered world of jobs.

We stand at a comparable watershed today. Again the future looks both dangerous and uncertain. Again we can see the shadowy outlines of the new post-job world, and again we are unsure that we can deal with the new life that faces us. And what do we do? We fight bitterly over the remaining pieces of the old world. We idealize the world of jobs and conveniently forget how boring and depressing most people found it. We forget how unfairly it treated women and minorities and how seldom its promises of success were actually fulfilled with promotion to the top of the heap. We denounce international agreements like NAFTA because they will "take away jobs" without any awareness that jobs are not so much being exported as they are disappearing into the great black hole of technical and economic change.

Although I have been emphasizing the individual and the organizational levels of action in what I have so far said, it is clear that society—in both its official governmental aspect and its unofficial private aspect—has a critical role to play too. Social institutions and agencies need not only to channel the forces of change but to provide buffers and nets to keep this second great job transition from being as traumatic as the first. These institutions and agencies are the only plausible source of assistance and education for the creation of a new generation of workers who are today jobminded but who must rapidly develop a whole new outlook on themselves and on work. We face the same task described by an unnamed British industrialist, quoted by the historian Herbert Guttman: "The spirit of [a new way of working] must become the general spirit of the nation and be incorporated, as it were, into their very essence. . . . It requires a long time before the personal, and a still longer time before the national, habits are formed."

So far I have addressed this situation with a wake-up call to you as an individual, an appeal to look at the current reality and to see that this is not just one of those periodic dips in employment but a major and permanent shift in how work is going to be done. Some individuals are already turning these difficulties into opportunities, and others will need little more than the call and some advice on how to answer it. Those individuals will form the critically important vanguard of a new workforce. Their turning in a new direction will turn others behind them, and their success in the new career paths will serve as a model to others. These trendsetters have a critical social role to play. But they cannot accomplish the necessary changes alone.

I have also spoken of the changes that organizations will have to make, because unless the trendsetters and their followers want to establish whole new organizations, existing organizations are going to have to change their ways for the post-job worker to be an asset to them. Many organizations will not change, however, and unless they have the luxury of a tax-based life-support system, they will sicken and die. Over the coming half century, we are going to see many once-invincible corporations disintegrate. But in their place new ones will grow. In the organizational world as in nature, new life grows out of the decomposing remains of the old.

Public Policy for a Time of Transition

It will take more than the acts of individuals and organizations to get the bulk of people through the great shift to the post-job world. The "habits" that the eighteenth-century British industrialist had in mind grow from deep roots that go down into the culture and the social psyche, and to change them requires a deep societal shift and leaders who understand the socioeconomic factors that will drive it. They are not just bits of behavior that could be itemized on a checklist or practiced before breakfast every morning.

The first thing we must do is to demand that our political leaders have the courage to abandon the fantasy that jobs can be recovered or re-created as they once could have been. We need to understand that there is no way to pump out more jobs, as though they were industrial products, and every time our leaders play into our old fantasy that that is possible, they do us an enormous disservice. The trouble is, of course, that promising more jobs is an effective electoral tactic. Furthermore, it sounds public spirited and humane.

"More jobs" is something that both liberals and conservatives can endorse—although the former will want the government to produce the jobs and the latter will insist that the private sector must do it. Politicians only appear to disagree in their debates over how best to create jobs—for they agree on the fiction that *anyone* can actually "create jobs" when the conditions of the modern workplace are making jobs dysfunctional. Until they stop spreading this fiction and begin to talk honestly about what the future holds for us, they are just letting us wander further and further from the road to recovery. Like strong medicine, the truth is not going to be pleasant. But without it, our condition will continue to worsen.

The second item on the public agenda is to get our leaders to stop pouring their energies into fighting over the jobs that remain and turn their attention to helping people deal with the fact that jobs are disappearing everywhere. Such fighting can be seen in the way that Arizona politicians, fearful of losing Hughes Missile jobs in Tucson, passed a tax-relief measure to hold onto them and also to attract new ones away from General Dynamics sites in California; San Diego, of course, lost everything that Tucson gained, and jobs were simply moved from one pocket to another.

Company leaders are doing the same thing. Shortly after the appearance the documentary *Roger & Me*, which pilloried General Motors for closing auto plants in Flint, Michigan, the automaker announced that the manufacture of vans would be moved from plants in Scarborough, Ontario, and Lordstown, Ohio, to a plant in Flint. Pure business, said GM; a pure shell game said the critics. The first act of legitimate leadership is to stop the shell game and deal forthrightly with the real reasons that people are losing their jobs. Until that is done, people are going to be seizing on one simplistic solution after another, blaming one scapegoat after another, and doing nothing to better the situation.

The third thing that our leaders need to do is to clear the path before us, so that we can catch up with the socioeconomic realities. Sometimes what it would take to do that seems so simple that one marvels at the dedicated stupidity that keeps it from happening. In the aftermath of the Los Angeles riots of 1992, the Industry Education Council of California, a nonprofit group of business, labor, and education leaders, came up with a plan to help people find work in riot-devastated areas. The plan was to start a newsletter to publicize work opportunities that were available in the areas that had been hardest hit by the riot. "Job fairs" and training sessions would supplement this information, and more than three dozen Los Angeles radio and TV stations offered to publicize these resources for free. Once the program had placed 2,400 people (three-and-a-half months of advertised openings), it would begin to pay for itself with the additional payroll taxes that it generated. Everyone agreed it was a terrific idea.

But when its coordinator, Kathy Masera, went to Washington for $2.6 million in startup money, the Bush administration Labor Department told her to go to the California Employment Development Department, which turned her down because the program would duplicate existing state efforts. (Such efforts had been invisible to the Industry Education Council's members.) When she went back to Washington for another try, the Labor Department told her that they couldn't help her because "they had already financed a similar tryout—just where and when, though, they couldn't say." After the 1992 election, things went a little better, although it still took months of congressional intervention to prod the Labor Department into action.

Barriers to helping people find work and to learning to work in new ways need to be removed at all levels of government. At the local level, this would mean doing away with outdated ordinances like Los Angeles's ban on all home-based businesses or Chicago's zoning rules that make it illegal to use a computer for commercial purposes in a home. Most zoning regulations need review, in fact, for they were drawn up with an image of "business" that presumed customer-heavy retailing or noisy and noxious manufacture. Today it may be neither, but the old rules still stand.

At the national level such regulations involve the unrealistic restrictions that are placed on the deductibility of home offices. The U.S. Supreme Court recently upheld the IRS refusal to permit a Virginia anesthesiologist to deduct the expense of his home office because he did not regularly meet clients there (and anesthetize them?) and because he regularly conducted business elsewhere. The fact that such an independent professional needs a central place at which to do financial recordkeeping and from which to conduct the telephone work that such a business requires counted for nothing. In fact, rather than tax penalties, the SoHo (single operator, home office) business needs tax incentives commensurate with the contribution that it is going to be making to local and national economies.

The point here does not really involve the details of the useful actions that government could take. Details are given only to suggest that there are, in fact, many things that public and private societal bodies could do. The main point is that the efforts of such bodies need to be reoriented away from jobs (government job statistics, community job listings, and employment department job-search seminars) and toward the work that needs to be done in the post-job world and the work arrangements that are emerging to take the place of jobs.

The old distinction between the organization (which was "the business") and the individual (who was "the employee") is no longer a useful one.

■ Individuals are businesses now, and organizations won't need nearly as many employees.

■ Business activity can expand enormously under these new conditions without creating a single new individual job.

■ Unless government-created "jobs" or other work situations can be integrated into ongoing business activities, they will disappear the minute their subsidy ends.

The old individual/business distinction is enshrined (I almost said "embalmed") in the tax laws, where businesses can deduct many expenses that an individual cannot. Tax rates rise and fall, but the individual and the business are always treated differently. It is t ue that the Chapter S corporation allows business income to be taxed as individual income, but until there are comparable ways for the individual to be taxed as a business, the inequities continue to make it difficult to develop You & Co. to its full potential.

Just as individuals need to forget jobs and look for the work that needs doing, so do societal agencies and institutions. Just as organizations need to refocus their efforts on work and stop trying to make the job the vehicle for the results they seek, so do societal agencies and institutions. Laws, regulations, and all kinds of public expenditures need to be rebuilt from the ground up on this new basis. How they will look when that has been done cannot now be foreseen, but they will look different. And they will move us forward into the twenty-first century and not back into the nineteenth.

But just getting out of the way of good ideas, important as it is, will not be enough. It is time to abandon the fiction long propounded by the Reagan and Bush administrations that business would do just fine—and create plenty of new jobs—if government just got out of the way. In fact, the new conditions of work require a coordinated effort and activities that are much more proactive and far-reaching. What stands in our way is not just this regulation and that, which can be killed or rewritten. What stands in our way is a whole system designed to serve the job.

So the fourth thing that our leaders need to do is to undertake a full-scale audit of the regulations we live under today, the social services we count on today, the taxes we pay today, and the health care we utilize today: all of them are based on the idea that having a full-time job is the normal human condition. People who do not have such jobs are socially defined by that fact ("temps," "the unemployed," "the self-employed," or "the independently wealthy"), and society has its rules for them as well. Jobs are woven into the fabric of our public policy and the laws we live under. This is the culture (a job culture, if you will) that resists all the superficial efforts that we make. We have a lot of unraveling and reweaving ahead of us, for until we begin to create a new set of assumptions and outlooks and expectations, the old culture will simply "bleed through" like an underlying pattern and obliterate our efforts.

So, as our fifth agenda item, we must resist the temptation to embrace pseudo-solutions that rearrange the details of the problem without solving it. Such a pseudo-solution is the shorter workweek, recently in vogue as an answer to European job shortages. Volkswagen has embraced it to forestall further layoffs, while French companies have tended to view it as a way to open up opportunity for new hires. The difficulty with the answer is a practical one.

Do the workers themselves absorb the costs in lower pay? If the goal is to spread the pain caused by current conditions, this might be a possibility—but so far, no group of workers has offered to pay the price. One could argue that considerably shortening the workweek, sharing existing jobs with those currently out of work, and reducing pay would create both the carrot and the stick that would get many workers moving down the road toward a job-free work life. Workers who took to heart the message of this book might well use the ten extra work-free hours a week to go through their D.A.T.A., articulate and market their product, and set up the wherewithal that You & Co. requires. And the smaller pay would be an incentive to get rolling.

If the worker does not embrace that opportunity, the price must still be paid. Does the employer absorb the costs and cut profits or raise prices? In a few high-margin businesses, cutting profits may be a fair option; raising prices is inflationary, and in many cases would be self-defeating since it would make the products uncompetitive and imperil the whole business. Or does the government subsidize the increased costs? As a temporary measure in unusual cases, subsidy might be justifiable, but in this day of budget crunches it is hardly a good long-term solution. And none of these solutions addresses the underlying problem: jobs are an inefficient and uneconomical way to divide work. Shared inefficiency is no answer.

Job creation is the wrong focus. Business creation is the right one. Not only does job creation encourage "business stealing," from one city, state, or country to another, it also misunderstands where expanding employment opportunities come from. They come primarily from the creation of new businesses. In a study of employment patterns in the metropolitan Dallas area, University of Texas political economist Donald A. Hicks found that 61 percent were created by new businesses, 25 percent by expanding small businesses, 10 percent by expanding big businesses, and a paltry 3.3 percent by new employers that moved into the region. Hicks's conclusions: forget "attracting new business"; focus instead on "creat[ing] an environment friendly to the formation of new businesses."

Besides the low taxes, good schools, accessible transportation and communication networks, and minimal red tape that obviously encourage business formation, local governments can directly assist those who want to start new businesses through the funding of "business incubators." These are places where a fledgling business can get the advice, support, and space it needs to get off the ground. There are almost five hundred incubators in the United States (the number fluctuates constantly, since their funding is often precarious). They tend to be located in low-rent areas because one of their main functions is to provide very inexpensive space to a business just getting started. A big incubator, like Minnesota's University Technology Center, has more than 125 businesses under its roof. Besides the low rent, such centers can provide the technical assistance—from lawyers, accountants, and consultants—that young businesses often do not know where to get or how to pay for.

Helping People to Recycle Themselves

It won't be enough to create new businesses, however, for really new enterprises are those that are increasingly job free, and they make demands that today's workers have difficulty handling.

Public and private nonprofit institutions need to refocus their efforts on providing the help that people need to develop the skills necessary to compete for the work that needs doing. These skills are not the same as the offerings of the "retraining" programs that are common today. Most retraining programs purport to foresee the technical, clerical, or professional fields that are going to expand in the future and then offer skill-based training to prepare people for jobs in those fields. The trouble with such programs is that when people graduate from them, the jobs turn out to be mighty scarce, both because foreseeing the economic future is very difficult (today's growing fields are all too often tomorrow's shrinking ones) and because the programs themselves are tied to a vanishing entity, the job.

A program that promises help but does not deliver it not only wastes scarce money but also feeds the growing bitterness and mistrust that arises when people keep trying to use old solutions for a new problem. It is understandable that individuals—particularly economically unsophisticated ones—continue to bark up the wrong, old tree. It is inexcusable that the government sponsors such actions. Training programs must be refocused on the real skills appropriate to the work situations of the post-job age. These skills fall into three categories.

The first skills that dejobbed workers will need are very basic: they will need to be literate, numerate, and (if you will permit it) computerate. Without these things, workers cannot even continue to learn; with the skills, they can understand enough to learn more. The more advanced machine or computer skills that most of today's retraining programs emphasize would be better provided by an employer or a trade association. In fact, the most successful programs are joint efforts between a source of training and a source of employment. In an article on Cincinnati's very successful cooperative education program, the *Wall Street Journal* noted that one key to its success "is something that is lacking in most state and federal job-training programs: an intimate, symbiotic relationship between local businesses that have jobs to offer and the educational institutions that are preparing workers for them."

Training needs to be related to clear work demands. Even the elementary skills of literacy, numeracy, and computeracy become meaningful only as they are focused on the demands of some actual work situation. To realize that you have to be able to understand a computer printout or make an intelligible oral report after a meeting or write a clear request for information and send it to another site on E-mail: these discoveries are far more motivating than even the most well crafted classroom lesson plan. So the first requirement for any skill-based retraining program is to link it with (or, better, embed it in) a real workplace where the trainee is responsible for real work that needs to be done.

The second kind of skill that the dejobbed world is going to require is the ability to manage oneself in a businesslike fashion. This takes us back to the idea of You & Co. and the notion that the best way to think about dejobbed work is to imagine that you are a business that operates in a market full of customers whose needs are changing. What are the skills that you are going to need to run that business? Time-management skills, goal-setting skills, communication skills, basic bookkeeping skills, project-management skills, and the fundamentals of office management.

Listed in this way, they sound like a curriculum beyond the reach of most workers. But that misrepresents them. They are simply an updated version of the basic skills that Mom and Pop use to run the corner store, that anyone uses to launch a new church group or run the PTA, or that high-school entrepreneurs use when they start a Saturday child-care or car-wash business. Too esoteric for the average person, you say? Every successful neighborhood drug dealer uses them. They are simply the skills you need to get organized and accomplish something.

The third cluster of skills that tomorrow's worker will need and public training facilities can provide is the kind needed to find work under the new conditions. Even under the old job paradigm, training in such skills was shortchanged—even though it paid off more liberally than did technical training. You can give one group of people job-search training for $300 to $400 each, while another group's technical retraining costs ten times as much. Yet both groups end up earning about the same amount over the years, and the job-search students actually out-earn the technically trained group by about $250 in the first year of employment because they were able to find work sooner.

For a number of reasons, the importance of work-search (*not* "job-search") training is going to be magnified as jobs diminish in importance. First, the job world puts a higher premium on formal qualifications (like graduation from a retraining program) than the dejobbed world will; where such qualifications matter less, your skill at searching becomes a larger factor in your success. Second, the old job-application process is well known, but how you "look for work that needs doing" isn't. When you were looking for a job, there were places to get résumés typed. The daily paper ran job ads. There were formal job applications to fill out.

So work that is not "packaged" into a job is harder to find and harder to secure. If job-search skills were valuable, work-search skills are going to be priceless. Such skills will include

- Understanding your own D.A.T.A.
- Seeing every situation, inside and outside an organization, as a market.
- Spotting change-created needs that are not currently being met in the market.
- Understanding the potential customer's present perception of that need.
- Assessing the current and potential competition for the task of meeting that need.
- Developing and being able to describe a personal product that will fill that perceived need—or rather that need as it may be redefined by the client with assistance by the work seeker.
- Assuring continuous quality improvement of the product as delivered to the client.

All in all, these are as far a cry from ordinary job-search skills as those were from the old-fashioned "answering an ad." A person who has learned them, however, is never again in the dependent role of job seeker, but is instead an independent business person who knows how to provide products and services in a world that has stopped packaging work into jobs.

Needed: Career and Business Development Centers

Government agencies have not done very well by people who are looking for work. The U.S. Department of Labor's Employment Service, the main federal employment agency, has managed to find work for less than one out of every five people seeking its assistance. Cornell labor economist John Bishop wrote a recent Brookings Institution study on the difficulty that workers have, not only finding work but even finding effective help in how to find work. He concluded that (in the words of a *Fortune* article on the topic) "the Employment Service would improve its performance if it were to simply list all job openings in convenient public places and on computer bulletin boards that would allow job seekers and employers to find each other."

That's a half-truth, of course, for it's precisely those "job openings" that are going the way of the dinosaur. But the true half of the point is that we do lack reliable information-distribution systems that work seekers can use to find clients and customers for their services and products. The best of the systems we do have are not governmental but private. They are places like Palo Alto, California's Career Action Center and San Francisco's Alumnae Resources.

These places help people to find work, not jobs. Each of them has around 70,000 visits by work seekers each year. Each of them maintains exhaustive lists of contact people in local organizations, runs workshops on how to manage your career as though you were a business, and provides ongoing education in the unmet needs in different economic sectors. They both use "alumnae" (and "alumni") to serve as models, mentors, and contacts for those currently seeking work. They provide the kind of self-assessment help that we discussed as "surveying your D.A.T.A.," and they offer both personal counseling and videotape-assisted training in how to market yourself in an interview. Although both were originally founded by and for women, who have always been poorly served by the job world, they now assist both men and women.

Both of them also offer courses in how to launch a business of your own, but neither yet takes what would seem to be the next logical step in providing help. That is to integrate their services with those of the business incubators we described earlier. Because job-mindedness has led us to separate business formation from looking for employment, the small-business incubator and the career-development center have been heretofore seen as separate institutions with very different purposes. But if you buy the argument that jobs are not the path to anyone's future and that the new kinds of work that replace them will have a lot in common with self-employment, then the two kinds of institutions begin to converge in both their aims and their clientele. They both are intended to help people to create new work situations, and so they could be profitably combined into a Career and Business Development Center (CBDC), where people would not only learn to find work but could also create an on-premises work situation for themselves and others. If the federal government wanted to move beyond being a clearinghouse for information and begin to help people create the work that they are now helplessly trying to find, it might well contribute funds to the efforts of cities and rural areas that wanted to set up CBDCs.

The CBDC could also foster creative efforts to build the tax base of a community like those followed by Steamboat Springs, Colorado, for example. Not all communities want big or highly industrial businesses. Steamboat Springs, anxious to protect its scenic assets and so distinctly unfriendly to conventional industry, has recently launched an effort to attract SoHo (single-operator, home-office) professionals. As we have already pointed out, fax machines, overnight mail, modems, E-mail, and access to public databases make it possible to conduct sophisticated professional activity in almost any location. Steamboat Springs has realized that recruiting ten such people to move there could add a million dollars to the local economy, and that does not even count the possibility that such a SoHo business could grow into a large organization in a few cases.

Replacing the Worn-out Safety Net

One of the most important things that policymakers need to do is to start transferring the security machinery from jobs to some more permanent basis. Take health care. We seem to be moving toward universal health coverage, which is a major step in the right direction, but we are still tying most of the cost for that coverage to jobs. America is the only major country that bases health care on jobs rather than on citizenship, and we do it because a World War II expedient (attracting new workers by offering health care as a benefit) was continued after the crisis passed.

Jobs have too much riding on them already. Health care needs to be detached from them and funded from general taxes. Since the money comes out of our pockets, either through what we pay for the employers' products or through what we pay in taxes, it won't cost more to fund it publicly. But it makes a huge difference practically, since job-based health insurance discourages employers from hiring more people and in that way increases the numbers of those who need governmental assistance, not just to pay their medical bills but to pay for food and housing as well.

Pension plans, likewise, need to be unplugged from jobs. (The growing use of employee-controlled 401(k) plans is a step in the right direction—but only a step.) Many corporate pension plans are badly underfunded, and the government agency that is supposed to guard workers against default in such cases is itself stretched beyond capacity. But even when they are well funded, corporate pension plans are irrelevant to more and more workers because the available jobs during the past decade have largely been at smaller companies, which are much less likely to offer the big-company pension plans. (They also, not coincidentally, are far less likely to carry health benefits than GM, Sears, IBM, and comparable big companies were.) Even worse, the job-based pensions were meant for people who worked for a single employer for a long time. Today's job-hopper has trouble qualifying for them, even if he or she works for a company that provides them.

Nor is the present social security system in much better shape. Current estimates by the Clinton administration suggest that it will be insolvent by 2036 and will be running deficits twenty years earlier than that. More pessimistic projections move the insolvency date to 2017. (Today's forty-year-old will turn sixty-five in 2019.) And these projections assume what in this day of budget crises is by no means assured: that legislators will keep their hands off these funds in the meantime. There is no easy solution to this problem, but an obvious avenue to explore is to encourage individuals to take more responsibility for their own retirement security. Individual workers who are setting up a You & Co. had better put a "company pension plan" at the top of the to-do list.

But that simply shifts all of the responsibility back to the individual. Society needs to help. Chile has taken an interesting step that we may want to follow: It has privatized its social security system, turning back to the recipients the responsibility for and control over the social security funds that they have accumulated. To such funds are added monthly retirement contributions that remain mandatory, and the resulting accounts are something like our IRAs. Such funds not only grow much faster than do traditional social security investments, but they also help the country's economy by raising the savings rate—so far, in Chile's case, by about a third. True, some individuals might invest unwisely, but there could be rules governing what types of investment such funds could make—rules that would minimize the chance of losing the worker's assets. Before we reject such an alternative as dangerous, we need to remember how many people are going to end up with little or nothing under our "safe" system of social security and corporate pension plans.

Even when an organization's pension funds are safe, the present regulations under which they operate make it difficult to face a dejobbed future with confidence. Composite careers and the number of employers tomorrow's worker will be working for over his or her career make the old vesting rules (it isn't your money until you've been here for x years) and the old requirements for full-time employment dysfunctional. Present pension rules raise problems for workers who want to roll over money from one pension plan to another. These things will make long-term individual security much harder to build than it needs to be. If pensions are not to be privatized, they must at least be fully portable. They could be pooled, as the Teachers Insurance Annuity Association does for college teachers, so that the individual can move from employer to employer without jeopardizing retirement security.

Then there is the need for a more realistic source of financial support while people are in transit from one work situation to another. We talk as though most people get an unemployment check when they lose a job, but during the recessions since World War II, only half of the jobless received unemployment benefits. During the recent—and uniquely devastating—recession, the figure fell below 40 percent. More than three out of five people got no unemployment benefits at all. And the figure is lower in the southern states, where a jobless person is a third less likely to receive such assistance than is a person in the northeastern states.

It used to be that European countries, with their nearly limitless unemployment benefits, represented the most attractive alternatives to our system. But mounting rates of unemployment and diminishing rates of growth have called into question whether those generous social-benefit systems can long survive. Workfare systems, in which people contribute some kind of productive labor in return for public support, are certainly an alternative. But the real need is for a system that would both subsidize those at the bottom of the income ladder and encourage them to keep working and earning.

In the end, only some form of income subsidy will fill that bill. Such a subsidy would also solve what will certainly be one of the pressing problems of a world in which steady employment at a long-term job gets less and less common. That problem is the need for temporary support when income levels fall, as they must in the dejobbed world. We need to detach such support from the idea that it is a "jobless benefit." Most people are going to be jobless. This benefit is, rather, an income supplement to buffer the drops in income that the self-employed are prone to.

It may be possible to make it at least partially self-funded, an "account" into which deposits are put during good times and from which they are withdrawn during hard times. Or perhaps this "deposited" money would be better spent purchasing "income subsidy insurance" from a private carrier. We are in a situation where there is a huge market for employment-insurance coverage, and insurance companies are likely to create products to meet the need as it grows.

It is too early to try to establish the details. At this point the important thing is to agree that some new kind of income buffering is going to be necessary, especially during the difficult period during which jobs are being replaced by kinds of work that are much more like self-employment. Such buffering would consist of a variable payout that would keep relatively constant the level of disposable income under circumstances where earnings fluctuate. At the upper income levels, these subsidies would go into effect only during those rare times when all earning stopped. In the middle range of incomes, they would serve to fill in the unexpected income "potholes" and control the fluctuations. And at the lower levels, they would constitute a constant supplement to (but never replacement for) what was being earned.

The Role of Unions

As the American workplace becomes more and more dejobbed, no institution has more to gain (or lose), more ways that it could help workers (or harm them), no greater chance of evolution (or extinction) than the labor union. Traditionally viewed as an opposing force to the conservatism of the business world, labor unions have usually been seen as politically liberal in their platforms. But today they are at least as reactionary as business groups are, for they are equally wedded to the archaic job world.

In responding to the way that industrialism was transforming work throughout the western world, labor unions ironically became the greatest defender of the job. Job descriptions became their sacred texts, for they were considered the workers' protection against exploitation. Labor contracts spelled out the regulations in stupefying detail. For example, the 1946 United Steel Workers contract not only specified exactly how much sand a shoveler could shovel per minute, but precisely what its moisture content could be.

It is time for unions to stop such practices. They not only stand in the way of more flexible work arrangements and a work style that is more in tune with the new economic realities, such actions also keep unions from playing a creative and useful role in the years ahead. Until unions abandon their focus on jobs, they will not only continue to lose members but they will not find their proper role. New times bring new problems, and new problems call for new solutions. Recall what we have been saying. Tomorrow's workers are going to be more "craft" based than job based. They are going to be more like independent business people (or one-person businesses) than conventional employees. They may work for more than one client at a time, and they will be likely to move back and forth across organizational boundaries—being employed fulltime for a while, then hired to do contract work, then hired to consult, and then brought back in-house (but part-time this time) on a long-term assignment.

This new kind of worker isn't a member of the proletariat or the laboring class, or even an hourly worker in a particular industry. This person is a portable resource with no fixed job identity. This person needs the information and the learning opportunities that alliance with other, similar workers could provide. This person needs something more like a medieval crafts guild than the labor union of 1860–1980.

Since hiring and work rules will be customized to each situation, what we've known as collective bargaining will be more or less irrelevant. But that does not mean that workers will not have common interests. It just means that those interests will be more often pursued in the halls of Congress than in the factory. Tomorrow's "unions" will be public-advocacy groups, serving the common interests of different kinds of workers. The American Medical Association, whatever its shortcomings, has served doctors in this way for decades. In fact medicine has been, at least until recently, built around the *practice* rather than the *job.*

Tomorrow's "unions" will be educational institutions, where workers turn when the demands of their work present them with something that they need to learn more about. Perhaps they will offer Continuing Education Units, as nurses' groups and other professional associations do. Such CEUs would be one of the *assets* that the dejobbed worker could use to enhance employability.

They will also be sources of consultative assistance, with more similarities to a computer users' group than to a traditional union. Where computer literacy is an element in the work, they may be even more like the users' group by providing many of their services on-line. Some of this consultative assistance will be technical—rating the new software in a professional field, surveying educational opportunities, providing case studies, and the like—but some of it will be business related. The new union can help independent workers protect their interests by showing them what to look for in a contract and how to insist on protective phrasing and terms.

Some of them may be out-and-out business "unions," where one-person businesses will turn for help. They will help members arrange to have a grievance against an employer mediated. They will be common purchasing pools where workers can procure insurance and investment counsel more cheaply than they can singly. They will be frameworks within which younger workers can be apprenticed to older workers, and within which workers without a good network of business and professional contacts can find a mentor.

The new union will share some qualities with today's professional association, where lawyers, history teachers, or social workers band together to further their shared interests. Like such groups, tomorrow's unions will put on annual meetings that are educational events. Today's union member may have nowhere to see the newest technology in his or her field, to hear individuals talk about the "Dos and Don'ts of Being a Contractor," to learn about areas of expanding economic opportunity, and to compare notes with others on the best insurance or retirement policies.

Finally—but not least—they will be communities of people, unaffected by the changing membership in any given workplace, where people will find the buddies and colleagues that used to be provided by the world of jobs. The local unit of a particular union will be especially important here, for it will give people with the same professional, technical, or business orientation a way to get to know and keep track of one another.

Unions need, in short, to be reinvented. That will probably happen first in the knowledge-based types of work, where traditional unions never made much headway and where the process of dejobbing is furthest advanced. There is less history there to contend with, and yet there is still a need for some kind of collective support. The learnings in such industries will certainly be transferable to others in which unions have traditionally been more powerful—but in which they are declining currently. For wherever the old job descriptions dissolve, people lose their need for the old-style unions. But they gain the need for new kinds of advocates, support, and counsel. They need "the union of tomorrow."

Conclusion

At the end of another great period of collective effort called The Crusades, the social institutions and the cultural forces that had coordinated and contained individual energies collapsed. Whole armies disintegrated into their component individuals and sub-groupings. Knights who had ridden forth under the banner of this leader or that rode back on their own. They were the "free lances" who made the late medieval world such a dangerous yet dynamic place.

It's no accident that today we're surrounded once again by free lances. The old rules are gone, and the new rules aren't clear. Security—so far as there is any—is largely something that we must build for ourselves. Identities are confused and changing. We know that ultimately we are on our own, and so we are ready to learn a new way of doing and being. We know that our organizations were designed to serve the needs of another world, so we are busy redesigning them.

But we also need a social order that provides for our new needs and that doesn't try to impose archaic obligations on us. We need new laws. We need new leaders. We need a new social principle, an alternative to both selfishness and selflessness. We need a new sense of the common good to justify the sacrifices that we'll need to make to help those who find the new world the most difficult. To create these things, we must begin by remembering that we are all in this together.

Getting Ourselves from Here to There

Man has a limited biological capacity for change. When this capacity is overwhelmed, the capacity is in future shock.
                                           —Alvin Toffler, *Future Shock*

One must be thrust out of a finished cycle in life, and that leap is the most difficult to make—to part with one's faith, one's love, when one would rather renew the faith and recreate the passion.

                                              —Anaïs Nin, *Diary*

The Change and the Transition

So far, we have been talking about *change*—an enormous change in how we work. Now it is time to talk about *transition*, which is not the same thing. A change is a shift in the world around us. A transition is the internal process we go through in response to that shift. Changes are events and situations; transitions are experiences. The end of jobs is a change. Like all far-reaching changes, it will set off a cascade of secondary changes: hiring procedures will change, pay systems will change, management styles will change, public policy will change. And each one of these changes will put the people that it affects *into transition*.

Regardless of the change that triggers it, transition has a predictable form. Whereas change has two stages—an "old way" and a "new way"—transition has three overlapping phases:

1. An *ending*, during which one disengages from and breaks the old identity with "the way things were."
2. A *neutral zone*, when one is in between two ways of doing and being, having lost the old and not yet having found a way to live with the new.
3. A new *beginning*, after which one again feels at home and productive in "the way things are" with a new identity based on the new conditions.

While change must be planned and managed with reference to the outcome that the change events produce, transition must be planned and managed with reference to this three-phase process that the person in transition goes through. It is not enough just to describe the outcome and say, "Now do it." It is necessary to deal effectively with the ending and the feelings of loss that it occasions; it is necessary to get through the difficult neutral zone; and it is necessary to become comfortable and effective in the new situation.

To deal effectively with the changeover to a dejobbed world and a jobless way of life, you and I are going to have to manage both the change and the transition. In the previous six chapters, we discussed the change—that is, the vocational destination of working-without-a-job—and we explored some of the ways in which you can get there. In this chapter, we will discuss the transition—that is, the process of disengaging from the old expectations, the old assumptions, and the old identity that the job world provided and required; and the process of dealing with the distressing emptiness of the neutral zone that must be crossed before you can make a new beginning.

One of our shortcomings as a society is that we have always been ready to make changes with little thought for the transitions that they will cause. We assume that if people understand the change outcome and accept its necessity, they will "adjust" to the change. If they don't adjust, we talk about how people "resist change." In fact, people resist change far less than we usually think. What they resist is transition. That is, they resist three very disturbing experiences:

1. They resist saying good-bye to the world that has given them their identity and their feelings of competence.
2. They resist the chaotic and confusing neutral zone, where everything is up for grabs and no one knows what the rules are.
3. And they resist taking the risk of trying something completely unfamiliar and staking so much on an untried way of being and doing.

Anyone who did not have at least misgivings about transition would be very unusual. Those who tell you that they thrive on transition usually mean that they thrive on somebody else's transition.

The transition to a world without jobs is going to take place on both the individual and the societal levels. That is, each of us is going to have to let go of a familiar world and cross the no-man's-land that separates us from tomorrow. Because the old world meant something different to each of us, the transition is going to vary somewhat from person to person. But because we are all members of a society that has endowed jobs with particular functions and significances, the collective transition will confront us with a common challenge. In each case, we need to develop a plan for getting "from here to there." In this chapter, we will first deal with what the societal transition is going to require, and then with what each of us will have to do to deal with our own personal transition.

The Underlying Societal Shift

The end of jobs is taking place throughout the developed world. It has gone furthest in the United States, but its symptoms are already evident in Europe and Japan. Because those societies are less individualistic than America, individual solutions to dejobbing are not so visible there as they are here. In other words, dejobbing is having mostly quantitative, rather than qualitative, effects. In Europe those quantitative effects (unemployment rates) are getting very serious, while in Japan they are rising but still, by our standards, low. But like us, those societies are being pushed beyond jobs by technology and the speed of change. Gertrude Stein once said that America was the oldest country in the world because it had entered the twentieth century first. In the same way, we are entering the twenty-first century ahead of other countries, but they are close behind.

Each country's experience, however, is shaped by its culture and its heritage, and to appreciate what the post-job world is going to mean to any particular society it is necessary to place it in context. Every society develops its own answers to a few basic questions, and those questions involve how to create wealth and how to allocate it in some way that is perceived to be workable and fair.

Relatively stable societies with strong traditions tend to divide up wealth and resources and then build semipermanent clusters of people around the resulting portions. Tribal groups do that, using clans and other extended-family groupings to assure that everyone has a place at the social table. Medieval Europe did that by parceling out land to feudal landlords, each of whom supported a little community of tenants and vassals who worked the land and took a share of the crop. Such systems were usually, by modern standards, inequitable, exploitive, rigid, and inefficient. But for centuries they worked well enough to provide their members with the necessities of not only physical, but also social and psychological, subsistence. These systems gave people an identity, a place, and a sense of belonging. If the social arrangements and economic responsibilities usually fell short of the espoused ideal of interpersonal respect and mutual support, they also usually met the expectations that they generated well enough so that little time was spent trying either to improve or to do away with them.

From the very beginning, the European settlers in America had different expectations. The stability of the traditional society had been based either on the fact that all the land was already taken (as in medieval Europe) or on the fact that no individual ownership of land was morally or legally possible (as in most tribal groups). In either case, the wealth was a fixed quantity and there was very little new private access to it. In America, however, the Europeans found land that seemed to be there for the taking. Lacking any appreciation for the native peoples' sacred relation to the land and motivated by the concept of private ownership, they took the land and began to work it. And in the process, they began to create wealth on a very large scale.

Every society must have an agreed-upon principle to govern the creation of wealth and another principle to govern the distribution of it. In the Europe left behind by the first white immigrants to these shores, the only real source of wealth creation had been international trade—and especially the importation of gold and silver from the so-called New World. People brought back such wealth and then converted it into the real coin of the realm, property. They bought their way into the landed aristocracy.

In seventeenth-century America, the land that stretched away beyond any horizon represented a wealth-creation system that surpassed anything the Old World had ever dreamed of. It was like finding gold in your backyard. The wealth-distribution system was equally obvious: you moved out to the edge of the settlement and took a piece of the "unowned" land. No other society in human history had ever created and distributed wealth in such a simple and apparently effective manner.

The End of the American Myth

Every socioeconomic system also generates an underlying myth, a story that defines the possibilities and the obligations of life in that particular time and place. The American myth, fostered by a seemingly inexhaustible supply of apparently free land, is the story of starting with nothing and ending up with comfort, affluence, and security. Its psychic dimension is the story of starting out as *nobody* and ending up as *somebody*. For the first two centuries after European settlers arrived on these shores, the story involved a place and a state of mind called the frontier. However discouraging one's present situation was, there was always the frontier. There you could begin over again. There, all accounts reverted to zero. There, all people toed the same starting line. There, yesterday's loser might be tomorrow's winner.

In a famous paper read to the American Historical Association meeting in 1893, Frederick Jackson Turner announced that the frontier was gone. Population densities had increased to the point where there were no longer significant blocks of unsettled land left. But the frontier remained a fact of the imagination in America long after it ceased to exist on any map. It survived partly because myths are rooted in a deeper psychic level than population figures can reach. But it also survived because it had imperceptibly blended with another story that was better grounded in the facts of the late nineteenth century. That other story, likewise, traced the path from poverty to wealth and obscurity to fame. That later story was the rags-to-riches tale of the young man (it was essentially a sexist tale) who started with a modest job and did so well at it that he was promoted . . . and promoted again . . . and again until he became the boss of the whole show.

Without missing a beat, the American myth left behind the frontier and moved to the bank, the store, or the factory. And in its new incarnation, the myth transformed the old promise into new terms: wealth was still limitless and access to it was still universal, but now it involved a job and not a piece of land. Anyone could begin with any job and work his way up to the top. Jobs became the stepping-stones for social advancement and personal fulfillment.

To get a job was to plug in to the system through which wealth was distributed in American society. To expand the pool of that wealth, the society simply needed to keep generating new jobs. It was true that periodic recessions caused the job level to fall temporarily, but as with any rising tide, the ebb was always followed by a greater flow. Like recessions, the gradual mechanization of American work took away jobs too. But the huge expansion of consumer markets offset those losses, and the tide kept rising.

Until now. For reasons detailed in the first chapters of this book, the tide has turned and jobs that are disappearing are not being replaced. As we saw, that does not mean that no work remains that needs doing. On the contrary, work needing to be done is all around us, but it is no longer so easy to box it into jobs.

Job seekers send out hundreds of résumés and they answer job ads in droves, but they report that the jobs are all taken. Then they try again. And again. They respond to the unconscious pull of the old mythic story that says that the job is the gateway to success, and they keep responding to it long after the jobs have disappeared—just as people kept looking for the frontier way of life long after there was no frontier actually left.

Losing a core social myth of this sort is much harder than losing any number of jobs: it undermines the very reality that people live in. The world doesn't feel the same any longer, and people don't feel at home in it. The shadows seem longer and the wind seems colder. People feel exposed and lost and confused. The loss of the job myth marks one of those dividing lines in history that makes an earlier period seem in retrospect to have been simpler and easier to live in—simpler even than the past really was. You can be sure that we will look back on the age of jobs in the same way that people of a century ago looked back at the world of the frontier farm. We will idealize it. Nothing makes it so clear that something is passing than the aura of meaning and comfort that begins to surround it like a halo of warmth and light. A telltale sign of the transition is the sense of mourning and disorientation that we feel as we grapple with the fact that jobs really are going away.

Mourning is something that we associate with the death of a loved one or with the discovery that we ourselves are going to die. But any large loss triggers mourning, and the end of jobs is indeed a big loss for everyone who grew up with the myth that the job train was the best way to reach success and happiness. As articulated by Elizabeth Kubler-Ross, mourning (she called it grieving) typically goes through five stages, and you can see all of them in people's reactions to the current job transition:

Denial

Hey, we're just going through one of those periodic readjustments! No big deal. Maybe that dejobbing stuff makes sense at Microsoft, but here at Industro National we've still got real jobs. Fewer of them, maybe. But real jobs. Except for the temps, of course.

Lotta temps . . . and part-timers. A bunch of contractors too. But that'll change when times improve and things get back on an even keel. After that, I plan to put in about eight more years, and then . . . retirement.

Anger

This is rotten! This job situation stinks! Where did all those good jobs go? Damn overseas competition! And Washington just let the jobs go! And what about our own senior management, giving themselves golden parachutes and all, while the stockholders get big bucks, and we (who gave our lives for this rust-bucket operation) get our health insurance cut back? I tell you, if I get the ax, I'm going to bust something on my way out the door! (And what sort of a book is this, anyway, announcing that there are no more jobs? I have a good mind to throw it in the trash!)

Bargaining

Now, look. Things don't have to be this way. If we all get together and . . . or how about the union? . . . then there's Clinton. Let's set up big tariff barriers to protect our jobs; and we could stop letting those immigrants into the country. Or we could expand our business with a big, new customer-service program; and we could do some strategic planning . . . and marketing . . . and shift to self-managed teams. There *has* to be some way out, some way to get things back the way they were! Hey, this is America, the land of job security. Give us another chance, and we'll show those damn foreigners! Say, I've got an idea. How about cutting back to a four-day work week?

Despair

What's the use? There aren't any jobs out there. I've looked. There's nothing to do except live off unemployment benefits and hope to hit it big in the lottery. I guess you never appreciate what you've got till it goes. I never knew how important a job was. But there's

nothing you can do about it when they all disappear. I
feel like hell. Weak. Useless. Some days it's real hard to
get up in the morning.
Then, and only after going through those four progressively
deeper stages of mourning, Kubler-Ross found that people come
out into a final stage that she called

Acceptance
Sure, I miss the old job, but I'm going to get on with
my life. You can't just sit around and try to get the past
back. I may be down, but I'm not out. This "Recycling
Your D.A.T.A." and "You & Co." stuff is a little
strange, but I know that some people are making it
work. I don't like this new situation, you understand—
I mean, all this "marketing" stuff! But I'm going to
give it my best shot.

As Americans move toward their different individual solutions
to the disappearance of jobs, you hear these feelings being ex-
pressed, and you probably feel some of them yourself. It is important to realize that the feelings are not only natural but that they
are the only real pathway through to the other side. Shakespeare
said, "He that lacks time to mourn, lacks time to mend." So we
must not block out what are really healthy reactions to losing the
future that our society has been promising people.

We need to find ways to talk honestly about what is really happening and what we are feeling about it. All of the research on
mourning makes it clear that the main danger comes from bottling up such feelings until they burst forth in some destructive
action. The research also demonstrates how destructive it is for
those in positions of power or prestige to feed people's natural
denial with hopeful talk about the job crisis being nearly over or
not being as bad as people think.

It is also important to mark endings in some official way. That
is probably why we still remember Frederick Jackson Turner's
speech. (How many American Historical Association presenta-
tions are still remembered a century later?) Ending-marker events
usually celebrate the contributions and benefits of the time that is
ending, just as a eulogy is part of the funeral through which we

bid farewell to a dead person. But it is psychologically wise to recall the less-than-glorious side of the departed situation, too. Wakes do that, with stories and remembrances that are comical or even bitter. The more fully a marker event can sum up the reality of what is ended, the more helpful it will be. Just what sort of marker event might be an appropriate way to bid farewell to the departed world of the job is something that we need to discuss publicly in both the political and the organizational arenas.

Getting through the Neutral Zone

Any loss of a whole world creates a dangerous (though also potentially exciting) interregnum, when the old order is gone but the new one is not yet really established. Such a time is bound to be full of confusion. The impulse to act out, to strike back, to scapegoat, to embrace simplistic solutions, to try to recapture lost innocence is very great during such a time. Our society's leaders need to help us to face and contain the disruptions that we are going to experience—are *already* experiencing, in fact—as we dejob our workplaces and our communities.

As Senator John C. Calhoun said during the period of social turmoil that preceded the Civil War, "The interval between the decay of the old and the formation and establishment of the new, constitutes a period of transition which must always necessarily be one of uncertainty, confusion, error, and wild and fierce fanaticism." Our social institutions need not only to bring themselves back into alignment with the new world of work, they also need to provide us with the temporary support we will need in order to cross from the old world to the new.

The first thing that we need during this difficult time between letting go and beginning over is to understand that our present turmoil is the result of the process we are going through and is not a sign that we have taken a wrong turn somewhere. We need to understand that, as Henry Thomas Buckle put it in his monumental *History of Civilization,* "every new truth which has ever been propounded has, for a time, caused . . . discomfort and oftentimes unhappiness." With time, Buckle noted, the "framework of affairs" incorporates the new way of thinking and adjusts

itself to it. Then the new way begins to make new developments
and breakthroughs possible. "But at the outset there is always
great harm. And if the truth is very great as well as very new, the
harm is serious."

The idea of the job as the right way to package the work of
the industrial age was a "new truth" in the nineteenth century,
and the transition through which it became the dominant work
setting caused great distress and unhappiness. Today it has become orthodoxy, and people defend it as though it were the
only good way to live and to work. The idea of the vendor-
minded worker running an individual *business* is another such
"truth," and we must see that the distress and unhappiness
that we are going through once again are coming from the
transition through which the truth is being incorporated socially and psychologically, not from some unfortunate property
of the truth itself.

People in the neutral zone can further be helped to endure the
chaos that they are experiencing if they are given tools to deal
with their condition and support while they are dealing with it.
The Business and Career Development Center will supply such
tools, and it will also provide the support of fellow learners who
share one's problems. It is hard to exaggerate how much ready
access to such centers would help people to work out viable personal alternatives to traditional jobs, or how much such assistance
would mitigate the societal effects of this enormous transition.

Another societal action that will help people through the neutral zone is to provide different kinds of temporary assistance
while people are in transit from the old way to the new. The
safety-net issues we talked about in Chapter 8 would be helpful,
but in this neutral zone between careers based on jobs and careers based on the work that needs doing, we need more. Transitional assistance—such as financial help with relocation, grants
for reeducation or retraining, and seed money for business
startup costs—could take many different forms:

- loans or tax credits for individuals;
- subsidies to startup businesses;
- subsidies to nonprofit institutions that assist such ventures;

- grants to support individual programmers who create life- and career-planning software; or
- publicly funded databases listing individuals and organizations with work that needed doing—databases that could be accessed either directly by computer users or indirectly through a visit to a CBCD, a community college, or a public library.

Financial assistance could also, of course, take the form of grants to ad hoc groups that would undertake projects to improve the transportation, communication, and education infrastructure on which business development depends. Whatever form it took, public funds would be well spent in any way that facilitated the transitions that the dejobbing of America will require us all to make.

Making the New Beginning

Ironically, the new beginning will be the easiest part of the transition to accomplish; the ending and the neutral zone are the most difficult and potentially dangerous. When we find it hard to make a new beginning, it is usually because we have not really made an ending. (As a bit of American folk wisdom puts it, "You can't steal second base and keep your foot on first too.") Or we find it difficult to make a new beginning because we have not taken the time in the neutral zone to achieve the reorientation and renewal that the neutral zone makes possible. We may, for example, be so anxious and confused by the neutral zone that we cannot see any possibility beyond "getting another job." In that case, even if we succeed, we have just postponed the real transition and aborted the chance for a real beginning.

One thing that will help people to make a genuinely new beginning will be contact with people who have already done that. In some fortunate cases, such people are close at hand and could serve as mentors to people who are emerging from the neutral zone and making their own new beginnings. Such mentoring could be encouraged by "entrepreneur-in-residence" programs at high schools or community colleges. In other cases the access would have to come indirectly through vignettes and case histories. These might be written and published regularly in newspapers or other periodicals, or else they could be the basis of an ongoing series of public television programs.

To make an effective new beginning, people need to have four things that begin with the letter *P*: a *purpose* for their efforts, a *picture* of their destination, a *plan* to follow, and a *part* to play.

Purpose: Any difficult undertaking becomes impossible when you lose your sense of purpose, when you forget why the effort is necessary. Then it becomes just drudgery. But with a clear and compelling sense of purpose, you can manage even the most difficult transitions.

Picture: The purpose needs to be supplemented with a picture of the outcome that you are seeking. Otherwise the neutral zone can become an utterly bewildering array of possibilities. Where is it, exactly, that you are going? How are you going to know when you are there?

Plan: Having a clear reason for the journey and an imaginable destination are both essential; but unless there is a route, a set of stages, a timeline, and a concrete starting point, the new beginning may never be more than a dream. A person needs to have a step-by-step plan for getting there.

Part: And, finally, there are the details of the part that one must play. For the journey is only a metaphor. What we are talking about is really an active project of self-renovation, and although others can help, the effort must ultimately be made by the individual or it won't be made at all. The individual needs a set of tactics and ideas and skills to accomplish the project.

These are the things that turn endings and neutral zones into new beginnings, and any person in transition needs help articulating and formalizing them.

During the first great job shift, elementary schools and Sunday schools turned out jobholders in the same way that those jobholders would later turn out mass-produced goods: mechanistically and in volume. Today, as we move away from mass production and the mass organization, we need to follow a process in creating the new worker that parallels what the new worker is using to create the new services and products that will shape tomorrow's economy. Just as each new worker must be an individual "business," so must the creation of that worker be an individual undertaking. Governmental agencies, educational institutions, communications media, and self-help groups can provide the resources and help us acquire the necessary skills. But we are going to have to create ourselves. Our model must not be the old factory production line, but the automatic teller machine, the self-serve gas station, or the do-it-yourself quilting store.

And Now, a Few Words to the Individual

Traditional societies once ritualized the transition process with rites of passage, but today we have to find our own ways to manage transition and to make it meaningful. John Rollwagen, the CEO of supercomputer maker Cray Research, tells a story about his predecessor and mentor, Seymour Cray, that suggests how one person did that.

> Seymour lived on a lake in Wisconsin, and he would pass the long winters there by building sailboats. Some of them were pretty big. In fact, the last one he built was 36 feet. He would build the boat in the basement and when the weather grew warm, he would drag the boat out to the lake and sail it around all summer. But at the end of the summer he wanted to dispose of the boat because he had so many ideas about the next boat he wanted to build. And so every fall, he would have a party—a cookout on the beach with a big bonfire. He'd encourage people to dance around the fire, and at a certain point they would burn the boat. Just burn her right up!

Rollwagen remarks that organizations, like individuals, need to clear the ground and the mind to provide the psychic space for the new way of doing things to emerge. The great Renaissance thinker Erasmus said the same thing more cryptically: "Only the hand that erases can write a true thing." And Picasso put it this way: "Every act of creation is first an act of destruction."

The point of the story about Cray is only incidentally that you might want to create your own symbolic transition ritual— though you might. It is to remind you how important it is to end the old before you try to undertake the new. You have to put the world of jobs behind you. That is not to say that (if you currently have one) you ought to quit your job. That job may well be a valuable interim vehicle that you use to take you to your new work destination. Actually, from a transitional point of view, it doesn't really matter whether you presently have a job or not: letting go of the *idea* of jobs is the ending that is important.

Such a transition does not happen all at once, of course. Think how slowly the agricultural world faded from dominance in this country. Think how slowly the idea of the frontier died out. When Frederick Jackson Turner used census statistics to show that the frontier no longer existed, some people still lived in "frontier conditions," and those conditions did not disappear for a long time. It is just that those conditions did not provide a good basis for life planning any longer.

Thus it is today with jobs. During a transition period like ours, jobs too will be around for a while, so if you still have one, hold on to it while you work on your alternatives. For quite some time many people will find a job to be a workable stopgap solution to the need for an income. But the only long-term solution is to rebuild your career and your life around strategies that work in a dejobbed environment.

There are some things that you can do to help yourself get through the three-phase transition process. Below, a number of them are listed in the form of questions. That is meant to encourage you not simply to note them for some imagined future use, but rather to stop and ask yourself how you are currently handling transition and what you need to do to handle it better.

As you consider each of these questions, realize that you are not being asked to think about letting go of a particular job, of full-time work, or of working for a particular organization. You are being asked to consider what it will be like to let go of *the whole cluster of attitudes, expectations, assumptions, self-images, and values that went with the idea of "having a job."* Whether you actually have a job at the moment or not, you need to let go of all those things because they are not going to help you deal with what lies ahead of you. They are going to get in your way. But at present they are part of you: the part of yourself that for years has lived in, counted on, and defined yourself in terms of the world of jobs.

Handling Your Endings Successfully

Yes☐ No☐   Have you decided what, for you, is over—and what isn't? What is it time for you to let go of and what can you hold on to? Endings have a way of feeling global, so it is important to identify what is still there. Also, without such sorting, you may be unclear exactly what it is that you are going to have to say good-bye to. What we've said about the psychological function of jobs is generic. What do they mean to you?

Yes☐ No☐   Have you used symbolic "boundary" actions and events to mark your clean break with the past and show that your present is really different from your past? How could you express this transition to the dejobbed life symbolically? Would it be letting your hair grow (or getting it cut short), burning your old résumés, writing a poem, cleaning out your closet and your file cabinet . . . or what?

Yes☐ No☐   Have you sorted your losses into those that you can *retain* (you don't have to lose contact with your old friends), those that you had better try to *replace* (like your income, if it has dropped), those that you can *rebuild* on a new basis (like your sense of vocational security, by focusing on employability), and those that you must simply *relinquish* (the idea that there are "good jobs" that will leave you fixed for life)? You have some options. A loss is just the first step in transition. What comes next depends on what you do with the first step. What are you going to do with your losses?

Yes ☐ No ☐   Have you actively (*pro*actively) sought all the information you need to deal effectively with your changes? Ignorance leaves you powerless. Before you accept that state, push a little. Stick up for yourself. (You'd do that for a friend, wouldn't you?) Is your present (or former) employer willing to do anything to make your transition easier—helping you to enhance your employability, for example? If not, what other sources of help are open to you?

Yes ☐ No ☐   Have you found symbolic "pieces of the past" to take with you into the future? These mementos will provide you with a symbol for what is valuable in the job world and in that chapter of your life. It might be a collection of items with the logos of all the places you have worked, an honor or recognition you got at some point in your career, or some object with strong associations with the job phase in your life.

Yes ☐ No ☐   Have you identified the continuities in your life and work situations and taken pains to strengthen them? The end of this kind of a career is a big thing, but not everything is over, and the continuities are important stabilizers for you during this turbulence. Be careful not to take them for granted or to forget that they are there.

Yes ☐ No ☐   Have you used this point of ending as an opportunity to step back and look at the path you've been following, to sum up, to understand how you got to where you are? What *is* the message for you in this change? People sometimes do this by writing autobiographically during a time of ending. They find it useful to get a clear picture of their lives at this point. It also helps to pull things together before releasing them. (It's hard to let go of what you don't have a good grip on.)

Yes ☐ No ☐ Have you taken this ending as a chance to look at past endings in your life? Have you unpacked any old baggage that you find that you are carrying? Old unfinished endings and unresolved losses will make this one much more difficult, for they will resonate with this one and make it feel even bigger than it is. If, for example, your job world is the gate to the imagined self-acceptance that a high executive job promises; if it is the way you've been planning to "show your parents" that you are really worth something—then you'd better let go of these fantasies first, or the job loss will be even more difficult.

Yes ☐ No ☐ Have you accepted the necessity for going through a time of "mourning" in dealing with your losses? The anger and depression you feel are not only natural, but they are part of the healing process. Don't deny them.

After you have completed each section of the questions, pause and think what action you might take to handle the particular phase of transition more effectively. (Do that now with endings.) With each potential action that you identify, write yourself a little note in your notebook. You are making a to-do list.

Then, Deal Successfully with the "Neutral Zone"

Letting go of an old, tried-and-true idea like jobs would not be so difficult if you could step right into an alternative. But in changes that affect us deeply, you can't move straight from the old way into the new. You move from the old way into a no-man's-land where there seems to be no way. When you do this, you will feel as though you lost your way, but this kind of a "lostness" is significant and meaningful. This is the neutral zone, the time-between-realities, which is both very confusing and very creative.

Marilyn Fergusson, in writing about social change, said, "It's not so much that we are afraid of change or that we are so in love with the old way. It's that in-between place that we fear. It's like being in between trapezes. It's Linus when his blanket is in the dryer: there is nothing to hold to." The irony is that the same up-in-the-air, nothing-to-hold-on-to quality that makes the neutral zone so confusing and anxiety producing is the same reason that it is very creative. Just because everything is up for grabs, there is much less standing in the way of a creative breakthrough than there is during more stable times. So, you're going to have two tasks during the neutral zone that you encounter after you've let go of jobs. First, you need to create the conditions that will make it possible for you to endure the neutral zone. And second, you need to do whatever you can to capitalize on this time when nothing is settled and anything is possible.

Begin your plan for making the neutral zone more livable with this information: The people who deal best with this in-between state are those who find ways to reestablish four things that endings often destroy: (1) control, (2) understanding, (3) support, and (4) purpose. Specifically, they find ways to re-create these things in new terms. If they can't actually re-create them, they redefine them, so that if their old form is no longer within reach, their new form is still available.

Control
Many people in transition feel like victims; things are "happening to them." Are you doing what you can to recover a sense of control in what feels like an out-of-control situation?

Yes☐ No☐   Have you looked for ways to gain access to the people whose decisions are creating the changes or who have the resources to help you through your transition? You can't make them cancel the layoff or expand government spending, you say.

Right, but have you tried to influence how they carry out their decision? You may be able to influence them more than you imagine. You may think you could never get an appointment with an executive or your state representative. Have you tried?

Yes ☐ No ☐   Have you established realistic levels of output for yourself and avoided undertaking unnecessary responsibilities? Are you avoiding unrelated and unnecessary changes, wherever possible? You're going to be especially burdened during this time. Don't set yourself up for failure by overcommitting yourself. If you do, the failure or shortfall will burden an already damaged self-confidence. You don't need that now.

Yes ☐ No ☐   Have you created checkpoints and short-range goals for yourself during the neutral zone? Nothing makes you feel more out of control than the experience of not being able to accomplish anything, and one of the characteristics of the neutral zone is that it lacks the kinds of natural milestones and landmarks by which you can chart your progress. Even artificial checkpoints ("when I've scheduled four interviews") and short-range goals ("by the end of the week, I'll have registered for that life-planning course") will give you a sense that you are accomplishing something and that the transition process is still moving forward.

Understanding

Things don't make sense during transition. The rules are changing. Your old understandings don't pertain anymore. To make

matters worse, you may not have understood why you were feeling what you were feeling. You need new understandings.

Yes☐ No☐   Have you learned all you can about the transition
             process, especially about this neutral zone? At
             best it is a confusing time, and the more you
             know about it and how it facilitates transition, the
             more bearable it will be—not easy, just less dis-
             orienting.

Yes☐ No☐   Have you actively sought the information you
             need and collaborated with others who share
             your need? One of the hardest things about the
             neutral zone is feeling as though you are in the
             dark and can't find the light switch. You can
             probably do more to help yourself (especially us-
             ing coaction) than you imagine. What can you do,
             individually or with others, to learn more about
             how dejobbed organizations really work and how
             vendor-minded individuals capitalize on that
             knowledge?

Yes☐ No☐   Have you pushed to gain an understanding of the
             resources available to you? These resources in-
             clude books, videotapes, and seminars, as well as
             individual counseling. Make sure that what you
             are trying to understand is the path forward. Un-
             derstanding "how to get my job back" or "how to
             find a job that pays just as much as the last one
             did" is a regressive exercise. Focus instead on un-
             derstanding how to leave jobs behind.

Support
People in the neutral zone need to realize that they are not alone
and that their reactions are not unique or weird. They need to
recognize that even though the old way of doing things is gone, at

least there are a lot of people in this boat together. (There are—including all of those currently employed in jobs. Most of them don't know they are in the boat, however. You are just ahead of the curve.) This kind of support is often difficult to find in the neutral zone, because support systems (both practical and interpersonal) may be one of the casualties of the nonstop change that organizations are going through today.

Yes ☐ No ☐   Have you joined others in planning group-building events and experiences, both at work and outside the workplace? If your support group has been damaged, it has to be repaired. If it is gone, you have to find a new one. Here is where professional associations, fraternal/sororal groups, and religious congregations have a critical and as-yet poorly developed role to play. Too often, the groups that are offering support (Forty Plus, many college-placement centers, and the like) are still tied to the outmoded paradigm of "job hunting."

Yes ☐ No ☐   Have you created temporary arrangements and agreements to get you through what feels like a "time in the wilderness"? You won't be able to rebuild your life quickly. But you can build some scaffolding to stand on while you do the rebuilding. Your present job, if you have one, is a "temporary arrangement." If you don't have one, finding an interim job may make sense. So may other short-term sources of money. This is also the time for some interim agreements between you and family members who may be very anxious about your situation (e.g., "We're not going to make a final decision on moving for at least six weeks").

Yes ☐ No ☐   Have you taken this gap in the pattern of your life to rethink what you want out of your life? With so much up for grabs now, more things are possible than at other times when you have reconsidered what you want to achieve. This is a time to let go and really brainstorm about all the things that you could do.

Purpose

Changes make irrelevant many of the purposes that once motivated you and gave meaning to what you did. That is one reason why you are likely to feel so lost in the neutral zone.

Yes☐ No☐   Have you built "getting yourself through the wilderness" into your personal agenda? That makes a lot more sense than wasting your energy trying to put the pieces back together again. The only way out of this wilderness is ahead. And besides, letting go of the fantasy that you can go back is a relief, and it will free up some energy too.

Yes☐ No☐   Have you revisited the question of personal purpose? What brings pleasure and meaning into your world? Why are you here on earth? What is your personal mission? People who can answer these questions are far less likely to be devastated by the neutral zone than people who cannot. Besides, the answers may show you where your path is going.

Yes☐ No☐   Have you converted this purpose into a "picture of how your work and life might be"? Hold that picture in your mind. This is your "promised land," and focusing your mind on it will do a lot to get you through your personal wilderness. The philosopher Nietzsche said that a person who has a *why* can deal with any *how*.

The neutral zone is also a time full of creative possibilities. In fact, one of the reasons to handle its frightening and enervating aspect well is to be sure that you maintain the energy and the motivation to capitalize upon the opportunities it offers. To judge how you are dealing with these opportunities, ask yourself the following questions.

Yes☐ No☐   Have you taken the time to step back and take stock, to challenge your old answers and ways of doing things, and to look for opportunities to head off in a new direction? Or are you rushing blindly ahead to "get through the change"? The neutral zone is the best time to take a fresh look at things: "Why *am* I doing that?" "*Is* it really as necessary to be employed full-time by one organization as I have always thought it was?" "What else *could* I do with these abilities of mine?" "Is it *really* so unrealistic to go for what I desire?"

Yes☐ No☐   Have you taken some time alone, preferably away from the regular settings of home and work? It doesn't need to be a long time. The point is that it's difficult to get a new view of things as long as you are surrounded by the old patterns. The old rites of passage took place in isolated locations, and even modern people instinctively gravitate toward such places when they need to think something through and when they need guidance.

Yes☐ No☐   Have you cultivated the habit of experiment during the neutral zone? Playing with the possibilities in little things may lead to experimenting with bigger things and to bigger payoffs. Drive home by a different route tonight, spend tomorrow's lunch time in a new way, wear something tomorrow that you usually don't wear. Or try doing some new thing that you've been thinking about.

Yes ☐ No ☐   Have you studied your own recent work and life
               experience for "clues" to new possibilities that
               might be explored? Look particularly at things
               that you didn't expect to work as well as they did,
               or things that you expected to work but didn't.
               Look at "coincidences" and the natural patterns
               events seem to be taking. Look at everything, in
               short, as though it contained a message for you.

Yes ☐ No ☐   Have you tried brainstorming? One way to get a
               good, new idea is to get a lot of new ideas. Ask
               others for their ideas—and don't kill the idea by
               saying, "I could never do *that!*" Ask a couple of
               friends to brainstorm possibilities with you. Sit
               down and write out ideas in stream-of-conscious-
               ness fashion for ten minutes.

Yes ☐ No ☐   Have you tried using that notebook you started as
               a place to record all the ideas and clues that you
               get? (What? You haven't started the notebook
               yet? Why not?) Use it as a place where you can
               think on paper. Neutral-zone creativity is ephem-
               eral, and its results can vanish without a trace if
               you don't catch them while you have them. Use
               the notebook, too, as a place to carry around clip-
               pings that you come across and phone numbers
               of people whom you want to talk to sometime.

Finally, Make a Successful New Beginning

Your last step is to find ways to turn the neutral-zone possibilities
into the next stage of your journey so that you can focus your
energies on a viable new beginning.

Yes ☐ No ☐   Have you converted the picture that you discov-
               ered in the neutral zone into objectives and then
               laid out a backward path from *there* to *here*? At
               each turn of the path, ask yourself, "What do I

need to have done to get this far?" Then go back and plan how you will do that. Step by step, work back until you are at your present situation.

Yes ☐ No ☐   Have you studied the planned route of your path and decided what knowledge and skill you need to acquire to follow it successfully? Put together a "learning project" to get that knowledge and skill. The project may be anything from an article you will read tomorrow to a degree that you will get three years from now. Be creative in designing these projects, and be sure to focus on how best to learn what you need to know—not on where they give a course or a program in your subject.

Yes ☐ No ☐   Have you found some low-risk settings in which to test and practice what you are learning? Find a mentor who can coach and advise you. Find places where you can watch others acting as you want to learn to act. In other words, don't just think of this as published information you are seeking. You want to know how to do something, how to be something. You want to learn how to have a whole new kind of work life.

Yes ☐ No ☐   Have you broken your learning/changing project into small increments and laid it out along a realistic timeline? Mark the completion of each segment with a little reward for yourself.

Yes ☐ No ☐   Have you regularly reviewed your plans and introduced "course corrections" whenever events and experiences show that your original plan needs to be modified? Remember, the whole rationale of "the end of jobs" is that there is so much change taking place that no one arrangement (e.g., job description) will work for very long. So don't build the same rigidity into your own goals that jobs have built into them. Be opportunistic. Sail with the wind. Focus your early efforts on achieving a few quick successes and use them to build your confidence in further steps.

Yes☐ No☐   Have you converted each of these actions-toward-a-new-beginning into some concrete first step that you can take during this coming week? Action ⟶ accomplishment ⟶ increased confidence: that is the sequence you need to initiate now.

Conclusion

Life is our teacher. Periodically it destroys how things have been and forces us to say good-bye to how we have done things and defined ourselves. The external details of the change may be unique and confusing, but the real transitional task is always the same: to let go of some reality or strategy or personal identity that characterized the previous leg of our journey. The question life asks is always, "What is it time for you to say good-bye to?"

We extrude our identities like shellfish, for protection, but in time the protective shell that they provide begins to cramp us. You and I have outlived old realities many times in the past, but our first impulse is almost always to try to add to or change them so that we can make them last longer. What we need to recognize—which is the larger point of the Cray story—is that endings are really a gift, a chance to begin again, an opportunity to create something that will be more nearly adequate to the people we have become and the changing world we inhabit.

That "something" is a new kind of life and career, one not dependent on a job. To create such a career, you may want to return now to Part Two of this book. Look again at the question of the markets that exist all around you. Where is the work that needs doing? What are the unmet needs? How is change creating new opportunities, even as it destroys the old ones?

Then go back over your D.A.T.A. I hope it is clear now what may not have seemed credible then: that the qualifications are really changing and that the new qualifications exist inside us rather than on our résumés. This may be a good time to go back over the exercises designed to help you articulate your

Desires: What do you really want at this point in your life?

Abilities: What are you good at?

Temperament: What is your natural style? How do you work best?

Assets: What incidental advantages do you have?

Out of these things, you and I need to shape the products that we "take to market," those things that you and I can provide to the customers who need such products. And based on our products, we need to reinvent ourselves as little one-person "businesses." We need to learn all we can about marketing, product development, sales, production, administration, contracting, and all the other hats we'll be wearing in rapid succession. Those hats will feel strange at first, but we will get used to them.

And then one day, you will catch yourself looking back and thinking that it is a little hard to recall just what it was like to "have a job," to argue about whether something was your job or not, to show up for work at the same time every day and hang on for eight or nine solid hours (regardless of what else was going on in your life or how you felt) until "quitting time." And you are likely to think that the transition to this new state of affairs was terribly difficult, but that you would hate to go back to the old way. You'll have a sense of why in the old days, self-employed people called jobs "wage slavery."

I say that you will probably feel these things, because they are what I feel. I used to have a job as a college teacher, but I left it and found that I had walked completely out of the job world. That was twenty years ago, and I have no desire whatever to return. I'm a bit ahead of you on the path, perhaps, but not so very far ahead, because I had to go cross-country for quite a while. There were no paths, no books like this to mark the way. I hope that this book saves you some of the time I spent figuring out the new rules. Happy journeying.

Afterword

When old words die out on the tongue, new melodies break forth from the heart; and where the old tracks are lost, new country is revealed with its wonders.

—Rabindranath Tagore, Indian philosopher

I know that for every door that closes, another door opens. But, man! These hallways are a bitch!

—T-shirt motto

This Book's Sources

This book project started less than two years ago when I began the actual writing, but in another sense it started twenty years ago when I left my teaching job and launched my own "composite career" with a product (transition-management seminars) that I created originally to fill my own personal need. But even longer ago it began as I watched my father struggle unhappily and unsuccessfully with the constraints of the job world, too frightened by his Depression-generated fears to abandon it, but too enamored of all the other kinds of work that might be done to fit into it successfully. While other fathers taught their sons to admire great, single-minded business tycoons, generals, artists, or politicians, he taught me to admire Albert Schweitzer—but not because he was a great humanitarian who dedicated himself to bringing modern medicine to central Africa. My father touted Schweitzer because he wasn't a slave to a job. He was a medical doctor *and* a clergyman *and* an organist *and* a philosopher *and* a missionary *and* the author of the then-definitive book on J. S. Bach. To get my father's vote, you had to operate outside the boundaries of any job box.

The Subject Is Taboo

Perhaps because the topic had so much personal meaning for me, I thought dejobbing was just something that I personally was going through. I was slow to realize how many people are being affected by dejobbing and how far-reaching its implications are. As I studied it, I realized that it was a necessary (though seldom acknowledged) ingredient in many other organizational prescriptions. Customer service, total quality, fast cycle time, organizational flexibility, mass customization, self-directed teams, and the constant pressure for reduced costs: abandoning jobs is the catalyst that is necessary for each of them to work as promised. Dejobbing is the unacknowledged but logical result of possibilities generated by the networked-PC revolution and by cellular phones and other pieces of portable information technology. Things like the decline of the "we'll-look-after-you" pension system, the battle over NAFTA, the new interest in universal health care, all the temping and subcontracting, and the persistent unemployment statistics were all related to the end of jobs.

I was also slow to appreciate the powerful emotions that discussing the end of jobs triggers. I remember a man at a speech I gave in Portland, Oregon, who grew more and more agitated and finally yelled, "What am I supposed to do about my mortgage payments? That's what I'd like you to tell me!" I felt terrible for him, and I tried to explain that I wasn't *recommending* the post-job career as something good in itself—only saying that it was being forced on us by social, technological, and cultural forces. It didn't even occur to me until he had left that it was not pursuing the post-job career but trying to hold on to a job-based career that was making his mortgage payments so difficult.

I remember the Ford Motor Company executive at a business-school development program, who huffily called the whole idea of dejobbing "crazy" and estimated that the chances of his company moving in that direction as "less than 2 on a scale of 1 to 10." I sympathized with him, remembering how hard it was for me to give up the job biases I had grown up with. I was almost as startled as he was to find that one of his fellow executives in the program rated Ford's odds at "over 8" and came up with a whole string of examples of places at the company where dejobbing was already happening. The Taurus design team was his first example. (The first man looked at the second as one might look at someone who had just desecrated a holy relic.)

I found audiences asking suspiciously whether the dejobbing of the American workplace wasn't just another way to do in poor people, who lacked fancy educations and lots of powerful contacts. I would reply that my reading of the present situation was that those people were being done in by *the job world* and that I doubted that things would get worse for them under the conditions I was describing. I sometimes found people reacting with the kind of hostility one might encounter if he questioned the value of democracy or publicly accused a family member of abuse. It was clear that dejobbing struck a nerve.

This defensiveness is related to the high level of denial that exists in the business press, where every uptick in the employment figures is greeted as though it were the news that we had finally balanced the budget. (This very week, headlines proclaimed that 1994 college grads were going to have an easier time of it than those of recent years because organizations "were finally hiring again." You had to read almost to the end of the story to discover that the projected increase in hiring was only 1.1 percent.)

The Real Issue: Jobs Favor the Privileged

I see the gulf between the rich and poor growing, but not because jobs are getting scarce. Rather, it's the inequities in how job work is rewarded. Jobs at the top of the organizational pyramid, jobs within professional preserves, and jobs in the media spotlight are obscenely overpaid with money that ought to be shared with the people with minimal jobs, who are on the edge of extinction.

Consider the case of Myan Jencks, a thirty-three-year-old woman, whose telemarketing job in Omaha does not provide health benefits, whose wages do not enable her to get out of debt, and who drives a rickety 1977 Chevy Malibu. Divorced, she sees her children only on weekends. She's one of those voices that we hear when we pick up the phone and learn that we've qualified for a special subscription price to some magazine that her tele-marketing firm is pushing that hour. She has to deal with irritated customers (like me, I have to admit) who resent her intrusion. But she bounces up after each verbal knockdown, like the weighted inflatable clowns that kids play with, because as an on-screen computer message reminds her and her coworkers, "Our first job—happy customers!" And in case she lets her frustration show, there's always the supervisor who monitors her phone. Many of the workers in her organization cannot take more than a single four-hour shift of this (she usually works two), and it would take between two and three shifts a day to earn $15,000–$20,000. But that is academic, since the average worker at her firm lasts only eleven weeks before quitting the job. And her firm is considered one of the good ones to work for in the industry!

It is *her job*, not the demise of the job, that is doing her in. If she could utilize modern communications technology to do her work from home, paid by the amount of work she actually does rather than those terrible four-hour shifts, it would have to be better than the job is. She would probably do more and get paid better, and she might even be able to get rid of the old car.

When people talk about the have-nots, they are referring to someone like Brian Deyo of Newport, Vermont, whose job at a hockey-stick factory provides rent and utilities and $20 a week for food. He was featured in a front-page *Wall Street Journal* article titled "Minimum Wage Jobs Give Many Americans Only A Miser-able Life." " 'Every day I'm making choices,' says Mr. Deyo, who has a wife and a chronically ill two-year-old daughter. 'Do I pay the rent and risk having the power cut? Or do we take a chance on both and buy food?' "At the time he was interviewed, he was taking a $5 gamble on a box of rifle shells in hopes of getting bear meat for the table.

What if his local high school or the town library had an evening Business and Career Development Center attached to it? What if there were someone there to walk him through a computer-based survey of his own personal D.A.T.A? It seems unlikely that the "personal product" that he would come up with would be "m k-ing hockey sticks." Maybe it would be turning out wooden toys at home or even making bearskin products. At present, he's simply clinging to a little piece of jetsam from the job economy. With help, he could do better.

Or what about Antonia Contereras, whose income provides the main support for a family of six? She worked her way up from a minimum-wage job at a computer components company to her present wage (after fourteen years of hard work!) of $6.60 an hour. Well, not her present wage exactly, since she and fifty co-workers went out on a six-week strike against their employer, Versatronex Corporation, a Sunnyvale, California, circuit-board builder. They won the right to unionize and bargain for higher wages. But they lost too, because the company found that higher job pay rendered its business unprofitable, and so it closed its doors.

Her efforts on behalf of herself and her coworkers tell me a lot more about her abilities and her temperament than her old job at the circuit-board company does. Like millions of other workers, she has seen no alternative but to hold on to the job and try to improve the wages it pays. But she is already a one-person "business," organizing people, helping them to fight for what they need, helping them work their way through all the labor regulations. What a waste it would be for her to go back to the assembly line! And yet, who could blame her as long as she saw no alternative to the old job or one like it?

The defenders of the job need to take another look at what they are defending. Whose interests are they serving? They certainly aren't looking out for the welfare of the disadvantaged, who are mighty poorly served by the job world. They aren't serving the interests of young people, who are having a terrible time getting jobs. (The percentage of twentysomethings living with their parents has doubled since 1960.)

As I said in Chapter 9, I believe that to a large extent they are defending and preserving a myth. That is not bad in and of itself, since myths are vital cultural artifacts. But this one has done its time. It served us well. It needs to be retired. And the defenders of the job need to see that there is an alternative—and to see that the alternative is already being lived out by millions of people who hardly realize that they are the vanguards of a great movement.

Working without Jobs Is No Picnic Either

This is not to say that the dejobbed world that is emerging is without its severe societal and psychological dangers. I have some serious misgivings about dejobbing and about what a future shaped by it is going to be like. I worry a good deal about that, not because I think that people (including the poor) cannot make a go of it but because it represents such a huge change that I am afraid we will rip ourselves apart making the transition to get from here to there. Social reaction and political fanaticism thrive during times of transition, and we can already see signs of increasing xenophobia and isolationism in all the industrialized countries.

I worry that without the counterweight of a solid sense of self and a clear grasp of personal values, individuals will not be able to withstand the centrifugal forces of the market. People willing to become whatever market opportunities will pay them to be either get pulled apart or become centerless, lacking any overriding purpose. That is why understanding and respecting one's own D.A.T.A. is so essential. "Opportunity" is empty unless it fits *you*.

I worry that the sense of craft and of professional vocation, both of which are ways to frame today's constant change, will break down under the need to earn a fee. An important countercurrent in the tide of the first great job shift was the Arts and Crafts movement, led in England by people like the art critic John Ruskin and the artist William Morris. It was brought to America late in the century, where it gave its name to a style of furniture and of domestic architecture, both of which emphasized high craftsmanship and a sensitive use of materials. I see some parallels between that and the spirit in contemporary desktop-publishing and industrial-design firms, which (not coincidentally) are at the forward edge of the movement beyond jobs.

I worry about the stress of constantly marketing oneself, which can take an awful toll on home and family, as the life s.ories of most entrepreneurs make all too clear. But I am heartened by he statistics which suggest that fewer and fewer people are willing to sacrifice personal considerations to organizational ones. And I can see in the increase in home-based workers a healing of the split between work and family that the job originally created. In the same way, I worry that people who are for hire (as today's independent worker is) lack a center to their lives, and yet I am encouraged that such workers are more likely than the old jobholders (who did one little piece of work again and again) to have a real relationship to the outcome of their labor. Karl Marx claimed that capitalism had destroyed that vital connection, but we can see now that it was the specialized job that did it.

I view the dangers inherent in dejobbing as the second great job shift's counterpart to the atrocious working conditions of the early factory- and office-based jobholders. These are the dangers and damages that await the first waves of people exposed to any great social change. The real issue is not how to stop the change but how to provide the necessary knowledge and skills to equip people to operate successfully in this new world, and how to build buffers and nets to keep the change from being so destructive. Such things will not be done by institutions and individuals who are idealizing their past and turning their backs on the reality of the present.

The world beyond jobs has its advantages and its prices. It offers more freedom, more control over one's time, more consistency with personal values, more self-expression, more flexibility, more chance to see the results of one's labors. But it also exposes people to nonstop change. It has all the economic instability of self-employment, and it can magnify self-doubt and disorganized habits. It destroys the sense of community that existed in many workplaces, and so it can be very lonely.

Having pursued it for twenty years, I can attest to both its pluses and minuses. I wouldn't trade it for any job I can imagine. I know myself far better than I'd ever have if I had stayed with a job. I have accomplished more than any job that I was qualified for would have allowed me to. I have earned more than any job I could find would have paid. And I can't wait to finish this book to discover where it is going to take me next.

Ducunt fata volentem, nolentem trahunt.

Those words by the Latin writer Seneca provide my final motto: "The fates guide those who go willingly; those who do not, they drag." We are moving beyond jobs today as surely as we moved into them almost two hundred years ago. At that time there was a very popular story about a man who went to sleep and awoke to find that enormous changes had taken place and that life had passed him by. Washington Irving's character Rip Van Winkle didn't fit into the job world that was just then emerging, for he had what his creator called "an insuperable aversion to all kinds of profitable labor," although he was always ready to lend a hand at the old communal tasks like barn raising. The modern Rips are in danger of repeating his mistake and of waking to find themselves old people in a world that they cannot any longer understand.

The new vocation is not in the field of electronics or genetic engineering or international trade. The new vocation exists within every field, for it requires not that one produce some particular new thing but rather that one develop a new way of being productive. The new vocation is living with the ambiguities produced by the disappearance of any meaningful economic slots to settle into; it is living with the tension between doing different things for different clients at the same time, without being able to unify everything under the rubric of "my job."

Not everyone will enter this world soon. The old world of jobs will still be around, the way that agriculture is still around. It will still be important, the way agriculture is. But agriculture also employs only 2 percent of our population today, although before the job tide rose it employed almost everyone. The job world is in for the same fate. If you are close to retirement, you may be able to hang in there and wait it out—although as a sixty-year-old myself, I find that option a sad and deadening one. But if you have more than a very few years of earning ahead of you—or if your job has already evaporated—I'd urge you to turn your face toward the future and set forth.

Notes

Preface

Page ix: *Three out of ten large American industrial firms* See Thomas A. Stewart, "Welcome to the Revolution," *Fortune*, December 13, 1993, 76.

Page x: *manufacturers "may have no choice . . . "* James C. Cooper and Kathleen Madigan, "Suddenly, the Job Engine Is Purring," *Newsweek*, June 21, 1993, 29–30.

Page x: *"Where Did My Career Go?"* See David Hage, Linda Grant, and Jim Impoco's lead article in the June 28, 1993, issue of *U.S. News & World Report*, 42–52.

Page x: *the condition will "last for many years."* Cited in George J. Church, "Jobs in an Age of Insecurity," *Time*, November 22, 1993, 35. © 1993 Time Inc. Reprinted by permission.

Part One

Page 1: Quotation from Lance Morrow, "The Temping of America," *Time*, March 29, 1993, 40–41. © 1993 Time Inc. Reprinted by permission.

Chapter One

Page 4: Quotation from Robert Howard, "An Interview with Xerox's Paul Allaire," *Harvard Business Review*, September–October 1992, 107–121.

Page 5: *only 18 percent of the lost jobs* Ronald Henkoff, "Where Will the Jobs Come From?" *Fortune*, October 19, 1992, 58.

Page 5: *In the summer of 1993* Cited by Jonathan Marshall in "Sliding Down the Income Ladder," *San Francisco Chronicle*, June 21, 1993, C8.

Page 5: *"Today, people who lose their jobs . . . "* Quoted in G. Pascal Zachary and Bob Ortega, "Workplace Revolution Boosts Productivity at Cost of Job Security," *Wall Street Journal*, March 3, 1993, A8. Reprinted by permission of the Wall Street Journal. © 1993 Dow Jones & Company, Inc. All rights reserved worldwide.

Page 5: *European companies are still overstaffed* Cited in Charles Burck, "The Pain of Productivity," *Fortune*, November 30, 1992, 22. The high unemployment rate in Europe doesn't include what one survey of the situation termed the "millions of . . . workers who get government paychecks under various programs that pay fishermen for not fishing, farmers for not farming and workers for not working." From "Recession Crimps Europeans' Good Life," *Honolulu Star Bulletin*, June 23, 1993, A21.

Page 5: *Japanese companies are already beginning to break their patterns* Job openings in Japan, which were 1.1 per job seeker in 1991, have fallen to 0.7 per job seeker today. The Japanese unemployment figures are artificially depressed, because the Japanese government pays companies not to lay people off. It is currently estimated that there are 1.5 million of these "in-house unemployed" workers who are not counted in the ِ ntistics. See Jacob M. Schlesinger, "Japan Begins to Confront Job Insecurity, ' *Wall Street Journal*, September 16, 1993, A20. Douglas T. Shinsato (in "J; pan Tries to Get the Size Right," *Wall Street Journal*, June 28, 1993, A14) tells of one manufacturer that is considering putting everyone on a temporary contract. Since employees become permanent workers in Japan after six months, that would mean giving everyone a five-month, twenty-nine-day contract, then terminating everyone for a day, and finally giving everyone a new five-month, twenty-nine-day contract. Some change from lifetime employment!

Page 6: *Automotive designers* Michael Williams, "Toyota Creates Work Contracts Challenging Lifetime-Job System," *Wall Street Journal*, January 24, 1994, A10. Reprinted by permission of the Wall Street Journal. © 1994 Dow Jones & Company, Inc. All rights reserved worldwide.

Page 6: *more than 1,000 mergers* Tom Abate, "On the Defensive," *San Francisco Examiner*, December 13, 1992, E1.

Page 6: *If you add the jobs lost since 1989* Lee Smith, "Can Defense Pain Be Turned to Gain?" *Fortune*, February 8, 1993, 84.

Page 7: *A recent editorial cartoon* Toles's cartoon originally appeared in *The New Republic*. It was reprinted on p. A18 of the July 1, 1993, issue of the *San Francisco Chronicle*.

Page 7: *very large job losses at hospitals* While the job losses in health have so far been much smaller than those in defense, they are likely in the long run to be just as large. See Lee Smith, "The Coming Health Care Shakeout," *Fortune*, May 17, 1993, 70–75.

Page 8: *the temporary-employment agency Manpower* Janice Castro, "Disposable Workers," *Time*, March 29, 1993, 43.

Page 8: *confidential Bank of America memo* Quoted in Zachary and Ortega, "Workplace Revolution," A8.

Page 9: *Temporary professionals are increasing* Ron Henkoff, "Winning the New Career Game," *Fortune*, July 12, 1993, 46–47.

Page 9: *The San Francisco firm M^2* See "Flexible Jobs on the Rise," *San Francisco Chronicle*, August 10, 1992, C1.

Page 9: *hiring a temporary executive* Claire McAuliffe, "Contingent Workers Deliver a Certain Advantage," *San Francisco Business Times*, June 11, 1993, 5.

Page 9: *Action Staffing* Louis S. Richman, "America's Tough New Job Market," *Fortune*, February 24, 1992, 57–58. © 1992 Time Inc. All rights reserved.

Page 10: *For every one thousand American jobs* Brian O'Reilly, "Looking Ahead," *Fortune*, December 14, 1992, 52.

Page 10: *paradigm* Joel Barker, *Paradigms: The Business of Discovering the Future* (New York: HarperCollins, 1992), 32.

Page 11: *Who knows what digitized images will do* I conducted an executive seminar at the Transamerica Corporation headquarters in California recently, and one of the participants—fully visible and actively participating over a videophone—never left his office in Connecticut. The airlines don't even know that they lost a ticket sale.

Page 11: *to informate* See Shoshana Zuboff, *In the Age of the Smart Machine* (New York: Basic Books, 1988).

Page 12: *informated work needs fewer people* Michael Hammer and James Champy, "The Promise of Re-engineering," *Fortune*, May 3, 1993, 96.

Page 12: *the ATM that gives us the cash we need* Both this and the case from Solectron are taken from Jaclyn Fierman, "What Happened to the Jobs?" *Fortune*, July 12, 1993, 41.

Page 13: *middle managers made up more than one in five* Eric Greenberg, "Upswing in Downsizings to Continue," *Management Review*, February 1993, 5.

Page 14: *WHDH-TV* Edward C. Baig, "Inching Out of the Stone Age," *U.S. News & World Report*, May 3, 1993, 68.

Page 15: The Peter Drucker quote is from his article, "The New Society of Organizations," *Harvard Business Review*, September–October 1992, 101.

Page 15: The Safi Quereshy quote is from "FYI," *Inc.*, July 1993, 13. Reprinted with permission of *Inc.* magazine. © July 1993 Goldhirsh Group, Inc. (617) 248–8000.

Page 15: The quoted passage is from Nuala Beck, *Shifting Gears: Thriving in the New Economy* (Toronto: HarperCollins, 1992), 68–69.

Page 15: *In 1989 that figure had risen to 51 percent* Megan O'Leary, "Mapping Out Global Networks, *CIO*, March 1992, 33. Quoted in Tom Peters, *Liberation Management: Necessary Disorganization for the Nanosecond Nineties* (New York: Knopf, 1992), 114. Or consider this: In 1982, about $100 billion a year was being spent on industrial equipment in the United States, while only $50 billion was spent on computers and communication equipment. In 1992, the industrial spending had risen to nearly $110 billion, while the computer/communications spending had leaped to $135 billion. From Stewart, "Welcome to the Revolution," 72.

Page 16: The quoted passage is from Rosabeth Moss Kanter, *When Giants Learn to Dance: Mastering the Challenges of Strategy, Management, and Careers in the 1990's.* (New York: Simon and Schuster, 1989), 304.

Page 18: *The steering-column design of a Pontiac Grand Am* Neal Templin and Joseph B. White, "GM Drive to Step Up Efficiency Is Colliding with UAW Job Fears," *Wall Street Journal*, June 23, 1993, A1.

Page 18: *It used to take up to twenty-five minutes* "The Metamorphosis of Hewlett-Packard," *The Economist*, June 19, 1993, 67.

Page 18: The automaker outsourcing statistics are from Alex Taylor, "What's Ahead for GM's New Team," *Fortune*, November 30, 1992, 61.

Page 19: For these and other examples of outsourcing, see Shawn Tully, "The Modular Corporation," *Fortune*, February 8, 1993, 107–108; Thomas Stewart, "There Are No Products-Only Services," *Fortune*, January 14, 1991, 32; Sharen Kindel, "Network Outsourcing: Let Your People Go," *Financial World*, June 9, 1992, 38; and Donna Brown. "Outsourcing: How Corporations Take Their Business Elsewhere," *Management Review*, February 1992, 15–20.

Page 19: Details of the Commodore-FedEx arrangement are from Stewart, "There Are No Products," 32.

Page 19: The Xerox-Ryder arrangement is described in Laurie M. Grossman, "Truck Cabs Turn into Mobile Offices As Drivers Take On White-Collar Tasks," *Wall Street Journal*, August 3, 1993, B1.

Page 20: Electronic Scriptorium is featured in Jyoti Thottam, "Entrepreneur Finds Monks Make Heavenly Employees," *Wall Street Journal*, July 12, 1993, B2. Reprinted by permission of the Wall Street Journal. © 1993 Dow Jones & Company, Inc. All rights reserved worldwide.

Page 20: The PC Connection and Rosenbluth Travel examples come from Brent Bowers, "Technology Allows Small Concerns to Exploit Distances," *Wall Street Journal*, March 23, 1991, B2. Reprinted by permission of the Wall Street Journal. © 1991 Dow Jones & Company, Inc. All rights reserved worldwide.

Page 21: The Quarterdeck example is from O'Reilly, "Looking Ahead," 62, 64.

Page 21: Arthur Andersen's move is described in David Morgan, "Arthur Andersen Sends Execs Home," *San Francisco Examiner*, June 29, 1993, E14.

Page 21: ValueQuest's story is told in Peter Coy, "Start with Some High-Tech Magic . . . ," *Business Week/Enterprise 1993* [undated special issue], 24, 32.

Page 21: Herman Miller's office is described in Julie Cohen Mason, "Workplace 2000: The Death of 9 to 5?" *Management Review*, January 1993, 18.

Page 22: IBM's space-saving program is the focus of Laurie Hays, "IBM Speeds Drive to Shed Real Estate As Part of Program to Trim Jobs, Costs," *Wall Street Journal*, June 18, 1993, A5B. Reprinted by permission of the Wall Street Journal. © 1993 Dow Jones & Company, Inc. All rights reserved worldwide. See also Mitchell Pacelle, "To Trim Their Costs, Some Companies Cut Space for Employees," *Wall Street Journal*, June 4, 1993, A1.

Page 22: The telecommuting statistics are from Cohen Mason, "Workplace 2000," 15.

Page 23: The IBM Credit quotations are from Hammer and Champy, "Promise of Re-engineering," 94–96.

Page 24: The Hallmark example and the San Diego Zoo material are from Thomas A. Stewart, "The Search for the Organization of Tomorrow," *Fortune*, May 18, 1992, 92–98. © 1992 Time Inc. All rights reserved.

Page 24: The reengineering article mentioned is Al Ehrbar, "Re-Engineering Gives Firms New Efficiency, Workers the Pink Slip," *Wall Street Journal*, March 16, 1993, A1. Reprinted by permission of the Wall Street Journal. © 1993 Dow Jones & Company, Inc. All rights reserved worldwide.See also Hammer and Champy, "Promise of Re-engineering," 94–96.

Page 25: The material about job turbulence is from David Birch, "The Rise and Fall of Everybody," *Inc.*, September 1987, 18–21. Reprinted with permission of *Inc.* magazine. © September 1987 Goldhirsh Group, Inc. (617) 248–8000.

Page 25: The computer-company turnover is described in Don Clark, "Jobs Coming and Going in Silicon Valley," *San Francisco Chronicle*, July 7, 1993, E1.

Page 26: The Peter Drucker quote is from Drucker, "New Society of Organizations," 97.

Page 28: These two Drucker quotes are from Peter Drucker, "Planning for Uncertainty," *Wall Street Journal*, July 22, 1992, A14. Reprinted by per-

Chapter Two

Page 29: The Malcolmson quote is from R. W. Malcolmson, "Ways of Getting a Living in Eighteenth Century England," in *On Work: Historical, Comparative, and Theoretical Approaches*, ed. R. E. Pahl (Oxford: Basil Blackwell, Ltd., 1988), 48.

Page 29: The Handy quote is from Charles Handy, *The Future of Work: A Guide to a Changing Society* (Oxford: Basil Blackwell, Ltd., 1984).

Page 30: The old factory-worker joke is retold in Joe Griffith, ed., *Speaker's Library of Business Stories, Anecdotes, and Humor* (Englewood Cliffs, N.J.: Prentice Hall, 1990), 182.

Page 31: The information about the changing meaning of *job* is taken from *Webster's New Universal Unabridged Dictionary*, 2d. ed. (New York: Dorset & Baber, 1983); *The American Heritage Dictionary of the English Language* (Boston: Houghton Mifflin Co., 1979); and the patriarch of English dictionaries, *The Oxford English Dictionary*, rev. ed. (Oxford: The Clarendon Press, 1933).

Page 33: The 1795 decision is described in E. P. Thompson, *The Making of the English Working Class* (London: Penguin Books, 1980), 72.

Page 34: For an analysis of the linguistic shift regarding jobs, see Raymond Williams, *Culture and Society: 1780–1850* (Garden City, N.Y.: Anchor Books, 1960), xi–xvi.

Page 36: An interesting subtext to the present thesis could be written about the implications for women of this shift to jobs. In the premodern economy, there were activities that were usually performed by men and others usually performed by women. Attitudes were what today we would call "sexist," and the sexual and physical abuse of women was terrible. But "women's work" was not, by and large, lower or more degrading than "men's work." The farmer and the farmer's wife had comparable hardships, and the work deemed appropriate to each gender existed side by side. It was only when it became "women's jobs" and "men's jobs" and when work was relocated into a hierarchically organized factory or office that pay and power differentials became so extreme. Then the male department director earned much more than the female secretary, the male principal more than the female teacher, the male hospital administrator more than the female nurse. In other words, jobs provided an essentially sexist society a very important new way to express and to reinforce male dominance.

Page 36: The Guttman quote is from Herbert Guttman, "Work, Culture and Society in Industrializing America, 1815–1919," in Pahl, ed., *On Work*, 134–35.

Page 36: The Thompson quote is from his essay "Time, Work-Discipline, and Industrial Capitalism," in *Past and Present*, no. 38 (1967): 57.

Page 37: The Pollard quote was quoted in Guttman, "Work, Culture, and Society," 127.

Page 37: The two Ure quotes are from Thompson, *Making of the English Working Class*, 394–95 and 397, respectively.

Page 37: These quotes from Thompson are from *Making of the English Working Class*, 450–51.

Page 38: The *Time* article is in the March 29, 1993, issue (pp. 40–41; © 1993

Time Inc. Reprinted by permission), and Tom Peters' response is in his weekly management column that appeared three weeks later ("It's Time to Turn U.S. Employees into Self-Reliant Business People," *Rocky Mountain News*, April 20, 1993, 35).

Page 39: The Ashenfelter quote is from Ehrbar, "Re-Engineering," A12.

Page 40: The information on the dejobbed environment at Microsoft is from Bob Flipczak, "Beyond the Gates at Microsoft," *Training*, September 1992, 43. Reprinted with permission of Training magazine. Copyright © 1992. Lakewood Publications, Minneapolis, MN. All rights reserved. Not for resale.

Page 41: This material on Microsoft Windows NT is from G. Pascal Zachary, "Agony and Ecstasy of 200 Code Writers Beget Windows NT," *Wall Street Journal*, May 26, 1993, A1. Reprinted by permission of the Wall Street Journal. © 1993 Dow Jones & Company, Inc. All rights reserved worldwide.

Page 42: *Most of them eventually return to the company* Alan Deutschman, "Odd Man Out," *Fortune*, July 26, 1993, 55.

Page 43: *alternate bouts of intense labour* Quoted in Guttman, "Work, Culture, and Society," 134.

Page 43: *Frequently . . . after several weeks* Ibid.

Page 43: For *Inc.*'s second annual survey, see the July 1993 issue, pp. 51ff. The material on IDEO is on p. 60. Quotes reprinted with permission of *Inc.* magazine. © July 1993 Goldhirsh Group, Inc. (617) 248–8000.

Page 43: The Walsh quote is from *Inc.*, July 1993, 92.

Page 44: The Hardwick quote is from *Inc.*, July 1993, 172.

Page 44: The Sweningson quote is from *Inc.*, July 1993, 63.

Page 44: The information about Intel is from Jay Stuller, "Why Not Inplacement?" *Training*, June 1993, 40. Reprinted with permission of Training magazine. Copyright © 1993. Lakewood Publications, Minneapolis, MN. All rights reserved. Not for resale.

Page 45: *Secretaries are becoming managers* Gareth Morgan, *Riding the Waves of Change: Developing Managerial Competencies for a Turbulent World* (San Francisco: Jossey-Bass Publishers, 1988), 103.

Page 45: The Peters quote is from Peters, *Liberation Management*, 25.

Page 45: The Vienne quote is from Véronique Vienne, "Make It Right . . . Then Toss It Away: An Inside View of Corporate Culture at Condé Nast," *Columbia Journalism Review*, July–August 1991, 29. Quoted in Peters, *Liberation Management*, 9.

Page 46: The Glines quote is from Stewart, "Search for the Organization of Tomorrow," 98.

Page 46: The Frey quote is from Robert Frey, "Empowerment or Else," *Harvard Business Review*, September–October 1993, 88.

Page 47: The Senge quote is from Peter M. Senge, *The Fifth Discipline: The Art and Practice of the Learning Organization* (New York: Doubleday, 1990), 18.

Page 48: The quoted definition of CRM, as well as information on how Southwest Airlines utilizes it, is from Connie Bovier, "Teamwork: The Heart of an Airline," *Training*, June 1993, 53–58. Reprinted with permission of Training magazine. Copyright © 1993 Lakewood Publications, Minneapolis, MN. All rights reserved. Not for resale.

Page 49: *It isn't coincidental* People's Express took dejobbing several steps further, of course, doing away with job boxes entirely. Plane crews might

sell tickets and help with baggage. Most students of that experiment have
concluded that the tremendous morale that that system engendered was
never allowed to flourish, however, because the airline's attempt to expand too quickly burdened what was otherwise an innovative and successful enterprise. I will be surprised if we do not see another People's
Express before long.

Page 49: The Peters quote is from Peters, *Liberation Management,* 204.

Page 50: My thinking on the new rules has been influenced by a speech
called "Motivating Workers in Critical Times" that Robert A. Jud gave at
the November 10, 1992, convention of the American Electronics Association. He calls it "The New Employment Contract," and its items differ
from mine, but the spirit is very much the same.

Part Two

Page 55: The former advertising executive was quoted in Castro, "Disposable Workers," 47.

Page 55: Quadracci was quoted in Peters, *Liberation Management,* 146.
Quad/Graphics is a half-billion-dollar-a-year printing company in Wis-
consin.

Page 56: *That's why AT&T . . . has stopped* Henkoff, "Winning the New
Career Game," 48.

Page 57: The excerpt is from Melvin Anshen, "The Management of Ideas,"
originally published in the *Harvard Business Review,* July–August 1969,
and reprinted in that journal in March–April 1993, p. 159.

Page 57: *the terms of work have been reframed* The idea that the assignment is
today's "natural unit of work" is suggested by Kenneth P. De Meuse and
Walter W. Tornow in their article, "Leadership and the Changing Psychological Contract between Employer and Employee," *Issues & Observations*
[Center for Creative Leadership] 13, no. 2 (1993): 4–6. I am indebted to
John Taylor, whose dejobbed work as an "information designer" is referred to elsewhere in this book, for calling my attention to the way *gig* is
being used by many independent professionals. The term comes originally from a jazz combo's one-night employment.

Page 57: employment *too has shifted its meaning* Again, this information is
taken from *The Oxford English Dictionary.*

Chapter Three

Page 63: *exploiting their own distinctive "core competencies"* "Peter Drucker's
1990's: The Futures That Have Already Happened," *Boardroom Reports,*
December 15, 1989, 7–10. Reprinted with the permission of Boardroom
Reports, 330 West 42nd Street, New York, NY 10036. Here Drucker
accurately predicted that "unbundling" would be one of the major forces
that would change organizations during the 1990s.

Page 66: I am indebted to John Iacovini for articulating this connection
between Moments of Truth and the end of jobs. "In the old days," he
notes, "you went to work and used your 'job' description as your guide
for doing your daily work . . . . With cycles of service and especially Moments of Truth, the notion of job description is undermined." Personal
communication.

Page 66: The Juran excerpt is from Joseph M. Juran, "Made in U.S.A.: A
Renaissance in Quality," *Harvard Business Review,* July–August 1993, 44.

Page 68: The Jonas excerpt is from Donald Jonas, "Lessons from Lechters:

How Lechters Built a Big, Big Business on a Narrow Niche," *Boardroom Reports,* August 1, 1993, 5. Reprinted with the permission of Boardroom Reports, 330 West 42nd Street, New York, NY 10036.

Page 69: *"The last iceman always makes money"* See Jack Willoughby's interview with Harrigan, "Endgame Strategy," *Forbes,* July 13, 1987, 181–82, and also his profiles (pp. 183–204) of firms and individuals who have successfully harvested the late crops in wooden cameras, harpoons, velvet, wooden propellers, leather belting for machinery, vacuum tubes, ice, and (yes, even) buggy whips.

Page 69: I'd even take the argument that *interface* is an important word another step: *interface* is to our society what *frontier* was to the nineteenth century. *Frontier* was a chauvinist concept that drew a line between civilization and noncivilization—even between the human and the subhuman. *Interface* far better reflects our growing sense that the cultural meetings of today are between comparable social systems that are, whatever their differences, of equal human significance.

Page 71: For information on IKEA, see Richard Normann and Rafael Ramirez, "From Value Chain to Value Constellation: Designing Interactive Strategy," *Harvard Business Review,* July–August 1993, 66–70.

Page 72: The information on Drew Melton is from Donna Fenn, "Bottoms Up," *Inc.,* July 1993, 58.

Page 72: The Harari excerpt is from Oren Harari, "Back to the Future of Work," *Management Review,* September 1993, 33. Reprinted by permission of Oren Harari, Professor of Management, University of San Francisco. He also tells stories about two other workers that are relevant to the topic of dejobbing, although that aspect of their activity is not what he is writing about.

Page 74: *"How can I meet those needs?"* What we are talking about is not simply "intrapreneurship," as that concept was popularized a few years ago by Gifford Pinchot in *Intrapreneurship.* He, too, was talking about employees acting like entrepreneurs *inside* the organization. But his intrapreneurs faced outward, creating new products and services for the external market on behalf of their organization. I am talking about turning the organization itself into a market and focusing an entrepreneurial spirit on the needs of the customers within the organization.

Chapter Four

Page 76: *The Fifth Discipline* (New York: Doubleday Currency, 1990), 18.

Page 85: For more by Haldane and Bolles, see Bernard Haldane, *Career Satisfaction and Success,* rev. ed. (New York: Amacom, 1988); and Richard Bolles, *What Color Is Your Parachute?* (Berkeley, Calif.: Ten Speed Press— slightly revised editions come out almost yearly).

Page 86: The Henkoff excerpt is from "Winning the New Career Game," 46.

Page 88: There are many useful books on temperament. The two to start with are Isabel Briggs Myers, *Gifts Differing* (Palo Alto, Calif.: Consulting Psychologists Press, 1980), and David Keirsey and Marilyn Bates, *Please Understand Me: Character and Temperament Types,* 3rd ed. (Del Mar, Calif.: Prometheus Nemesis, 1978). In this chapter I use the term *temperament* in its everyday meaning: the person's characteristic manner of thinking, feeling, and behaving. I am not limiting it to the narrower meanings that have grown up around the application of particular typological theories.

Page 93: The Bell Labs study is described in Robert Kelley and Janet Caplan, "How Bell Labs Creates Star Performers," *Harvard Business Review,* July–August 1993, 128–39.

Page 93: The McKenna quote is from Regis McKenna, "Marketing Is Everything," *Harvard Business Review,* January–February 1991, 65–75.

Page 94: The Express Project is described in John Seely Brown, "Research That Reinvents the Corporation," *Harvard Business Review,* January–February 1991, 110–11.

Page 96: The information about Lopez is from "Breaking Away," *Inc.,* October 1993, 84.

Page 97: The Captain Marryat quote was quoted in Oscar Handlin, ed., *This Was America . . . As Recorded by European Travellers* (Cambridge: Harvard University Press, 1949), 202.

Chapter Five

Page 100: The Schaen quote was quoted in Castro, "Disposable Workers," 47.

Page 100: The Morin quote was quoted by Henkoff in "Winning the New Career Game," 46.

Page 101: See the story of Farrow and Walden Paddlers in Edward O. Welles, "Virtual Realities," *Inc.,* August 1993, 50–58. Reprinted with permission of *Inc.* magazine. © August 1993 Goldhirsh Group, Inc. (617) 248–8000.

Page 101: *Reflecting on his own temperament* I have applied the D.A.T.A. template to Farrow's situation after the fact to show how it fits in a real case; I do not suggest that it was the way in which he actually explored his situation and made his decision.

Page 102: Bressler is described in John Huey, "Where Will Managers Go?" *Fortune,* January 27, 1992, 52.

Page 103: Snyder is described in Paul Blythe, "Sleuthing, She Wrote," *Modern Maturity,* February–March 1992, 16.

Page 103: Ferrington is described in Henkoff, "Winning the New Career Game," 47–48.

Page 103: The description of Taylor is based on my interview with him.

Page 109: The Koller excerpt is from Alice Koller, *An Unknown Woman* (New York: Bantam, 1991), 282.

Page 111: The Mercer survey is cited in Anne B. Fisher, "Don't Count On Your Pension," *Fortune,* 1994 Investor's Guide, 139. © 1994 Time Inc. All rights reserved. Fisher notes that "the list [kept by the federal Pension Benefit Guarantee Corporation (PBGC)] of the top ten underfinanced pension plans reads like a roll call of once secure employers, including General Motors, Chrysler, Westinghouse, Uniroyal, Goodrich and TWA." Plans that have already run out of money have exceeded the PBGC reserves by $2.5 billion, and 15,000 additional corporations have a total pension deficit of $51 billion.

Page 111: *Layoffs are taking place* As I am writing this, the fate of the Clinton health plan is still unclear, but its passage will not change the basic issue: fewer and fewer people are going to be able to benefit from employer-funded health coverage.

Page 111: The material regarding Skonie is based on my interview of her at the training firm she founded, called Skonie Associates, in Sausalito, California.

Page 113: *Something over 6 percent of the workforce*   Juliet B. Schor, *The Overworked Americans: The Unexpected Decline of Leisure* (New York: Basic Books, 1991), 31. See also Diane Crispell, "Moonlighting Serenade Lures Many Workers," *Wall Street Journal*, December 18, 1991, B1; and Ann Wylie, "Moonlighting Serenade," *America West*, November 1992, 75.

Page 113: The Bozzotto quote is from Schor, *The Overworked Americans*, 22.

Page 114: McGraw's moonlighting is described in Kathryn Harris, "Torch Song Lawyer," *Forbes*, December 10, 1990, 298–300.

Page 114: McBride is described in Wylie, "Moonlighting Serenade."

Page 114: The material on Lyn Snow is based on my interview of her at her studio in 1993.

Page 114: Wylie, "Moonlighting Serenade."

Page 115: The Gendron quote is from an editorial in *Inc.*, October 1992, p. 11. Reprinted with permission of *Inc.* magazine. © October 1992 Goldhirsh Group, Inc. (617) 248-8000.

Page 116: The information on woman-owned businesses is cited in "The State of Woman-Owned Start-Ups," *Inc.*, November 1993, 34.

Page 116: The information on Hirsh is from Suzanne Alexander, "Jane Hirsh Saw the Future and It Was Generic," *Wall Street Journal*, October 12, 1993, B1. Reprinted by permission of the Wall Street Journal. © 1993 Dow Jones & Company, Inc. All rights reserved worldwide.

Page 117: *our "course or progress through life"*   In the heyday of jobs, it was common to say that a worker who did not want (or see any way) to rise upward in the organizational hierarchy did not have a career, just a job. Needless to say, that way of looking at things is made meaningless by the changes we are describing. In the new-old sense, we all have "careers." But far fewer of us are going to have "jobs."

Page 117: *Career doesn't mean "rising in the world"*   Like the idea of the self-managed career, the idea of the career-without-vertical-promotions is a perennial one that is returning to prominence. A recent *Fortune* article (Jaclyn Fierman, "Beating the Midlife Career Crisis," September 6, 1993) is described in the front of the magazine thus: "How to succeed without really rising. Flattened organizations and their ambitious employees are finding new paths to job satisfaction and personal growth." Beverly Kaye has been writing and speaking about such careers for more than a decade. See her "Up Is Not the Only Way" in *Supervisory Management*, February 1980, 2–9.

Page 117: *You need to compose your career*   Mary Catherine Bateson uses that metaphor in her wonderful study of women's lives, *Composing a Life* (New York: Plume Books, 1990). Her thesis is that "women's lives offer valuable models because of the very pressures that make them seem more difficult. Women have not been permitted to focus on single goals but have tended to live with ambiguity and multiplicity. It is not easy. But the rejection of ambiguity may be a rejection of the complexity of the real world in favor of some dangerously simple . . . model." (p. 184) She notes that "this quality of broadly focused concern and interruptibility [that running a household requires] enables some important skills and hobbles others. There are tasks that really do require extended narrow concentration, but there are others that require a willingness to shift gears rapidly and think about more than one thing at once. Corporations, institutions, even nations are sometimes led successfully for a time by individuals who focus on single goals, but this narrowness is destructive in the long term. It is like the problem of monocrops: researchers develop a genetically uniform strain of wheat or tomatoes to maximize some single characteristic and then arrange for the planting of unvaried acres of that crop—which could potentially be wiped out by a single plague." (p. 179) Copyright © 1989 by Mary Catherine Bateson. Used by permission of Grove/Atlantic, Inc.

Chapter Six
Page 118: Quote from Christine is from Jonathan Marshall, "Sliding Down the Income Ladder," *San Francisco Chronicle*, June 21, 1993, C1.
Page 118: The Ehrlichman quote is from John Ehrlichman, "Who Will Hire Me Now?" *Parade Magazine*, August 29, 1993, 4.
Page 119: The Baratti quote is from Ehrlichman, "Who Will Hire Me Now?"
Page 119: The Cantine quote is from Kenneth Labich, "The New Unemployed," *Fortune*, March 8, 1993, 40. © 1993 Time Inc. All rights reserved.
Page 121: The Whitehead quote is from Gilbert Seldes, ed., *The Great Quotations* (Secaucus, N.J.: The Citadel Press, 1983), 738.
Page 122: The Schram quote is from Griffith, ed., *Speaker's Library of Business Stories*, 47.
Page 124: The Drucker quote is from Drucker, "Planning for Uncertainty," A14. See also the interview with him that appeared in *Boardroom Reports* ("Peter Drucker's 1990's," December 15, 1989), where he identifies what he considers the most important contemporary trends and closes with the statement, "The trends that I have described above are not forecasts (for which I have little use and scant respect); they are, if you will, conclusions. Everything discussed here has already happened; it is only the full impacts that are still to come. . . . [Few Americans, however,] have yet asked themselves: 'What do these futures mean for my own work and my own organization?' " (p. 10) Reprinted with the permission of Boardroom Reports, 330 West 42nd Street, New York, NY 10036.
Page 126: The Mackay quote is from Jay Conrad Levenson, *Guerrilla Marketing Newsletter*, September–October 1993, 3.
Page 133: The Welty quote is from *The Quotable Woman* (Philadelphia: The Running Press, 1991), 152.
Page 133: *But all of them provide continuities* Even a grievance is a kind of distorted dream, for as Eric Hoffer has said, "To have a grievance is to have a purpose in life. A grievance can almost serve as a substitute for hope; and it not infrequently happens that those who hunger for hope give their allegiance to him who offers them a grievance." From W. H. Auden and Louis Kronenberger, eds., *The Viking Book of Aphorisms* (New York: Dorset Books, n.d.), 163. To lose a grievance can be as difficult as losing a dream, for it forces one to reevaluate everything.
Page 135: *perhaps the organization is more like flowing water* For a study of the "permanent whitewater" metaphor, see Peter Vaill, *Managing as a Performing Art* (San Francisco: Jossey-Bass, 1989), especially pp. 1–32.
Page 135: The Wheatley book is Margaret J. Wheatley, *Leadership and the New Science* (San Francisco: Berrett-Koehler, 1992). This is the best book

currently available on how contemporary scientific theory might provide a new metaphorical basis for thinking about how organizations work.

Chapter Seven

Page 143: The Sculley quote is from *Odyssey: Pepsi to Apple* (New York: HarperCollins, 1987), 265.

Page 143: The Skonie quote is from a personal interview.

Page 144: *"these figures were even worse"* Greenberg, "Upswing in Downsizings," 5.

Page 144: *"every time you'd get a big batch"* The words are those of a worker at Schmid Laboratories in South Carolina and are quoted by Clare Ansberry in "Workers Are Forced to Take More Jobs with Few Benefits," *Wall Street Journal*, March 11, 1993, A9. Reprinted by permission of the Wall Street Journal. © 1993 Dow Jones & Company, Inc. All rights reserved worldwide.

Page 144: The Beer book is Michael Beer, Russell A. Eisenstat, and Bert Spector, *The Critical Path to Corporate Renewal* (Cambridge: Harvard Business School Press, 1990), 12.

Page 146: The Kelly quotes are from Fenn, "Bottoms Up," 60.

Page 146: The Baker quotes are from Peters, *Liberation Management*, 38.

Page 146: The Hauk quote is from Tom Ehrenfeld, "School's In," *Inc.*, July 1993, 66. Reprinted with permission of *Inc.* magazine. © July 1993 Goldhirsh Group, Inc. (617) 248–8000.

Page 146: The Wiegand quote is from Jay Finegan, "People Power," *Inc.*, July 1993, 62. Reprinted with permission of *Inc.* magazine. © July 1993 Goldhirsh Group, Inc. (617) 248–8000.

Page 147: The Berggren quote is from Mary Graham Davis, "Hiring the Overqualified," *Management Review*, August 1993, 36–37. By "transforming," he means an organization that is in the process of redefining itself to be capable of the tasks that the future will bring.

Page 148: "Secrets of Superior Customer Service" is by Robert L. Desatnick and it appears in *Boardroom Reports*, September 15, 1993, p. 3. Reprinted with the permission of Boardroom Reports, 330 West 42nd Street, New York, NY 10036.

Page 149: The Anshen quote is from Anshen, "Management of Ideas."

Page 150: *"We report to each other."* Peters, *Liberation Management*, 25, 92.

Page 151: The information about Corning is from Amal Kumar Naj, "Some Manufacturers Drop Efforts to Adopt Japanese Techniques," *Wall Street Journal*, May 7, 1993, A1. Reprinted by permission of the Wall Street Journal. © 1993 Dow Jones & Company, Inc. All rights reserved worldwide.

Page 151: The excerpt describing the Indus Group is from Leslie Brokaw, "Thinking Flat," *Inc.*, October 1993, 88. Reprinted with permission of *Inc.* magazine. © October 1993 Goldhirsh Group, Inc. (617) 248–8000.

Page 152: The Cypress Semiconductor excerpt is from Robert Tomasko, "To Really Boost Productivity . . . Eliminate Jobs," *Boardroom Reports*, August 1, 1993, 6. Reprinted with the permission of Boardroom Reports, 330 West 42nd Street, New York, NY 10036.

Page 152: The Wiegand quote is from Finegan, "People Power," 62.

Page 152: For more information about the changing nature of *assignment*, see De Meuse and Tornow, "Leadership and the Changing Psychological Contract," 4–6. They conclude that "assignments should perhaps be

looked at as the more natural unit of work [than jobs]. Assignments recognize more the dynamic and contextual nature of work as defined by the
changing needs of the organization."

Page 153: The information from Rich Martin is based on my interview with
him in Folsom, California.

Page 153: The Handy material is from "The Shamrock Organization," *The
Age of Unreason* (Cambridge: Harvard Business School Press, 1992),
87–115.

Page 156: The McGovern quote is from Leslie Brokaw, "Getting Back the
Fever," *Inc.*, September 1992, 84. Reprinted with permission of *Inc.* magazine. © September 1992 Goldhirsh Group, Inc. (617) 248–8000.

Page 156: The material about Chesapeake Packaging Company is from John
A. Case, "A Company of Business People," *Inc.*, April 1993, 86.

Page 157: *The "office" full of people*   The delocalization of the office parallels
the demise of the job and the rise of the virtual or amoebic organization.
"We have lost touch with the reasons why we have offices in the first
place," argues Duncan Sutherland, vice president of the Ohio furniture-
design firm Fitch Richardson Smith. "Offices now are looked at as a . . .
cost of doing business and as necessary evils rather than enabling tools
that allow an organization to leverage its intellectual potential." Cohen
Mason, "Workplace 2000," 14–18.

Page 158: The truck-driver excerpt is from Grossman, "Truck Cabs Turn
into Mobile Offices," B1.

Page 159: *Not so with the socio-cultural infrastructures*   Noel Tichy talks of the
three dimensions of organizational change as being the technical, the
political, and the cultural. I am substituting *social* for *political,* only because the latter term can be confusing because there are also public-
policy issues involved here, and many people will use *political* to refer to
them. He explains how change in any one of these dimensions triggers
change in the others too, and demonstrates how important it is to keep
the three areas moving in parallel. See his book, written with Mary Anne
Devanna, *The Transformational Leader* (New York: John Wiley & Sons,
1986).

Page 163: The Moravec and Tucker quote is from Milan Moravec and Robert Tucker, "Job Descriptions for the 21st Century," *Personnel Journal,*
June 1992, 22–25.

Page 164: The Kanter quotes are from Rosabeth Moss Kanter, "The New
Managerial Work," *Harvard Business Review,* November–December
1989, 89 and 85, respectively.

Page 164: The Drucker quote is from "The Post-Capitalist Executive: An
Interview with Peter F. Drucker," *Harvard Business Review,* May–June
1993, 116.

Page 164: The Kiechel quote is from Walter Kiechel III, "How We Will
Work in the Year 2000," *Fortune,* May 17, 1993, 46. © 1993 Time Inc. All
rights reserved.

Page 164: The Hammer quote comes from Michael Hammer and James
Champy, "The Future of Middle Managers," an interview in *Management
Review,* September 1993, 52.

Page 165: The Marshall excerpt is from her article, "Vision and Values at the
Edge of Chaos," in "Vision and Complexity, A Memorial Discussion Dedicated to David R. Gaster," *The Chaos Network* [newsletter] 5, no. 3 (August 1993).

Page 166: The Peters quote is from Peters, *Liberation Management*, 40.

Page 166: The material and quotations by Case in this and the following paragraphs are from Case, "A Company of Business People," 79–93.

Chapter Eight

Page 173: The Gendron quote is from "FYI," *Inc.*, October 1992, 11. Reprinted with permission of *Inc.* magazine. © October 1992 Goldhirsh Group, Inc. (617) 248–8000.

Page 173: The Handy quote is from Handy, *Future of Work*, 28.

Page 175: *"The spirit of [a new way of working]"* Quoted in Guttman, "Work, Culture, and Society," 126.

Page 176: The information about Arizona politicians' attempts to keep defense jobs comes from "Ashes of the Cold War," "Frontline" [a PBS news feature program], May 4, 1993.

Page 177: *a pure shell game* Gayle Hurmuses, "The Last Days of Local 303," *Toronto Globe and Mail*, May 1, 1993, D5.

Page 177: The whole account of this fiasco involving the Industry Education Council of California is taken from Susan Dentzer, "Beware the Immovable Object," *U.S. News & World Report*, June 28, 1993, 53.

Page 178: *doing away with outdated ordinances* Richman, "America's Tough New Job Market," 61.

Page 180: The information on Europe's efforts to shorten the workweek is from Terence Roth, "Europe Ponders the Shorter Workweek," *Wall Street Journal*, November 17, 1993, A13.

Page 181: The Hicks study is described in Louis S. Richman, "How Jobs Die—and Are Born," *Fortune*, July 26, 1993, 26. © 1993 Time Inc. All rights reserved.

Page 181: Material on business incubators is from Dee DePass, "Hatching a Business Dream: Incubators Can Give Entrepreneurs a Chance to Grow," *Minneapolis Star Tribune*, October 31, 1993, 1D.

Page 182: The *Wall Street Journal* article is Ralph T. King, Jr., "Job Retraining Linked Closely to Employers Works in Cincinnati," *Wall Street Journal*, March 19, 1993, A1. Reprinted by permission of the Wall Street Journal. © 1993 Dow Jones & Company, Inc. All rights reserved worldwide. Needless to say, I think that what the organization has to offer is "work," rather than "jobs." But the point remains valid.

Page 183: *Every successful neighborhood drug dealer* It would be worth studying the drug business as a model for employment-expansion products. It employs disadvantaged and often poorly educated people, utilizes sophisticated technology, maintains a complex communications system, manages large amounts of money, and provides access to "the American Dream" to large numbers of people for whom "a good job" is pure fantasy. Unfortunately, it is also illegal, dependent on a vicious and degrading product, and the source of both crime and social misery. But those terrible facts should not blind us to this lesson: disadvantaged people often work very effectively outside the parameters of a job.

Page 184: The numbers regarding work-search training are from King, "Job Retraining."

Page 185: The Employment Service statistic is from Louis S. Richman, "The Dark Side of the Job Churn," *Fortune*, August 9, 1993, 24.

Page 185: Bishop was quoted in Richman, "The Dark Side." The electronic possibilities are growing all the time. Forty major corporations have recently helped to fund the nonprofit Online Career Center, Inc., which uses the Internet to circulate news of openings and résumés. Here is a recent listing by Lilly Research Laboratory in Indianapolis: Seeking a pharmacologist to help in "investigating the role of mediators of arachidonic acid in inflammatory diseases such as asthma and AIDS, and . . . anti-tumor activity of monoclonal antibody-drug conjugates. . . . " Not exactly a job description! Quoted in "E-mail Might Help Improve Your Employment Picture," *Minneapolis Star Tribune,* October 31, 1993, 1D.

Page 185: The Career Action Center is located at 445 Sherman Avenue, Palo Alto, CA 94306 (415–324–1710); Alumnae Resources is located at 120 Montgomery Street, Suite 1080, San Francisco, CA 94104 (415–274–4700).

Page 186: For more information about Steamboat Springs, see a Business Report called "Lone Eagles: The Ultimate Commuters," in *American Demographics,* August 1993, pp. 10–13.

Page 187: *attracting new workers by offering health care*   See Milton Friedman, "The Folly of Buying Health Care at the Company Store," *Wall Street Journal,* February 3, 1993, A14. It is worth remembering that the largest HMO in America was also created for the same reason at the same time. Kaiser Healthcare was intended originally for Kaiser Steel workers, but it outgrew its original purpose and has become one of the prototypes for the kind of health system that a dejobbed society needs.

Page 187: The social-security insolvency dates are from Carolyn L. Weaver, "Baby-Boom Retirees, Destined to Go Bust," *Wall Street Journal,* August 26, 1993, A12.

Page 188: The information about the Chilean social-security system is from Wilton Woods, "The Latin Way to Boost Savings," *Fortune,* November 1, 1993, 26.

Page 189: Statistics about unemployment compensation are from James Aley, "Docking the Unemployed," *Fortune,* November 15, 1993, 28.

Page 190: Suggestions such as the variable payout have been made in David L. Birch, "Musical Jobs," *Inc.,* November 1987, 18; and in Beck, *Shifting Gears,* 117–18.

Page 190: The United Steel Workers contract is described in Case, "A Company of Business People," 82.

Chapter Nine

Page 196: The distinction between *change* and *transition* and how to deal successfully with the latter is the topic of several of my previous books. *Transitions: Making Sense of Life's Changes* (Reading, Mass.: Addison-Wesley, 1980) deals with personal transition, and *Managing Transitions: Making the Most of Change* (Reading, Mass: Addison-Wesley, 1991) deals with organizational transition.

Page 196: *Those who tell you that they thrive on transition*   There is a Calvin and Hobbes comic strip that makes the point well. The little boy announces that he thrives on change, and his tiger-companion replies, "You? You threw a fit this morning because your mom put less jelly on your toast than yesterday." Calvin replies, "I thrive on making *other people* change."

Page 198: *No other society in human history*   The effectiveness was only apparent, however, since it was achieved at the expense of the native peoples who lived on the land. The United States is still living down the real costs—in the form of social bitterness and human suffering—of the way in which European Americans created and distributed wealth.

Page 200: For more on mourning, see Elizabeth Kubler-Ross, *On Death and Dying* (New York: Macmillan, 1969).

Page 203: The Calhoun quote is from *A Disquisition on Government* (1850).

Page 206: *an ongoing series of public television programs* One could argue that just as the first great job shift depended on elementary schools to create a new breed of worker, so the second great job shift will find its best educational medium and venue to be public and cable television.

Page 207: The Cray excerpt is from Patricia A. Galagan, "On Being a Beginner: An Interview with John Rollwagen," *Training & Development*, November 1992, 32. © November 1992 by the American Society for Training and Development. Reprinted with permission. All rights reserved.

Page 212: The Fergusson quote is from Marilyn Fergusson, *The Aquarian Conspiracy* (Los Angeles: Tarcher, 1979), 34.

Page 214: For a more extended discussion of the neutral zone, see the chapter titled "The Neutral Zone" in my book *Transitions: Making Sense of Life's Changes*.

Afterword

Page 226: The Myan Jencks case is described in Dana Milbank, "Telephone Sales Reps Do Unrewarding Jobs That Few Can Abide," *Wall Street Journal*, September 9, 1993, A1.

Page 226: The article by Tony Horwitz featuring Brian Deyo appears on p. A1 of the November 12, 1993, issue of the paper.

Page 227: Antonia Contereras is described in Tom Abate, "Heavy Load for Silicon Valley Workers," *San Francisco Examiner*, May 23, 1993, E1.

Page 229: *the forward edge of the movement beyond jobs* I am indebted to the consultant Kim Barnes for suggesting this parallel to me.

Bibliography

Abate, Tom. "On The Defensive." *San Francisco Examiner,* December 13, 1992, E1.

Alpert, Mark. "Jumping Ahead by Going High Tech." *Fortune,* October 19, 1992, 113–114.

Ansberry, Clare. "Workers Are Forced to Take More Jobs with Few Benefits." *Wall Street Journal,* March 11, 1993, A1.

Anshen, Melvin. "The Management of Ideas." Originally published in *Harvard Business Review,* July–August, 1969; reprinted in the magazine, March–April, 1993, 159.

"Ashes of the Cold War." "Frontline," PBS news program, May 4, 1993.

Baig, Edward C. "Inching out of the Stone Age." *U.S. News & World Report,* May 3, 1993, 68–70.

Barker, Joel A. *Paradigms: The Business of Discovering the Future.* New York: HarperCollins, 1992.

Bateson, Mary Catherine. *Composing a Life.* New York: Penguin Plume Books, 1990.

Beck, Nuala. *Shifting Gears: Thriving in the New Economy.* Toronto: HarperCollins, 1992.

Beer, Michael, V. Eisenstat, and Bert Spector. *The Critical Path to Corporate Renewal.* Cambridge: Harvard Business School Press, 1990.

Bennett, Amanda. "Path to Top Job Now Twists and Turns." *Wall Street Journal,* March 15, 1993, B1.

Birch, David L. "Musical Jobs." *Inc.,* November 1987, 18.

―――. "The Rise and Fall of Everybody." *Inc.,* September 1987, 18.

Bleakley, Fred R. "Many Companies Try Management Fads, Only to See Them Flop." *Wall Street Journal,* July 6, 1993, A1.

Bovier, Connie. "Teamwork: The Heart of an Airline." *Training,* June 1993, 53–58.

Bowers, Brent, "Technology Allows Small Concerns to Exploit Distances." *Wall Street Journal,* October 15, 1991.

Brokaw, Leslie. "Thinking Flat." *Inc.,* October 1993, 86–88.

Brown, Donna. "Outsourcing: How Corporations Take Their Business Elsewhere." *Management Review,* February 1992, 15–20.

Brown, John Seely. "Research That Reinvents the Corporation." *Harvard Business Review,* January–February 1991, 105–111.

Bulkeley, William M. "Get Ready for 'Smart Cards' in Health Care." *Wall Street Journal*, May 3, 1993, B7.

Burck, Charles. "The Pain of Productivity" [about Gerhard Schulmeyer]. *Fortune*, November 30, 1992, 22.

Burdman, Pamela. " 'Flexible' Jobs on the Rise." *San Francisco Examiner*, August 10, 1992, C5.

Byrne, John A., with Richard Brandt and Otis Port. "The Virtual Corporation." *Newsweek*, February 8, 1993, 98–103. Case, John, "A Company of Business People." *Inc.*, April 1993, 79–93.

Castro, Janice. "Disposable Workers." *Time*, March 29, 1993, 43–47.

Church, George J. "Jobs in an Age of Insecurity." *Time*, November 22, 1993, 34–39.

Clark, Don. "Jobs Coming and Going in Silicon Valley." *San Francisco Chronicle*, July 7, 1993, E1.

Cooper, James C., and Kathleen Madigan. "Suddenly, the Job Engine Is Purring." *Newsweek*, June 21, 1993, 29–30.

Crispell, Diane. "Moonlighting Serenade Lures Many Workers." *Wall Street Journal*, December 18, 1991, B1.

Davis, Mary Graham. "Hiring the Overqualified." *Management Review*, August 1993, 35–38.

"The Death of Corporate Loyalty." *The Economist*, April 3, 1993, 63–64.

De Meuse, Kenneth P., and Walter W. Tornow. "Leadership and the Changing Psychological Contract between Employer and Employee." *Issues & Observations* [Center for Creative Leadership] 13, no. 2 (1993): 4–6.

Dennis, Helen, and Helen Axel. *Encouraging Employee Self-Management in Financial and Career Planning*. Conference Board Report No. 976. New York: The Conference Board, 1991.

Dentzer, Susan. "Beware the Immovable Object." *U.S. News & World Report*, June 28, 1993, 53.

Drucker, Peter. "The New Society of Organizations." *Harvard Business Review*, September–October 1992, 95–104.

———. "Peter Drucker's 1990's." *Boardroom Reports*, December 15, 1989.

———. "Planning for Uncertainty." *Wall Street Journal*, July 22, 1992, A14.

———. "The Post-Capitalist Executive: An Interview with Peter F. Drucker." *Harvard Business Review*. May–June 1993, 115–122.

Dumaine, Brian. "The New Non-Manager Managers." *Fortune*, February 22, 1993, 79–86.

Dyson, Esther. "Coordination Technology." *Forbes*, August 8, 1988, 96.

Ehrbar, Al. " 'Re-Engineering' Gives Firms New Efficiency, Workers the Pink Slip." *Wall Street Journal*, March 16, 1993.

Ehrenfeld, Tom. "School's In." *Inc.*, July 1993, 65–66.

Ehrlichman, John. "Who Will Hire Me Now?" *Parade Magazine*, August 29, 1993, 4.

Fenn, Donna. "Bottoms Up." *Inc.*, July 1993, 58–60.

Fierman, Jaclyn. "What Happened to the Jobs?" *Fortune*, July 12, 1993, 40–41.

Finegan, Jay. "People Power." *Inc.*, July 1993, 63–64.

Flipczak, Bob. "Beyond the Gates at Microsoft." *Training*, September 1992, 37–44.

———. "Unions in the '90s: Cooperation or Capitulation." *Training*, May 1993, 25–34.

Friedman, Milton. "The Folly of Buying Healthcare at the Company Store." *Wall Street Journal*, February 3, 1993, A14.

Galagan, Patricia A. "On Being a Beginner: An Interview with John Rollwagen." *Training & Development*, November 1992.

Gendron, George. Editorial in *Inc.*, May 1993, 9.

————. Editorial in *Inc.*, October 1992, 11.

Greenberg, Eric. "Upswing in Downsizings to Continue." *Management Review*, February 1993, 5.

Guttman, Herbert. "Work, Culture, and Society in Industrializing America, 1815–1919." In *On Work: Historical, Comparative, and Theoretical Approaches*, ed. R. E. Pahl. Oxford: Basil Blackwell, Ltd., 1988.

Hage, David, Linda Grant, and Jim Impoco. "White Collar Wasteland." *U.S. News & World Report*, June 28, 1993, 42–52

Hammer, Michael, and James Champy. "The Future of Middle Managers." Interview. *Management Review*, September 1993, 51–53.

————. "The Promise of Re-engineering." *Fortune*, May 3, 1993, 93–97.

Handy, Charles. *The Age of Unreason*. Cambridge: Harvard Business School Press, 1992.

————. *The Future of Work: A Guide to a Changing Society*. Oxford: Basil Blackwell, Ltd., 1984.

Harris, Kathryn. "Torch Song Lawyer." *Forbes*, December 10, 1990, 298–300.

Hays, Laurie. "IBM Speeds Drive to Shed Real Estate As Part of Program to Trim Jobs, Costs." *Wall Street Journal*, June 18, 1993, A5B.

Heizl, Mark. "Auto Worker Goals in Canada Differ from UAW's List." *Wall Street Journal*, May 5, 1993, A5.

Henkoff, Ronald. "Where Will the Jobs Come From?" *Fortune*, October 19, 1992, 58–64.

————. "Winning the New Career Game." *Fortune*, July 12, 1993, 46–49.

Howard, Robert. "An Interview with Xerox's Paul Allaire." *Harvard Business Review*, September–October 1992, 107–121.

Howe, Kenneth. "B of A Cut in Job Hours Follows Trend." *San Francisco Chronicle*, February 11, 1993, D1.

Huey, John. "Where Will Managers Go?" *Fortune*, January 27, 1992, 50–60.

Hurmuses, Gayle. "The Last Days of Local 303." *Toronto Globe and Mail*, May 1, 1993, D5.

Jonas, Donald. "Lessons from Lechters: How Lechters Built a Big, Big Business on a Narrow Niche." *Boardroom Reports*, August 1, 1993, 5.

Jud, Robert A. "Motivating Workers in Critical Times." Speech given at the November 10, 1992, convention of the American Electronics Association.

Kanter, Rosabeth Moss. "The New Managerial Work." *Harvard Business Review*, November–December 1989, 85–92.

————. "Shape of Companies to Come." *Business* [England], September 1989, 80–85.

————. *When Giants Learn to Dance: Mastering the Challenges of Strategy, Management, and Careers in the 1990's*. New York: Simon and Schuster, 1989.

Kaufman, Steve. "Downsizing's Ripple Effect." *Training*, November 1992, 12–14.

Kerr, John. "The Best Small Companies to Work For in America." *Inc.*, July 1993, 51–53.

Kiechel, Walter. "How We Will Work in the Year 2000." *Fortune*, May 17, 1993, 38–52.

Kilborn, Peter T. "New Jobs Lack the Old Security in Time of 'Disposable Workers.' " *New York Times*, March 15, 1993, A1.

Kindel, Sharen. "Network Outsourcing: Let Your People Go." *Financial World*, June 9, 1992, 38.

King, Ralph T. "Job Retraining Linked Closely to Employers Works in Cincinnati." *Wall Street Journal*, March 13, 1993, A1.

Koller, Alice. *An Unknown Woman*. New York: Bantam Doubleday Dell, 1991.

Koretz, Gene. "Tiny Employers Weigh Some Big Hiring Plans." *Business Week*, June 21, 1993, 24.

Labich, Kenneth. "The New Unemployment." *Fortune*, March 8, 1993, 40–49.

Lewis, Geoff. "The Portable Executive." *Newsweek*, October 10, 1988, 102–112.

McAuliffe, Claire. "Contingent Workers Deliver a Certain Advantage." *San Francisco Business Times*, June 11, 1993, 5.

McCune, Jenny C. "Tomorrow's Factory." *Management Review*, January 1993, 19–22.

McKenna, Regis. "Marketing Is Everything." *Harvard Business Review*, January–February 1991, 65–75.

Magnet, Myron. "Why Job Growth Is Stalled." *Fortune*, March 8, 1993, 51–58.

Malcolmson, R. W. "Ways of Getting a Living in Eighteenth Century England." In *On Work: Historical, Comparative, and Theoretical Approaches*, ed. R. E. Pahl. Oxford: Basil Blackwell, Ltd., 1988.

Marryat, Captain. "Visit to America." In *This Was America . . . As Recorded by European Travellers*, ed. Oscar Handlin. Cambridge: Harvard University Press, 1949.

Marshall, Jonathan. "Sliding Down the Income Ladder." *San Francisco Chronicle*, June 21, 1993, C8.

———. "Troubled Cities Put Services Out to Bid." *San Francisco Chronicle*, June 3, 1991, A1.

Marshall, Lisa. "Vision and Values at the Edge of Complexity." *The Chaos Network* [newsletter] 5, no. 3 (August 1993): 2–4.

Mason, Julie Cohen. "Workplace 2000: The Death of 9 to 5?" *Management Review*, January 1993, 14–18.

"The Metamorphosis of Hewlett-Packard." *The Economist*, June 19, 1993, 67–68.

Moravec, Milan and Kristen Anundsen. "You May Have to Work at It, but Think of Your Job As 'Role.'" *San Jose Mercury News*, June 14, 1993, 12D.

Moravec, Milan, and Robert Tucker. "Job Descriptions for the 21st Century." *Personnel Journal*, June 1992.

Morgan, David. "Arthur Andersen Sends Execs Home." *San Francisco Examiner*, June 27, 1993, E14.

Morris, Charles R., and Charles H. Ferguson. "How Architecture Wins Technology Wars." *Harvard Business Review*, March–April 1993, 86–96.

Morrow, Lance. "The Temping of America." *Time*, March 29, 1993, 40–41.

Naj, Amal Kumar. "Some Manufacturers Drop Efforts to Adopt Japanese Techniques." *Wall Street Journal*, May 7, 1993, A1.

Normann, Richard, and Rafael Ramirez. "From Value Chain to Value Constellation: Designing Interactive Strategy." *Harvard Business Review*, July–August 1993, 65–77.

O'Reilly, Brian. "Looking Ahead." *Fortune*, December 14, 1992, 52–66.

Pacelle, Mitchell. "To Trim Their Costs, Some Companies Cut Space for Employees." *Wall Street Journal*, June 4, 1993, A1.

Patch, Francis, Dan Rice, and Craig Dreilinger. "A Contract for Commitment." *Training & Development*, November 1992, 47–51.

Peters, Tom. "It's Time to Turn US Employees into Self-Reliant Business People." *Rocky Mountain News* (Denver), April 20, 1993, 35.

———. *Liberation Management: Necessary Disorganization for the Nanosecond Nineties*. New York: Alfred A. Knopf, 1992.

Richman, Louis S. "America's Tough New Job Market." *Fortune*, February 24, 1992, 52–61.

———. "The Dark Side of Job Churn." *Fortune*, August 9, 1993, 24.

———. "How Jobs Die—and Are Born." *Fortune*, July 26, 1993, 26.

———. "Why the Economic Data Mislead Us." *Fortune*, March 8, 1993.

Savage, Charles M. *5th Generation Management: Integrating Enterprises through Human Networking*. Bedford, Mass.: Digital Press, 1990.

Schor, Juliet B. *The Overworked Americans: The Unexpected Decline of Leisure*. New York: Basic Books, 1991.

Scism, Leslie. "Some Firms, Seeking Further Cost Cuts, Trim Jobs from Finance Departments." *Wall Street Journal*, May 25, 1993, A2.

Senge, Peter M. *The Fifth Discipline: The Art and Practice of the Learning Organization*. New York: Doubleday, 1990.

Sherman, Stratford. "The New Computer Revolution," *Fortune*, June 14, 1993, 56–80.

Shinsato, Douglas T. "Japan Tries to Get the Size Right." *Wall Street Journal*, June 28, 1993, A14.

Smith, Lee. "Can Defense Pain Be Turned to Gain?" *Fortune*, February 8, 1993, 84–96.

———. "The Coming Health Care Shakeout." *Fortune*, May 17, 1993, 70–75.

Stewart, Thomas A. "The Search for the Organization of Tomorrow." *Fortune*, May 18, 1992, 92–98.

———. "There Are No Products—Only Services." *Fortune*, January 14, 1991, 32.

———. "Welcome to the Revolution." *Fortune*, December 13, 1993, 66–76.

"Suicide Soaring among Marines; Stress over Cutbacks Is Cited." *San Jose Mercury News*, April 22, 1993.

Swanson, Roger. "On the Electronic Plantation." *This World* (magazine section of the *San Francisco Chronicle*), March 21, 1993.

Taylor, Alex. "What's Ahead for GM's New Team." *Fortune*, November 30, 1992, 58–61.

Templin, Neal, and Joseph B. White. "GM Drive to Step Up Efficiency Is Colliding with UAW Job Fears." *Wall Street Journal*, June 23, 1993, A1.

Thompson, E. P. "Time, Work-Discipline, and Industrial Capitalism." *Past and Present*, no. 38 (1967): 57.

———. *The Making of the English Working Class*. London: Penguin Books, 1980.

Thottam, Jyoti. "Entrepreneur Finds Monks Make Heavenly Emloyees." *Wall Street Journal*, July 12, 1993, B2.

Tichy, Noel M., and Stratford Sherman. *Control Your Destiny or Someone Else Will: How Jack Welch Is Turning General Electric into the World's Most Competitive Corporation*. New York: Doubleday, 1993.

———. "Walking the Talk at GE." *Training & Development*, June 1993, 26–35.

Toffler, Alvin. *The Third Wave*. New York: Bantam, 1984.

Tomasko, Robert. "To Really Boost Productivity . . . Eliminate Jobs." *Boardroom Reports*, August 1, 1993, 4.

Tucker, Robert, and Milan Moravec. "Do-It-Yourself Career Development," *Training*, February 1992, 48.

Tully, Shawn. "The Modular Corporation." *Fortune*, February 8, 1993, 106–116.

———. "Your Paycheck Gets Exciting." *Fortune*, November 1, 1993, 83–98.

Uchitelle, Louis. "Job Loss in Recession: Scratch Those Figures." *New York Times*, May 7, 1993, C1.

Weber, Joseph. "Farewell, Fast Track." *Business Week*, December 10, 1990, 192–200.

Welles, Edward O. "Virtual Realities." *Inc.*, August 1993, 50–58.

Williams, Raymond. *Culture and Society: 1780–1850*. Garden City, N.Y.: Anchor Books, 1960.

Willoughby, Jack. "Endgame Strategy." *Forbes*, July 13, 1987, 181–82.

Woods, Wilton. "The Latin Way to Boost Savings." *Fortune*, November 1, 1993, 26.

Wylie, Ann. "Moonlighting Serenade." *America West*, November 1992, 75.

Wysocki, Bernard, Jr. "American Firms Send Office Work Abroad to Use Cheaper Labor." *Wall Street Journal*, August 15, 1992, A1.

Zachary, G. Pascal. "Agony and Ecstasy of 200 Code Writers Beget Windows NT." *Wall Street Journal*, May 26, 1993, A1.

Zachary, G. Pascal, and Bob Ortega. "Workplace Revolution Boosts Productivity at Cost of Job Security." *Wall Street Journal*, March 10, 1993, A1.

Zuboff, Shoshona. *In the Age of the Smart Machine: The Future of Work and Power*. New York: Basic Books, 1988.

Index

About the Author

William Bridges is the author of seven previous books, including the best-selling *Transitions* and *Managing Transitions*. A former literature professor whose own career change first plunged him into the dejobbed world twenty years ago, he was originally trained at Harvard, Columbia, and Brown, where he received his Ph.D. in American Civilization in 1963. He founded William Bridges & Associates in 1981 to help organizations and individuals deal more successfully with transition. His training programs, speeches, and consulting have been utilized by several hundred organizations, including Pacific Bell, Baxter Healthcare, Intel, Apple Computer, Kaiser Permanente, Procter & Gamble, Hewlett-Packard, the U.S. Forest Service, Chevron Corporation, Kal Kan Foods, and McDonnell Douglas Astronautics. *The Wall Street Journal* listed him recently as one of the top ten independent executive development presenters in the country. He is currently working on a series of television programs based on the theme of this book.

For more information on his publications and services, contact:
William Bridges & Associates
38 Miller Avenue, Suite 12
Mill Valley, CA 94941
Telephone: (415) 381–9663
Fax: (415) 381–8124